THE
KENNEDY
LEGACY

JACK, BOBBY AND TED
AND A FAMILY DREAM FULFILLED

★ ★ ★

VINCENT BZDEK

palgrave
macmillan

First published in hardcover in 2009 by PALGRAVE MACMILLAN® in the US—a division of St. Martin's Press LLC, 175 Fifth Avenue, New York, NY 10010.

Where this book is distributed in the UK, Europe and the rest of the world, this is by Palgrave Macmillan, a division of Macmillan Publishers Limited, registered in England, company number 785998, of Houndmills, Basingstoke, Hampshire RG21 6XS.

Palgrave Macmillan is the global academic imprint of the above companies and has companies and representatives throughout the world.

Palgrave® and Macmillan® are registered trademarks in the United States, the United Kingdom, Europe and other countries.

ISBN: 978-0-230-62386-6

Library of Congress Cataloging-in-Publication Data is available from the Library of Congress.

A catalogue record of the book is available from the British Library.

Design by Letra Libre

First PALGRAVE MACMILLAN paperback edition: August 2010

10 9 8 7 6 5 4 3 2 1

Printed in the United States of America.

To Mom and Dad and the epic family they brought into being

CONTENTS

ACKNOWLEDGMENTS

Shortly after Senator Ted Kennedy collapsed from a seizure in May 2008, I hurried to several bookstores in Washington in search of something to read about Kennedy and his lifelong contributions to the Kennedy legacy. I soon discovered that no book about Ted had been written in the last ten years—years that have been among his most important and most accomplished. That's when my editor at Palgrave Macmillan, Jake Klisivitch, called up and suggested we simply put together a new book about the Kennedys that placed Ted at the center of the family narrative. In other words, the idea of this book is wholly Jake's. He rode herd on the project from outline to printing press with infectious confidence and good humor—this book is as much his as it is mine.

Kennedy campaigns have always been large family projects, and the creation of this book certainly mimicked the Kennedy approach. My father and mother, both accomplished journalists themselves, were crucial in improving the manuscript and listening to ideas, questions and gnashings of teeth. They've edited me and my work for more than 40 years, ever improving both. My wife Kelsey, a clinical psychologist, insisted that the book explore the emotional universe of the Kennedy family as much as the politics. Without her help, none of what the Kennedy family has been through psychologically would have made much sense. Kelsey also kept our family from flying apart during an intense year of writing, and gave the story that follows much of its coherence and design. Her father, the Rev. Cal French, with his long history in Washington, helped arrange many of the most important interviews for the book and gave us all his unconditional support.

To say that Anna Ghosh of Scovil Galen Ghosh has been a wonderful literary agent is to somewhat understate how important she was to this book. Anna not only made the writing of the book possible in a pragmatic way, she also *crystallized* its vague ideas into themes, narrative and chapters. In other words, Anna is the person who gives airy nothingness a home and a name.

At the *Washington Post*, I'd most like to thank editors Phil Bennett and Len Downie for their generous support. Len, a Kennedy aficionado and accomplished author in his own right, edited the manuscript with a gimlet eye, making certain the final story had a much tauter thread. Editor Emeritus Ben Bradlee, a close friend of John Kennedy, read through the book as well and shared many of his best Kennedy stories with me, enlivening the manuscript mightily. The *Washington Post's* eminence grise of politics, David Broder, took the time to explain Ted Kennedy's place in history to me. Senior political writer Dan Balz pointed me in a dozen right directions and made sure I talked to the people who know Ted Kennedy best. *Washington Post* photography editor Michel Ducille and his staff generously allowed me to use some of their images, many of which have never before appeared in a book. And special thanks to Rick Atkinson, a former *Washington Post* editor and Pulitzer Prize-winning author. Rick has spent a considerable amount of time covering the Kennedys and shared his expertise and insights with me.

Several members of the Kennedy clan graciously agreed to speak with me about the family legacy during the Democratic Convention in Denver in 2008. They are Kerry Kennedy, Vicky Kennedy, Joe Kennedy III, Ethel Kennedy and Robert Kennedy Jr. I interviewed Ted's son, Patrick, for the *Washington Post*, and found him insightful and articulate about his work and the Kennedy legacy. He's also a generous conversationalist and passionate public servant.

A vigorous nod of the head to my sources for this book, many of whom lent me a considerable amount of their time illuminating the Kennedy spirit. I'm especially indebted to Vice President Walter Mondale, Senator Al Simpson, Senator Orrin Hatch, Senator Harris Wofford, Representative Jim Ramstad, Representative Mike Enzi, Majority leader Steny Hoyer and President Barack Obama's chief of staff, Rahm Emanuel. Many onetime Kennedy family aides spoke to me at length about the family, including Ted Sorensen, former speechwriter for John Kennedy; Ken Feinberg, Ted Kennedy's onetime chief of staff; Bob Shrum, his longtime speechwriter; Dr. Jay Himmelstein, a former health care staffer; Melissa Wagoner, Ted's press secretary; Anthony Coley, Ted's spokesman; Dave Bowen, a health care specialist for Ted; Kerrie Bennett, an aide to Patrick Kennedy; and Tom Southwick, former Kennedy press secretary.

Thomas Oliphant, the author and longtime *Boston Globe* columnist who has covered the Kennedys most of his life, helped me frame the larger themes of the book. Carol Chodroff, a human rights advocate who has worked closely with the Kennedys, gave me a greater appreciation for the range of what the Kennedys have accomplished as a family. The great Marcus Raskin, a national security aide for John F. Kennedy, beautifully explained the Kennedy brothers' relationship to war. And much thanks to Janet Heininger, Senior Fellow for the Edward M. Kennedy Oral History Project, whose advice proved priceless, and to Alan Khazei, co-founder of City Year and architect of Kennedy's national service program.

I'm also grateful to the folks at the John F. Kennedy Library and Museum who were so vital to my research, including librarian Ronald E. Whealan, research archivist Stephen Plotkin, research assistant Sharon Kelly and above all, audiovisual archivist Maryrose Grossman, who selected many of the fabulous images for the book.

A salute to Yasmin Mathew and her crew at Macmillan for their patience and perfectionism in overseeing the production of the book. Jennifer Simington masterfully copyedited the manuscript and Debby Manette proofread it on a very tight deadline. Many thanks to Sarah Thomas for getting this book in front of people and to editorial assistant Colleen Lawrie for making sure it all came together.

The book also would not have made it to completion without the friendship and support of Carrie and Mike Hillegass and Betsy Babbington.

Finally, I'd like to make a special mention of Tom Cronin, presidential scholar, author of many books on politics, and former Ted Kennedy delegate, and one of my most treasured undergraduate professors. Tom's inspiring talks about the inherent nobility of public service are really the founding fathers of this book. My hope is that Tom's optimistic spirit—Kennedyesque in the best sense of the word—can be found lodged in every page of this book.

PROLOGUE

THE LAST HURRAH

The courage of life is often a less dramatic spectacle than the courage of a final moment; but it is no less a magnificent mixture of triumph and tragedy.

—*John Fitzgerald Kennedy*

August 25, 2008: With just two hours to showtime, Ted Kennedy and the speech of a lifetime languished uncertainly on a hospital bed. Exhausted, experiencing excruciating pain, Kennedy waited in a nondescript room at the University of Colorado Hospital in East Denver as the setting sun torched the sky behind the Rocky Mountains. He was just a few miles away from the convention hall, but it was beginning to feel like a million. He lay unnoticed by hospital workers, hoping against hope that doctors would clear him to make the speech. His wife, Vicki, was with him, and the last-minute ironies of their long, difficult trek were not lost on them. A very sick, 76-year-old Kennedy, fighting an arduous fight against brain cancer, had secretly made it all the way across the country in a chartered plane to be at the Democratic National Convention. During a long summer of chemotherapy and radiation treatments, he and his former speechwriter, Bob Shrum, had worked diligently on the speech he wanted to give. He'd endured a sleepless night after his arrival in Denver and fought off the effects of the altitude only to have the excruciating pain of a mysterious new ailment stop his last-ditch dream in its tracks.

After successful surgery in June to remove the tumor from his brain, Kennedy had called family members together at his white clapboard house in

Hyannis Port to tell them all that he was determined—no, hell-bent—on giving his speech in August. Family members remember emotional, difficult conversations about the wisdom of such a trip. Kennedy's wife, his doctors, his children and his aides warned that the speech could very well kill him. Some pleaded with him not to go to Denver at all, even for an appearance. They argued adamantly that the risk to Kennedy's health wasn't worth it. After two seizures in May, Kennedy had been diagnosed with malignant glioma, which is fatal for 50 percent of its sufferers by the end of a year's time. If he went to Denver, family members feared, it could be his last speech. Everyone close to Kennedy sensed that a curtain was slowly closing on both his life and a 50-year-long political drama in American history. And they did not want him to hurry that finale. They had been making their case for rest and caution for eight weeks, all during the "shock and awe" phase of his treatment. Kennedy repeatedly acknowledged his family's concerns about his health during those two months, largely agreed with them that going to Denver was reckless, and then vowed that he was going to do it anyway. "It was a risk to his health," said Shrum, "but he really wanted to do this."[1] Said another friend: "He gave every ounce of courage to attend that convention."[2]

Doctors were at first concerned that the pain he was experiencing after his arrival on Sunday, August 24, was due to his cancer or the chemotherapy and radiation treatments. Radiologists were reluctant to let him fly during treatment because the pressurized air in the plane cabin can wreak all sorts of havoc on the immune system of a weakened body. Kennedy's doctors were also concerned that Denver's mile-high altitude might complicate his condition, making his lungs and heart work harder as they coped with the reduced oxygen in Colorado's thin air. One of Kennedy's close associates said the senator had suffered a serious setback in July after he flew to Washington to cast a crucial vote on a Medicare bill.[3] Doctors had pleaded with him not to make that trip, either.

Kennedy had been taken straight to the University of Colorado Hospital from the plane for a routine check. At the hospital Sunday night, less than 24 hours before he was scheduled to give his surprise speech, doctors discovered what was causing Kennedy's pain. In addition to all his other health concerns, the senator had a case of kidney stones. The new ailment had nothing to do with his cancer, it was just bad luck and worse timing. The pain of passing kidney stones, it is said, feels something like childbirth, and doctors were almost certain the speech was off. Kidney stones are typically treated with morphine or other powerful painkillers—drugs that make it difficult to stand up, let alone deliver a rousing speech.

"We got there, and we went through a perilous period," said Shrum, who had flown out with Kennedy. "I mean I stayed in my hotel room basically for 24 hours in case he needed me, eating room service food, playing with text and trying to figure out what we were going to do." When Shrum heard about the kidney stones, he cut the speech Kennedy had planned to deliver in half to make it easier to get through, and he also wrote a three-sentence version, which he sent over to Kennedy's hospital room. Kennedy told Shrum that he wasn't going to let a few kidney stones keep him from speaking. "He said, 'I'm not getting up in front of the Democratic Convention to deliver three sentences.'" They had been working together in Hyannis Port for three weeks on the speech, and Kennedy had something he wanted to say.

Kennedy was treated for the kidney condition early Monday, the day of the speech, but the pain didn't abate right away. The problem didn't resolve itself until the middle of the night Monday.[4] At about 5 P.M., two hours before the speech was scheduled, family and friends were not at all sure he had the strength to give it. Kennedy still "just wasn't feeling well,"[5] and "there was a second round [of discussion] about 'is he going to be able to do it?'" Caroline Kennedy said. Kennedy finally told his wife that he was going to deliver the speech regardless. He rested until the last possible moment, then got up out of his hospital bed at 5:15 and rode by ambulance to the Pepsi Center.

"There was nothing that was going to keep him away," said Caroline, who knew her uncle was determined to follow through despite concerns of his friends and family. "He knew it all along. There was no way he was not going to do it." After the ambulance ride, Kennedy was taken by golf cart through the convention hall to a VIP room backstage. There he waited as Caroline took the stage to introduce a video tribute to her statesman uncle. Out on the floor, word was filtering through the hall that an army of Kennedys would take the stage at the end of the tribute, including the revered matriarch of the family, Bobby's widow, Ethel Kennedy. Convention-goers were quizzing each other about which Kennedys might show up, jogging their brains to remember the names of all of Bobby's 11 children. Word had started to leak out that Ted was in Denver, but thousands of people in the hall still didn't know.

An elaborate, two-tiered stage that looked as if it consisted almost entirely of video screens jutted far out into the floor space at the Pepsi Center. That meant the floor was more crowded than usual, and conventioneers were packed tightly against each other as they listened to Caroline. More than 15,000 members of the media—10,000 more journalists than delegates—were in Denver for the convention as well, and many of them were crowded into the lower seats just above the floor. Ten rows of giant blue risers, all bristling with video cameras, stair-stepped up the stands facing the stage. More than 100 cameras watched as Caroline made her usual graceful entry to sustained applause and the strains of Neil Diamond's "Sweet Caroline," a song that had been written for her.

JFK's last child had been left alone by America after the tragedies that had befallen her father, uncle and brother. For once in a celebrity-crazed country, a public figure was granted her privacy. As a consequence, she had preserved a kind of quiet dignity about her. This expressed itself as an unspoken moral authority as she took the stage in a simple blue dress.

But in 2008, Caroline assumed a high profile in the country's political slipstream. After Barack Obama won the Iowa caucus, she made an enthusiastic endorsement of his candidacy, saying she hadn't been as excited about a politician's potential to lift the country's sights since her father had run. She penned an editorial for the *New York Times* explaining her rationale back in January, and it stood as a strong testimonial to the little-known candidate at just the time he needed it the most. She went on after that to campaign vigorously for Obama, and she and Ted became perhaps his most visible high-profile supporters early in the campaign, anointing him the newest standard-bearer of the Kennedy legacy. When Obama won the nomination, he tapped Caroline to lead his efforts to pick a running mate. And here she was, again in the public eye she had shied away from for so long, paying homage to her uncle at what was likely his last Democratic convention ever.

The floor suddenly blossomed with hundreds of Kennedy signs. Delegates pumped them up and down enthusiastically, creating a blue spray of "K-E-N-N-E-D-Y"s above their heads. "I am here tonight," Caroline began, "to pay tribute to two men who have changed my life and the life of this country: Barack Obama and Edward M. Kennedy. Their stories are very different, but they share a commitment to the timeless American ideals of justice and fairness, service and sacrifice, faith and family."

The video tribute that followed was a poignant voyage through the Kennedy legacy, beginning and ending with images of Ted Kennedy at sea. The highlight of the eight minutes was footage of a much younger Ted Kennedy, grizzled at the temples, pounding the lectern during one of his rafter-ringers on health care. "Long as I have a voice in the United States Senate," Kennedy intoned from giant screens throughout the hall, "it's going to be for that Dem- *(pound)* ocratic *(pound)* plat- *(pound)* form *(pound)* plank *(pound)* that provides decent *(pound)* quality *(pound)* health care *(pound)* for NORTH AND SOUTH, East and West, *(drowned out by cheers)* FOR ALL OF AMERICA . . . as a matter of right *(pause for effect)* and not privilege."

The 20-year-old speech still got a standing ovation. As the tribute wound down, people there had the sense of being present at a monumental kind of ending in America's political history. "It kind of felt like this grand finale," said Kennedy's son Patrick. But it was a different kind of ending for many of those in the hall who had been affected by the Kennedys. This ending was tinged by sadness, as so many Kennedy endings are, but it was also under-girded by a satisfying sense of completion. Finally, it seemed, the life of one of the sons of Camelot had not been cut short.

And he still had enough fire in his belly to deliver a rousing valedictory.

With Vicki holding him by his left arm, Kennedy shuffled gingerly out to the podium for his twelfth Democratic convention. The crowd erupted out of their seats as he came into view, and he acknowledged their "hurrahs" and applause by hoisting his left arm crookedly up in the air. Dozens of teary-eyed delegates claimed they were utterly surprised when Ted walked out. He let a wide Irish smile take over his swollen face as he arrived at the lectern. The delegates all stayed on their feet as they slapped their hands to-gether, and the blue Kennedy sign garden bloomed again. With the spot-lights occasionally revealing patches of his scalp where he'd lost hair during radiation treatments—as if he were proudly displaying, just for this one night, the visible scars of a lifetime of battle—the last Kennedy brother began his speech. "My fellow Democrats, my fellow Americans," he began. "It is so wonderful to be *here*."

★ ★ ★

The Kennedy brothers delivered many memorable addresses in the 60 years they were part of the landscape of American politics. "Ask not what your country can do for you, ask what you can do for your country." "The torch has been passed to a new generation." "There are those who look at things the way they are and ask why, I dream things that never were and ask why not?" "Let every nation know, whether it wishes us well or ill, that we shall pay any price, bear any burden, meet any hardship, support any friend, op-pose any foe, in order to assure the survival and the success of liberty." "*Ich bin ein Berliner*." "Like my brothers before me, I pick up a fallen standard." "The work goes on, the cause endures, hope still lives and the dream shall never die."

Eleven of the top 100 American speeches of the twentieth century were delivered by the Kennedy brothers, according to a ranking by several histori-ans. They are words that have stood the test of time. Yet for pure grit alone, Ted Kennedy's speech to the 2008 Democratic convention probably has to be counted among the brothers' most dramatic. Democratic operatives had sworn that, if he were by some miracle to show up for the convention, it would be for a wave and a smile, not a speech. Instead, Ted Kennedy gave a full-throated rallying cry for Barack Obama and the reinvigoration of the Democratic Party. His tone wavered a bit in the upper registers at times, but otherwise the instrument that had brought the Senate down so many times was its usual *basso profundo*.

"For me, this is a season of hope," he declared despite his ill health. "I pledge to you that I will be there next January on the floor of the Senate," offering support to the new president, a promise he kept. Occasionally, as he had in the past when evoking the memory of his brothers, he teared up a little. In the crowd, monitors repeatedly caught his niece Maria Shriver crying during the speech, and tears could be seen on the faces of hundreds of delegates. Other family members in the hall—his children, Edward Jr., Patrick and Kara; his brother Bobby's widow, Ethel Kennedy; Bobby's son, Robert F. Kennedy Jr.; and a raft of fourth-generation Kennedys—all held their collective breath as Ted delivered his speech. The looks on many of the faces in the wings seemed to say, Hurry, get through this, and just make it to the end. Shrum made sure the 10-minute version of the talk was loaded into the teleprompter rather than the 20-minute one, a concession to the kidney stones. But Kennedy delivered all 10 minutes in full voice, and almost every sentence was met with cheers.

And, as he has in nearly every major speech for the past 30 years, Kennedy spoke again of "the cause of my life," the delivery of "decent, quality health care as a fundamental right and not a privilege."

He compared 2008 with 1960, when his brother called Americans to higher purposes. "We are told that Barack Obama believes too much in an America of high principle and bold endeavor, but when John Kennedy called of going to the moon, he didn't say it's too far to get there. We shouldn't even try. Our people answered his call and rose to the challenge, and today an American flag still marks the surface of the moon.

"This is what we do. We reach the moon. We scale the heights. I know it. I've seen it. I've lived it. And we can do it again."

His passion rose and the crowd revved as he barreled toward another memorable finish. "He actually got stronger as his speech went on," said his son Patrick, who was on stage with him just as he had been as a 12-year-old in 1980 when his father delivered his best-remembered line, "the dream shall never die." In his closing, Ted Kennedy echoed both that speech and his brother's 1961 inaugural address. "This November," he said, "the torch will be passed again to a new generation of Americans, so with Barack Obama and for you and me, our country will be committed to his cause. The work begins anew. The hope rises again. And the dream lives on."

★ ★ ★

"The man never quits," said a longtime friend, retired senator Alan Simpson (R-WY). "He's indefatigable. He's a fighter." Dogged perseverance—whether it's fighting political battles, overcoming personal shortcomings or coping with family tragedies—became something of Ted Kennedy's signature after a half-century in the political limelight. Ted was only 12 when his oldest brother, Joe, died in a warplane explosion during a secret mission over Europe. Ted lost his sister "Kick" in a plane crash when he was 16. His brother, the president, was assassinated when he was 31. He himself broke his back and nearly died falling from a crashing plane when he was 32. And Ted was only 36 when Bobby, the would-be president, was slain. A year after that day in California, just after a party to salute some of Bobby's campaign workers, Ted Kennedy's car went off a bridge and the woman in the passenger seat drowned.

The catalogue of death and suffering didn't stop there for Ted Kennedy. In the decades that followed, Ted's oldest son lost his leg and nearly his life to cancer. Ted lost three of his nephews: one to a heroin overdose, another to a freak skiing accident, and JFK's son, John Jr.—the next generation's brightest hope—to yet another airplane crash. And finally, after years of desperately fleeing from death much of his life, the last Kennedy brother faced his own for 14 months. But there is something about the Kennedys that, after 50 years and all that misfortune, simply refuses to fade. There is still something fierce burning at the heart of the Kennedy legacy.

Patriarch Joseph Kennedy Sr., the father of John, Bobby and Ted, first sculpted that legacy three generations ago. His political clout helped Franklin Delano Roosevelt win the presidential nomination in 1932 and usher in the New Deal. John Kennedy's public service idealism in the 1960s drew an entire generation of inspired young people into politics. His invocation of a New Frontier restored the country's optimism about itself and led directly to a man landing on the moon nine years after he was elected. Robert Kennedy broadened the legacy into to a deep compassion for the disenfranchised. And then Ted Kennedy struggled for 46 years to make the Kennedy legacy a permanent piece of America's superstructure.

"The younger brothers Bobby and Ted were infected by one particular aspect of John, which was his idealism. . . . Bobby was the suffering idealist. And Ted became over time the pragmatic idealist," said Joe Klein, a columnist with *Time* magazine. Generally, Americans are much more familiar with the enormous toll the task of being the surviving Kennedy brother took on Ted than with his own contributions to that legacy. Chappaquiddick, numerous affairs, drunken outings, and arrogant tirades most defined Ted Kennedy during a long fall from grace during the 1970s and 1980s. In the 1990s he was dismissed as an arcane throwback to old-school liberalism, out of touch with today's politics.

A worshipful mystique forever surrounds his slain brothers, despite their flaws, but Teddy lived long enough for the nation to see a Kennedy at his best and at his worst. Despite tabloid headlines and the sneers of conservative pundits, though, he still managed to keep the Kennedy legacy relevant. And today, it seems we are in another Kennedy moment. The traditional liberalism he has long stood for has made a comeback. In his last months, standing ovations in the Senate, honary degrees, endless expressions of personal appreciation and knighthood were what defined Ted Kennedy. For 50 years, in a life filled with tragedies, embarrassments, controversy and triumph, he has done the one thing his brothers never got the chance to do: He persevered.

Perseverance may well be Edward Kennedy's crowning contribution. He was the only real constant in the half-century construction of the Kennedy legacy. In stubbornly keeping on, he managed to keep alive something many of JFK's and then Bobby's contemporaries thought died with those men in the 1960s. "When Bobby was killed, my generation was almost critically wounded," Senator Walter Mondale said five years after that night. "As a matter of fact, I don't know, we may never get over it." What those kinds of sentiments about JFK and Bobby deny is all the good that's been done in their names since. More than anyone else, Ted took their deaths and tried to alchemize something positive out of them. For 49 years, Ted's guiding purpose was to keep aflame the torch of sacrifice, optimism and public service that JFK first lit in 1960. What they dreamed, he built, law by law. And he helped by legions of people inspired by his brothers, an entire Kennedy Generation.

Yet in the Kennedy pantheon, Ted is still the overlooked son, "the runt of the litter," "the baby of the family," the one who has never quite risen to the stature of his martyred brothers. It may be finally time to rethink that legacy. John and Robert captured the country's imagination, but it was Ted who has most improved people's reality. If Ted himself had ever been elected president, his influence would not have lasted so long. In many ways, because of his longevity and single-minded dedication to the memory of his brothers, Ted became a greater politician and left a greater legacy than either John or Bobby. John always called Ted the best politician of the family. In nearly five decades of behind-the-scenes Senate work, he finished much, though not all, of his brothers' unfinished dreams. "This is the most consequential legislative career in the country's history,"[6] said Thomas Oliphant, who as a correspondent and columnist for the *Boston Globe* has chronicled Kennedy's career. "It probably had more impact on more people than many presidents. In actual, measurable impact on the lives of tens of millions of working families, the elderly and the needy, Kennedy belongs in the same sentence with Franklin Roosevelt."

Whether you agree with Kennedy or not, he made flesh the progressive idealism of John and Bobby—and he made that idealism last. Back in 1998 political commentator Molly Ivins told biographer Adam Clymer that, "To tell the truth, Ted Kennedy has had a greater impact on this country than either of his famous brothers."[7] No other Kennedy can claim a 47-year legacy. Few senators can, either—he was the third-longest-serving senator in the history of the chamber. JFK had his 1,000 days in the White House. RFK had his 82 days on the campaign trail. Ted Kennedy's days in the Senate numbered more than 17,000. Political columnist David Shribman put it this way: "His brothers' words are in large letters on the sides of buildings and in the hearts and memory of a nation. But the youngest brother is the fine-print Kennedy. His words are in the fine print of the nation's laws."[8]

Kennedy cast more than 15,000 votes and wrote more than 2,500 bills. His fingerprints are on most of the major social programs that have been launched in the last 40 years. "He has done more for human happiness than anyone in Congress," said Carol Chodroff, a human rights attorney who works closely with Kennedy. He made his maiden speech in the Senate in support of the Civil Rights Act of 1964, which outlawed segregation in theaters, restaurants, hotels, swimming pools, libraries and public schools. He continued as a strong advocate for civil rights during the 1960s, 1970s, 1980s, 1990s and the current decade, helping to ensure passage of the Voting Rights Act and substantially improving the rights of the handicapped, women in the workplace, immigrants and refugees. He introduced the bill that created the Martin Luther King Jr. holiday. He got 18-year-olds the right to vote.

He campaigned for universal health insurance for 30 years, and from his hospital bed last year was orchestrating efforts to pass a bipartisan health-care reform plan in early 2009. Along the way toward his elusive goal he dramatically increased cancer research funds, created portable health insurance for workers, hammered through a patient's bill of rights and instituted closer government supervision of health maintenance organizations.

The mountain of achievements he compiled or played a significant part in include the creation of Medicare, the family and medical leave bill, national service legislation, worker retraining laws, freedom of access to abortion clinics, the lifting of the abortion gag rule, women's health legislation including fetal tissue research, and student loan reform. Ted Kennedy helped create

Meals on Wheels for senior citizens. He won greater justice for Native Americans, created a host of programs to combat hunger in the United States and abolished the poll tax. His immigration bill in the 1960s changed the very complexion of America, replacing a black-white divide with a multi-hued diversity of immigrants. He also had a strong history of gun control efforts—including early support for the Brady bill and opposition to the National Rifle Association dating from 1968.

His causes were large and small and crossed party lines. Working closely with President George W. Bush, he pushed through the controversial No Child Left Behind law intended to improve standards at public schools. In the 1990s, he and Republican Orrin Hatch cosponsored a bill to give health insurance to nine million uninsured children. Hatch and Kennedy rewrote the country's sentencing laws, ending parole in the federal prison system. In the 1980s, he and Republican senator Alan Simpson crafted immigration reform together. He and Senator John McCain did it again in the 1990s. He forged a balanced budget bill, helped Ronald Reagan deregulate the airlines and single-handedly blocked the confirmations of two Republican nominees to the Supreme Court, G. Harrold Carswell and Robert Bork.

Some have called him the Imperial Senator who ran a kind of shadow government out of the Senate. His involvement in foreign affairs, for example, was little known but broad. It was his activism that pushed the world toward a condemnation of apartheid in South Africa. He was the one who initiated the sanctions that eventually forced the end of second-class citizenship for blacks in that country. *New York Times* journalist Adam Clymer said Kennedy's influence "has extended from Vietnam to the Soviet Union, from Bangladesh to Chile, from Biafra to China, from South Africa to Ireland."[9]

His persistence kept the Kennedy flame burning long and bright enough to hand the torch off to Barack Obama. "I would not be sitting here as a presidential candidate had it not been for some of the battles that Ted Kennedy has fought," Obama said in one of his campaign speeches. "I stand on his shoulders." More than anything, the sanctity of that torch was the reason Ted Kennedy was so determined to make it to Denver. "He wanted to be here to demonstrate that this was another epic moment in the history of this country, when there was a real passing of the torch to a new generation," his son Patrick said. After bearing the torch for so long, Ted Kennedy had come to own it, and he wasn't going to let anyone else pass it along.

★ ★ ★

Many of the people who heard Kennedy's speech in Denver believed they were witnessing the last major address a Kennedy would ever give at a national convention. The events of 2009 would only serve to confirm that a fascinating chapter in America's political and cultural life was coming to a close. On August 11, 2009, Ted's sister Eunice Shriver, the founder of the Special Olympics, passed away at the age of 88, followed by Ted himself less than a month later. An endless stream of politicos and commentators called Ted's death on August 25, 2009, the end of an era. With his father gone, Ted's son Patrick would decide to leave politics as well. And in early 2010, Ted's Senate seat was taken over by a Republican, Scott Brown, which meant that at the end of the same year, for the first time since 1946, there would be no Kennedy in Congress. Without Ted's stewardship, the Kennedys' direct role in the country's political life is clearly coming to an end. As a result, perhaps the real measure of the Kennedy legacy can finally be taken.

The brothers' three stories can be seen as essentially one now, each successive brother striving to fulfill the interrupted promise and finish the unfinished life of the brother before. This book is the story of the birth of that legacy three generations ago, how it was built, when it nearly died, what caused it to spark again, and to whom it is being passed. It's a story of a brotherhood, really, in four acts. Act I charts Joe Jr.'s influence on the brothers as they were growing up. Act II is the road to John F. Kennedy's inspiring presidency, as seen from Ted's front-row seat; Act II is also Robert Kennedy's five brief years as the family standard bearer, including his tenure in the Senate with his brother Ted and the memorable 82-day campaign that redefined what the Kennedy legacy was all about. And Act III is Ted's 40-plus years in the Senate as keeper of the flame. It is the story of how a flawed, sometimes self-destructive, death-haunted man forever embedded into the country's DNA the ethos of idealism treasured by all three brothers. In the final assessment, the last Kennedy brother, the one who was least likely to succeed, may have succeeded beyond any other.

ACT I

JOE, JACK, BOBBY AND TEDDY

1

THE BLOWTORCH

The way it worked was the old man would push Joe, Joe would push Jack, Jack would push Bobby, Bobby would push Teddy, and Teddy would fall on his ass.

—*Garry Wills,* The Kennedy Imprisonment

The House of Kennedy was built at the dinner table.

"One of my most vivid childhood memories is of our family gatherings around the table at dinnertime," Ted Kennedy recalled.[1] "Conversation was lively and interesting, prompted by questions from my mother and father about events of the day. With nine of us eager to impress our parents as well as one another, it was hard to get a word in unless you had something interesting to say."

The dining room was classroom as much as eating-place. One family friend remembers a map on the dining room wall that Joe Kennedy would unfurl to make geopolitical points to his children. The dining room was where Joe and Rose Kennedy first engaged their children's minds in politics and current affairs, where the nine siblings all struggled to carve out their unique roles within the family hierarchy. It was also where their competitive instincts were honed, their rivalries were worked out and the ties that bound them so tightly to each other were rewrapped nightly. It was a verbal bath for visitors, a nonstop bull session supercharged with curiosity, energy and enthusiasm. Charles Spalding, a friend of John's who was often invited to dinners with the family, summed it up this way: "You watched these people go through their lives and just had a feeling that they existed outside the usual laws of nature; that there was no other group so handsome, so engaged. There was endless action . . . endless talk . . . endless competition, people drawing each other out and pushing each other to greater lengths. It was as simple as this: the Kennedys had a feeling of being heightened and it rubbed off on people who came in contact with them. They were a unit. I remember thinking to myself that there couldn't be another group quite like this one."[2]

Seventeen years separated Joe Jr., the oldest, from Teddy, the youngest, and the sheer number of children—enough to field a baseball team—required a mealtime battle plan. By the time Teddy was old enough to join the family for dinner, Rose had divided her brood into two distinct tiers. The younger children—Teddy, Pat, Jean and Bobby—had an earlier mealtime at the little table. Eunice was the swing child—sometimes she ate at the little table, sometimes the big. She became a kind of pivot for the family, swinging back and forth between the older and the younger and between the boys and the girls as well. She was at home in either subtribe, equally proficient with dolls and dress-up as with tennis and sailing. Though Rosemary was the oldest girl, she joined the young children's table, too, where Rose felt she would be more comfortable because of her developmental disabilities. Rosemary was slower than the other warp-speed Kennedys, and at the time the family believed her to be retarded, though evidence now suggests she had a mental illness of some sort, perhaps severe depression.

The older children ate later at the big table with the adults. "These three—Joe Junior, Jack and Kick—were like a family within a family, a charmed triangle," said one Kennedy friend. Kathleen had been nicknamed "Kick" when she was a small child because her exuberant personality reminded her father of a high-spirited pony. "They were the pick of the litter, the ones the old man thought would write the story of the next generation." Historian Doris Kearns Goodwin called them "the golden trio." While they were growing up, the younger children of the little table lived forever in the shadow of the children of the big, a status not altogether unwelcome, especially for Teddy. The intense pressure Joe Sr. put on his children to succeed was somewhat deflected by the older kids, allowing Ted and the other young ones to fly a little lower under the radar.

The ritual of the family meal took precedence over everything—schoolwork, sports, play and friends. Dinner started at a fixed time every night, and Rose broached no tardiness. If a child was late, as Jack often was, he missed a course. The children all stood when Rose made her entrance, and remained standing until she had taken her place. A cook and maid prepared the meals; a butler and the family waitress served them. Sometimes the Kennedys went through 20 quarts of milk a day. Rose posted news items on a bulletin board and children were expected to bone up on them before dinner. Joe Kennedy "would always assign a subject—Algeria, for example—to one child and instruct him to find out all he could on the subject," said one of Jack's personal secretaries. "Then he would tell the other children to do the same so they could question the first one who made his report and see how much he really knew. Both father and mother tried to develop alert minds in their children by giving them mental exercise."[3]

"We learned early that the way to be an active part of dinner conversation was to have read a book, to have learned something new in school, or, as we got older, to have traveled to new places," said Ted. "Our parents opened our nine young minds to the world that way, and it's been a wonderful lifelong gift."[4]

"I can hardly remember a mealtime," Bobby Kennedy reflected, "when the conversation was not dominated by what Franklin Roosevelt was doing or what was happening in the world." During World War I, a friendship had sprung up between the two men when Joseph Kennedy, an assistant general manager of Bethlehem Steel, started doing business with Roosevelt, who was assistant secretary of the Navy at the time. Kennedy was an early supporter of Roosevelt for the presidency, seeing in him not the radical socialist revolutionary many people feared, but rather an energetic reformer who saw just what changes the country needed to lift itself out of the Depression. Kennedy also supported Roosevelt's early stance against involving America in the troubles brewing in Europe, but that early agreement, and their friendship, would dissolve as Hitler became more and more of a threat and Roosevelt girded the country for war.

Joe would bring home politicians, scholars, actors and other leading lights to talk to his children at the dinner table. Charles Lindbergh came to dinner, as did Henry Luce, owner of *Time, Life* and *Fortune,* and his wife, Clare Booth Luce, a celebrated journalist and playwright. Mrs. Luce came away with a particularly memorable impression of the Kennedys. "Where else but in Gothic fiction," she wrote, "where else among real people, could one encounter such triumphs and tragedies, such beauty and charm and ambition and pride and human wreckage, such dedication to the best and lapses into the mire of life; such vulgar, noble, driven, generous, self-centered, loving suspicious, devious honorable, vulnerable, indomitable people . . . no wonder the American public, their audience—for that matter much of the world—has been fascinated by them."[5]

One night the Kennedy kids quizzed Dorothy Tubridy, a visitor from Ireland, about their Irish heritage—culture, painting, writing and geography. "It was very stimulating, very interesting conversation because they were all terribly intelligent and well educated and very enthusiastic about everything," Tubridy recounted.[6] "It was Joe's idea to expose his young brood to men and women of accomplishment, hoping, I think, that their elements of greatness would be seen and studied by the children," said Supreme Court Justice William O. Douglas, a friend of Kennedy's.[7] Joe was so proud of his dinner table salon he even had the gall to invite Gloria Swanson, Hollywood's most celebrated actress, to dine with his wife and children at the same time he was conducting a well-documented affair with her. Rose handled the occasion with her usual stoic denial that anything was ever amiss in her marriage, treating Swanson as if she were merely a glamorous business associate.

Joe encouraged his children to stand up for their own opinions and ideas and to argue against his at the table. "He encouraged them to thoroughly discuss why they felt certain ways, and he encouraged them to disagree with him,"[8] recalled Jack's friend Lem Billings. He wanted the children to develop their own views and backbones. He would carefully explain both sides of some great issue of the day, and his view on the issue, and when he was finished, the boys all felt free to disagree, respectfully. "He never wanted them to agree with him," said Billings.

Joe set up each of his children with a million-dollar trust fund, according to Lem, "because he wanted them to be independent [so they] could thumb their nose at him when they came into their money." "The truth is that they couldn't possibly be around the old man without being interested in damn near everything," said one dinner-table visitor.[9] A family friend added, "It wasn't like any other dinner table."[10]

If one of the children's friends at the table interjected, however, Joe often cut them off cold. The children's friends were welcome in the house, but their opinions at the dinner table were ignored. The Kennedy family was a closed circle. Joe bred an us-against-the-world mentality into his children in reaction to the prejudice he'd encountered as a Catholic in an old-money Protestant town. Joe was still treated as an outsider despite his massive wealth. He was once turned down for a country club membership because he was Catholic, and the hurt lingered. "The origin of the Kennedy sense of family is the holy land of Ireland, priest-ridden, superstitious, clannish," wrote Gore Vidal. "It flourished a powerful sense that the family unit is the only unit that could withstand the enemy, as long as each member remained loyal to the others, regarding life as a joint venture between one generation and the next."[11]

The sexism often associated with the Kennedy brothers was taught at the dinner table, as well. Joe usually ignored Rose's questions at dinner, too.

Though the family matriarch led the table salons when Joe was gone, often focusing on geography to take advantage of her deep love of travel, she played a supporting role when Joe was home. Joe just wasn't as interested in the opinions of his daughters, or Rose, as much as he was in the views of his four boys. "He paid more attention to the boys," the Kennedys' nurse, Louella Hennessy, remembers.[12] "The father liked to get together with the older boys, and he'd draw the details of their peccadilloes out of them, and they'd all laugh," a friend of Ted's recalls. "The old man kept track of everything they did. If he sensed something, if he had some kind of clue but not the story complete, he'd pretend he knew all about it and more often than not he'd worm the rest out of them fast enough," said another.[13]

The Kennedy compound at Hyannis Port, Massachusetts, faces the sea rather than the village, creating a private Kennedy peninsula on Nantucket Sound, walled off from the world by a ten-foot hedge. Hyannis Port itself has no city center, no geography of community, and the only pier belongs exclusively to the Kennedys. The cluster of clapboard houses is more an outpost than a town, a "faraway nearby" kind of place that shares the stunning geography of Cape Cod but remains isolated from it all the same. Joe Kennedy wanted it that way. He taught his children that the standards and measures of the Kennedy family itself were the only ones that mattered. His fortress of solitude was a self-contained training compound for competition against the Brahmin world.

It was also a bastion of masculinity, punctuated by touch football games on the compound's sprawling lawns, sailing contests in Nantucket Sound, marathon tennis matches and open-sea swimming. Joe Jr., Jack, Bobby and Ted ruled the household like brother kings, and competed like them, too. Right behind Joe Sr. as a motivating force was Joe Jr., his oldest son. The competition within the family to live up to Joe and the older siblings was fierce.

Many aspects of the Kennedy brothers' personalities show the influence of the older siblings as much if not more than the parents' because Rose and Joe Kennedy were away a lot when the boys were growing up. The older children, Joe, Jack and Kathleen, taught the younger children swimming, sailing, tennis and studying. They were often godparents for the younger children, as well, an unusual arrangement in Catholic families. Jack Kennedy, at age 14, wrote home from school when Teddy was born. "Dear Mother, It is the night before exams so I will write you Wednesday. Lots of Love. P.S. Can I be Godfather to the baby?" Teddy kept the letter framed on his office wall.

Joe Jr. became a kind of substitute parent for all of the children. He was clearly the favorite of Joe Sr. and Rose, the very best their parents could have hoped for in a child. He was 6 feet 2 inches tall with movie star looks and a strapping, athletic build. His dark blue eyes pulsed with vitality, and everything he pursued, he pursued to the hilt, especially his role as big brother to eight. "You know I'm the oldest of my family," Joe once explained in all earnestness to a friend. "And I've got to be an example for a lot of brothers and sisters." Jack thought Joe's principal contribution to the Kennedy legacy was his brotherly love. "I have always felt that Joe achieved his greatest success as the oldest brother," Jack once said. "Very early in life he acquired a sense of responsibility towards his brothers and sisters, and I do not think that he ever forgot it. He would spend long hours throwing a football with Bobby, swimming with Teddy and teaching the younger girls how to sail. . . . I think that if the Kennedy children amount to anything now or ever amount to anything, it will be due more to Joe's behavior and his constant example than to any other factor. He made the task of bringing up a large family immeasurably easier for my father and mother, for what they taught him he passed on to us and their teachings were not diluted through him but strengthened."[14]

In her memoirs, Rose wrote, "If you bring up the eldest son right, the way you want others to go, that is very important, because the younger ones watch him. . . . If he comes in and shakes hands with the guests, the others will watch him in the doorway and they'll come in and do the same thing. If he works at his studies and his sports until he is praised, then the others will follow his example."[15]

There was a unique bond between the oldest and the youngest, father-to-son in nature. Joe would hoist Teddy up on his shoulders when he saw him, and shower him with kisses like a parent would. He would always visit Teddy's room first when he got back from school, and he decided to call the family's new sixteen-foot sloop *The Teddy*. "My brothers, in addition to my parents, were the most important influences in my life . . ." Ted said privately to a friend. "I think of my brothers every day."[16]

As they were growing up together in Brookline and Boston, the four Kennedy brothers quickly staked out distinct roles that would stamp them for the rest of their lives. In short, Joe Jr. was the family's star, Jack its wit, Bobby its soul and Ted its laugh. Joe was the most combative of the four, Jack the most reflective, Bobby the most intense and Teddy the most agreeable. Joe lapped up politics; Jack, history; Bobby, religion; and Ted the company of others. "Joe Jr. could tell you all about Franklin Roosevelt's cabinet, Jack Kennedy about Sir Walter Raleigh and Marlborough, Bobby about the lives of saints and their feast days," said Richard Mahoney, author of *Sons and Brothers: The Days of Jack and Bobby Kennedy*. Ted, with his easygoing gregariousness, made everyone smile.

"Since Bobby was less outgoing, he and his father tended to have quiet conversations," said Hennessey.[17] "Even at thirteen and fourteen, Bobby was a deep-thinking boy and very close to his mother. Then Teddy would come in and the atmosphere in the room would completely change, for Teddy was like the sunshine, lighting up everything in sight and keeping his father young. Through the corridors, you could hear them laughing as Teddy jumped up and down on his father's bed until he was exhausted." "He always seemed to be laughing," said sister Eunice Kennedy Shriver. "He was just constantly cheerful."[18]

★ ★ ★

When Ted Kennedy was six years old, Joe Jr. deliberately threw him out of a sailboat into Nantucket Sound when he didn't answer the command "jib." Ted was too young to understand what a jib was, but that didn't matter in the competitive brotherhood in which he grew up. Teddy wasn't quite sure he would survive in the chilly water, but Joe dove in and tossed him back into the boat. "And then he told me not to tell my parents," said Ted. "Which I didn't. I certainly wouldn't risk the wrath of an older brother."[19]

When Bobby Kennedy was three and a half years old, he also went sailing with some of his brothers and sisters on Nantucket Sound. All of a sudden, he decided to jump into the water himself and go for a swim, something he hadn't yet learned how to do. He hadn't needed any push from Joe, who pulled him back into the boat. Then Bobby jumped in again, determined to teach himself to swim or die trying. Jack Kennedy, who had watched from shore, a bit aloof to the goings-on, used to love to tell the story, adding the observation: "It either showed a lot of guts, or no sense at all, depending on how you looked at it."

When Jack once lost a racing contest out on the sound while Joe Sr. watched from his second-story porch, known in family lore as the bullpen, Jack "caught a half hour lecture from the 'old man' on our return to shore," said a friend who had crewed for Jack. "There was no sense, he claimed, in going into a race unless you did your damnedest to win, an endeavor at which we had failed miserably. He was really angry with us."[20]

From the earliest ages, Joe entered the children in the town's swimming and sailing races and expected them to win. "The big thing we learned from Daddy: Win, don't come in second or third, that doesn't count, but win, win, win," said Ethel.[21] Joe was careful, however, to enter his children in different age categories in local contests so they didn't swim against each other. "He didn't like his children to be second best," said Lem Billings, a close friend of Jack's.[22] "Of course, the children were aware of this constant pressure. They knew that everything he did was because he loved them . . . so they automatically felt that they wanted to win." Joe's children were expected to remain stoical about setbacks, suppressing tears when things didn't go their way. Jack, Joe and Kick began semisarcastically spouting a family motto: "Kennedys never cry."

The competitive spirit had its downside, of course. Though their fierce drive to win at all costs was usually aimed outside the village of Kennedy, Joe Jr. and Jack engaged in such a fierce rivalry for supremacy within the family that it frightened the other siblings at times. Joe was the golden child, but he often bullied the second-oldest son, who endured a sickly childhood and retreated into books when he couldn't keep up with the pace Joe set. Joe had a quick temper and an aggressive streak. The other children were more afraid of him than of their father, and only Jack dared challenge his authority, and he did so at his peril. Hank Searls recalls a particularly vivid case study. When Joe Jr.'s favorite meal, roast beef and orange meringue, were served for dinner, Searls remembers Joe Jr. "would flash the grin at a maid, and ask for his piece early, just to look at it. It would be placed on display on his plate. One noon, Jack snatched it, stuffed it into his mouth, and took off at a dead run. With Joe in pursuit, he dived off the breakwater into Lewis Bay. Joe waited, in implacable anger, until his brother finally emerged, shivering with cold, and then there was a free-swinging brawl, for keeps. The lesson was clear to Jack: To embarrass young Joe before an audience was a dangerous affair."[23] In another episode, the two brothers raced around the block on their bicycles in opposite directions, coming directly at each other at the finish. Neither brother was willing to peel off, so the two crashed head-on. Joe walked away uninjured; Jack ended up with 28 stitches.[24]

Jack eventually conceded the spot of stronger, bolder and more powerful to his brother, but he never conceded smarter. Jack had scored higher on an IQ test when he was very young, though even Rose, when confronted with the numbers, still insisted that her perfect Joe was smarter. Because of his troublesome back and his frequent illnesses, including a brutal bout of scarlet fever, Jack developed an interior life that his brother Joe didn't have, losing himself in stories about knights and sailing ships and heroes of all stripes. Later his father encouraged both his sons to publish their Harvard theses as books, but only Jack actually did. *Why England Slept*, an analysis of England's slowness to arm against the threat of Hitler, was published when he was all of 23, and became a national best seller.

Jack told James M. Cannon of *Newsweek* magazine that his older brother "set an example in an atmosphere which meant pressure. Whatever there was in me, that pressure helped to bring it out. He set a standard of activity and commitment. I followed. In college I had something of a mediocre record, you might say, until that first book. The book, which I might well not have written except for pressure to do well, brought out latent ability that I had. . . . So if you say what was Joe's influence, it was pressure to do your best. Then the example that Joe and I had set put pressure on Bobby to do his best. The pressure of all of the others on Teddy came to bear so that he had to do his best. It was a chain reaction started by Joe, that touched me and all my brothers and sisters."

But Teddy was held to a different standard by his father. All his life, he heard this father admonish Joe, Jack and Bobby that they could do better, harshly criticizing them if they failed to live up to their potential. He pushed Teddy, too, but he was also much more forgiving of Teddy's lapses and faults. Ted remembers how often his father told him what a smart kid he was, always encouraging him and complimenting him more than he ever complimented Joe, Jack and Bobby. Yet in comparison to his brothers Ted always felt inadequate. Along the way, Ted concluded that, although his father loved his company and sunny disposition, Joe Sr. didn't think Ted had as much serious intellectual potential as his brothers did, and therefore wasn't worth pushing as hard. In a memorial book about his father called *The Fruitful Bough*, Ted wrote, "Dad wanted us to be natural, and able to smile no matter how tough things were. He wouldn't let any of his children feel sorry for himself, and expressed his frequent dislike of 'sour-pusses.' Yet he was also quick to scold a child who tried to smile too readily, or to charm his way through life. 'Remember,' he would say, 'a smile and a dime can only get you a ride on a streetcar. You are going to need a lot more than that to get somewhere in life.'"

All three younger brothers felt inadequate in comparison to their older brothers. Yet there is no evidence their father had anything but the highest regard for all of them, and a fondness for Teddy that was visceral and real. Joe Kennedy genuinely expected all four sons to be president. He gloated that he would outdo the Adams family, which had only two presidents. When Joe Jr. was born, his maternal grandfather "Honey Fitz" Fitzgerald, former mayor of Boston, told a reporter: "Well, of course, he is going to be President of these United States . . . his mother and father have already decided." At the time, most of Joe's contemporaries thought his boasts preposterous. But if it hadn't been for Joe Kennedy's outsized dreams for them, his sons certainly wouldn't have risen to the heights they did. Ted Kennedy put it this way: "He was this extraordinary figure that was trying to keep the blowtorch on you in terms of your own kind of abilities and was quite willing to point out your deficiencies, and challenge you to do better."[25]

The Kennedy brothers are unique in American history, just as Joe predicted they would be. The three brothers who survived World War II all ran for president, just as Joe had hoped. Each served in the Senate, and each made a permanent mark on the country, through both triumph and tragedy. No other members of the illustrious family have risen to the heights of political achievement as these three brothers. Why was it these three succeeded above all others? The short answer is that behind these Kennedys burned the unrelenting ambition of their unique, driving father, who put their futures above his own. "In my book he is the greatest practicing psychologist," said Jean's husband, Steve Smith. "He had focus all the time, way ahead of things, even in his hopes."[26] Joe gave his sons the drive, courage, money and open doors they needed to make history. Certainly other sons of the great men of their day had opportunities equal to the ones they had, and the wealth as well. Franklin and Teddy Roosevelt's sons surely did, to cite one example, but who has heard of any of them? Or Winston Churchill's sons—why didn't any of them rise to the heights their father did? Historian Goodwin points out that the second generation of a wealthy family usually squanders what the first gained, too spoiled by their own good fortune to maintain the hunger throughout their lives that gave the strivers before them their edge. A father can pass on his wealth, but passing on his motivation, born of struggle and hardship, is a more challenging thing. But that wasn't the case with the Kennedy sons. The second generation was more driven and more accomplished than the first. The Kennedy brothers were able to somehow defy the rule of the rich. "Joe gave them a gene that pushed them," said Ben Bradlee, the former *Washington Post* editor who was close friends with Jack. "Give the old man some credit." From a vantage point of 50 years of hindsight, in a country awash in Kennedys descended from Joe and Rose, the patriarch's transplanted ambition appears to be the secret ingredient that made John, Bobby and Ted into history-makers.

"Practically everything can be achieved with will power and a dedicated heart," Joe told an interviewer years later, after his son was president. "Failure usually results when one lets his guard down. I can truthfully say that my wife and I have never forgotten our sacred obligation to our family. And that's about all."[27]

2

AN ARMY OF MOTHERS

My babies were rocked to political lullabies.

—*Rose Kennedy*

Saturday night in the Kennedy house was weight-check night. Rose Kennedy had all her sons and daughters line up at the scale and, one by one, she logged their weights on index cards. If scrawny Jack's weight was down two weeks in a row, Rose gave him larger portions at mealtime and often added extra fats, sugars and creams to his diet. If Rosemary was just a tad too plump, she cut back the sweets and breads. Gaining weight was a physical expression of a lack of will and discipline in Rose's book, not a hereditary condition. She'd been able to shed every pound she gained after each of her nine pregnancies, and she expected her children to look lean and sleek, just as Joe wanted. After dinner, each child was allowed one indulgence: They could each choose a single sweet from a giant box of chocolates she kept near her bed.

Rose also kept a record of her children's illnesses, doctor checkups, eye exams, inoculations and orthodontist appointments on her 3 × 5 cards. (The famous Kennedy smile was more a product of teeth straightening than good genes.[1]) Her card file became one of the best-known, most-imitated child management gimmicks in the world, thanks to Joe, who talked national publications into doing stories on the Kennedy family and its unique child-rearing program. *Reader's Digest* described the Kennedys as "one of the most interesting family groups in the world."[2] *Parents Magazine* called

them "the natural expression of a fundamentally happy family, each young-
ster a personality at peace with himself." Rose called her cards and her system not a matter of "American efficiency," but of "Kennedy desperation."[3]

"I looked upon child rearing as a profession," Rose wrote in her memoirs, "and decided it was just as interesting and just as challenging as anything
else and that it did not have to keep a woman tied down and make her dull or
out of touch. . . . [I saw it] not only as a work of love and duty, but as a profession in the world and one that demanded the best that I could bring it."
She consulted journals on child rearing, brought in experts and adhered
strictly to their recommendations. She studied the books, pamphlets and
magazines of the day that tried to inject motherhood with a kind of scientific
exactitude.[4] *The New Housekeeping,* then a best-selling publication, gave her
the idea for the index cards.

What the indomitable Rose Kennedy contributed to the Kennedy legacy
was rigid Catholic discipline. Her sons wrestled this work ethic into their
personalities and used it to achieve their father's grand visions for them.
Telling them they must succeed was one thing; showing them how to do so
step by step was another. Joe was an attentive, involved, loving parent, more
so than Rose in many ways. And maids, nannies and servants did much of
the nitty gritty of mothering, keeping Rose and her children at somewhat of
an emotional distance from each other. But Rose is the one who developed
the manners, organizational skills and behind-the-scenes habits of hard
work and diligence that carried her sons to such great heights. "She was a
tough, constant, minute disciplinarian with a fetish for neatness and order
and decorum," said Jack's friend Lem Billings.[5] Joe was the strategist in the
family, Rose the tactician. "For all of us, Dad was the spark, and Mother was
the light of our lives," said Ted. "He was our greatest fan; she was our greatest
teacher."[6]

"Mother was a strict disciplinarian," Ted remembered. "Lunch was at
one, prompt. If you were late, you missed the course. Every Thursday we
went to the public library to get books. We had tennis lessons, swimming
lessons, all of us for seven years. . . . You had to be in the house when the
lights went on. We had to pick our clothes. We had to appear at a meal table
five minutes early. We were computerized at an early age, but fortunately by
a very compassionate computer."[7] Rose believed that if she ingrained habits
of mind and body deeply enough in her children those habits would last forever, and nothing could uproot them. Certainly that steely-eyed discipline
saw Ted Kennedy through many of his rougher seas, and even in his seventy-
sixth year was still very much in evidence. In the summer of 2008, Kennedy
continued to work like a well-organized ox while recovering from his brain

tumor. Instead of simply resting and recuperating in a hospital bed, he set up shop in Hyannis Port, where he met every day with aides, issued dozens of statements, kept in touch with colleagues in the Senate, chaired meetings with staffers via videoconference and successfully pushed through several bills and amendments. "He gets more done from the Cape than most of us do in a week," said Alan Khazei, co-founder of City Year, a Boston-based youth community service group.[8] Over the years, colleagues and staffers say, no matter how many private complications Ted happened to be juggling, he had an extraordinary capacity, just like his mother did, to keep the trains running on time.

★ ★ ★

Rose packed her discipline with the moral muscle of the Catholic Church. Her faith was a real, palpable force throughout her 104 years, the thing that brought her back from her grief after each Kennedy tragedy, and the source of the service ethic she so deeply embedded in her children. No place meant more to her than St. Francis Xavier Catholic Church in Hyannis, with its heavy oak pews, rough-hewn stone walls, soaring ceilings and stained-glass stations of the cross. Rose went to church every day and twice on Sunday. A short drive from the house, St. Francis was the place where she retreated to recharge her spirituality and sustain herself through the hardest sorrow.

"I have come to the conclusion that the most important element in human life is faith," Rose said near the end of her life.[9] "If God were to take away all his blessings—health, physical fitness, wealth, intelligence—and leave me but one gift, I would ask for faith. For with faith in Him, in His goodness, mercy, love for me, and belief in eternal life, I believe I could suffer the loss of my other gifts and still be happy—trustful, leaving all to His in-scrutable Providence." Each meal, Rose would choose a different daughter or son to say grace. The children would march to church on Sunday at St. Fran-cis in their velvet-collar wool Chesterfield coats, prayer books and rosaries in hand. "We would talk about the sermon, what did the priest say and what the gospel was about when they got home at dinner," Rose remembered. "And if they didn't pay attention one Sunday they'd pay attention the next Sunday."[10]

"Every day we prayed at home or in church, and often both places," said Ted. "My sisters and brothers all attended formal classes in religion and re-ceived the sacraments in our church."[11] Through her faith, Rose instilled in her children a deep concern for others, especially those less fortunate. "My family's religious views also demanded dedication to the needs and concerns of the least among us, and my parents passed that gift of faith on to all of their children," said Ted. The faith Rose taught emphasized the message of service in the Gospel of Matthew: *For I was hungry and you gave me food, I was thirsty and you gave me drink, a stranger and you welcomed me, naked and you clothed me, ill and you cared for me, in prison and you visited me.* "That sense of community and compassion, the belief that we are all in this together," Ted Kennedy said, "has echoes in every moral system, whether religious or secular, and is at the heart of the great promise of America."[12]

Rose's devotion to her Catholic-inspired service ethic has been indelibly imprinted on the country through her sons and daughters. It's easy to hear an echo of Rose's social justice Catholicism in her son John's "ask not what your country can do for you, ask what you can do for your country" call for service in his inaugural address. Rose's concern for the least of her brothers infuses the Peace Corps, begun after John challenged students at the University of Michigan to do something for their less-fortunate counterparts in developing countries. During his presidential campaign, Bobby visited ghettos, Indian reservations and slums, preaching a gospel of service to "those who can't help themselves." Ted, in the summer of 2008, put the finishing touches on a national service bill he cobbled together with Republican senator Orrin Hatch of Utah. Service is an integral piece of the Kennedy legacy, and it's the piece that comes most directly and forcefully from Rose.

Many biographers and historians have made the case that the Kennedy legacy of self-destructive behavior, especially the womanizing, can be traced to Rose's strictness, her reserve, her absences and all the boarding schools her children attended. One book, *Reckless Youth,* went so far as to call her borderline abusive. But none of the children alive today share that view. When *Reckless Youth* came out in 1992, the surviving children felt they had to speak up. "Mother was a powerful and loving presence in our lives," Jean, Eunice, Pat and Ted wrote together in a *New York Times* editorial entitled "A Grotesque Portrait of Our Parents." She was "a deeply involved parent," they wrote, "a constant friend when we were growing up and an inspiring and gifted teacher who made American history come alive at the dinner table, in our trips to Plymouth Rock, the Old North Church and Concord Bridge. The dominant value that all of us continually felt in growing up was the importance of each of us in the family. Dad and Mother set high standards for us, and their love and support for each other and for us made those standards livable and reachable."

The book made much of a comment Jack uttered when he was nine years old as the children gathered on the front porch to say goodbye to their mother at the start of a three-week trip to California. "Gee, you're a great mother to go away and leave your children alone," Jack taunted.[13] He did resent her frequent trips away, often crying when she left, although such trips were not unusual for upper-class mothers in the 1920s. And Jack's natural temperament— informal, irreverent, playful—was the opposite of his mother's, so there was always some friction between the two. But in their editorial, the siblings pointed out that nowhere did the book quote the best-known phrase Jack Kennedy used to describe his mother when he was older, that she was the "glue that held our family together." "That is exactly what she was," the siblings wrote, "as anyone who knows anything about our family will attest." And Jack Kennedy said in later years that the best quality he inherited from his family was curiosity, which came directly from his mother. He began to join his mother on some of her trips when he was older, and told his friend Lem Billings that while she was traveling "her eyes were so bright and so gay and her enthusiasm so contagious that she could not help but attract everyone who came into contact with her."[14]

Rose did treat the boys differently from the girls, believing as most mothers believed at the time that a woman's highest ideal ought to be the betterment of her family. "A mother knows that hers is the influence which can make that little precious being to be a leader of men, an inspiration, a shining light in the world. Women may excel in business," she said. "They may be leaders of society. They may be famous beauties. But these goals are ephemeral. You have only to compare a woman who is a great beauty, a famous writer, or a renowned scientist twenty-five-years ago, and visit her now. But a woman engrossed in her family twenty-five-years ago, now sees them grown-up, fulfilling worthwhile goals, adding luster to her name. She feels still needed, still loved, still a vital part of life, and that is the important thing."[15]

Rose also treated Ted differently from her other sons. "I admit that with Teddy I did things a little differently than I did with the other children," Rose wrote in her memoirs.[16] "He was my baby and, I think every mother will understand this, I tried to keep him my baby." More than any of the children, Ted was the good son, doting on his mother as she had doted on him. As an adult, Ted spent much of his time at Hyannis Port rather than his own house on Squaw Island.[17] He attended diligently to all the mandates of being the last Kennedy son. It was Ted who made the most effort to visit his mother at the Kennedy getaway in Palm Beach. "Whenever he could, he got down here to see his mother," said James Connor, a Palm Beach police office who moonlighted for the Kennedys.[18] "I mean he would go out and party, don't get me wrong. But I mean this was usually after his mother had gone to bed. And he would bring girls to the damn house. But the Senator came down mainly to see his mother. I mean, he really loves his mother. He cherishes her. I mean, he's the baby."

Former *Washington Post* editor Ben Bradlee, a longtime friend of the Kennedy family, said Ted was so much younger than the other boys that not much was expected of him. Four sisters insulated Ted from the rough-and-tumble-competition between Jack and Joe. As a result, Ted was showered with affection, most of it from women. "It was like having an army of mothers around me," Ted said.[19] "While it seemed I could never do anything right with my brothers, I could never do anything wrong so far as my sisters were concerned." As a result of being treated with so much affection he learned to be sensitive to the emotional needs of those around him. Not expected to be the breadwinner of the family, or even one of its leaders, he was trained instead to be responsive to the emotional climate of any family situation. His role was to brighten the day, to respond to the needs of the women in the family when no other male did and to show the world compassion and empathy and goodwill. And he kept that role throughout his life. Ted was the "people person" of the family, the most emotionally intelligent brother. "He'd try to bring everyone together by making them laugh," Eunice said.[20] He was the good-natured grease that sometimes kept the whole Kennedy machinery from grinding its many gears to a halt.

But he could also be the most emotionally fragile, not having grown the armor for battle the older brothers did in their endless competitions. And there was a loneliness about Ted in his early years, friends say. Ted was transferred around to so many different private schools that humor became his only defense. "That was hard to take," he said of the many different schools. "I finally got through school where I spent some time trying to find out where the dormitory and gym were located."[21]

Ironically, loneliness was a quality all the younger Kennedy brothers shared, and it kept them close to each other. Ted said years later that he tried to hide his loneliness because his brothers had also gone to boarding school "and they were lonesome, too, so I shouldn't complain."[22] Each brother developed a fierce individuality as a consequence, but each was intimately dependent on the other brothers as well. "My brothers and sister were all away, and dad and mother were in New York," Ted said years later about his early years. "Bobby was the one who used to call me up to see how I was getting along. On the two or three weekends I was able to get off from school, if I couldn't go home, he'd spend the weekend with me. I'll never forget how we used to go to that big empty house at Cape Cod—just the two of us rattling around alone."[23] Friends say it was hard to know where one brother left off and the other began sometimes. John, Bobby and Ted were so dedicated to each other and to the family, and so involved with each others' lives over the years, it was as if they were one über person made up of three. "They were like a warrior force," historian Doris Kearns Goodwin remarked, "combining in one person all their persons' goals."[24]

Rose was gentler with Ted than she was with the other boys, but she also kept a tender place in her heart for her firstborn daughter, Rosemary. Rose's namesake child was mentally retarded, according to family members, although one doctor who treated her said she may have suffered from an undiagnosed mental illness, such as severe depression. "She lived with our family for many years, and caring for her became the responsibility of us all," Ted Kennedy wrote in *America Back on Track*. "We lived with her disabilities day in and day out, and tried to make sense of why some people are healthy and others, through no fault of their own, are not. My parents' intense love and care for Rosemary was a lifelong lesson for the rest of us."

When psychologists diagnosed retardation and recommended the family send her to an institution, both Rose and Joe recoiled at the idea. "What can they do in an institution that we can't do better for her at home—here with her family?"[25] So the Kennedys all pulled together and cared for Rosemary themselves—with the help of a special governess and private tutors. Rosemary had a profound impact on the whole family, giving them a center point for their us-against-the-world unity and imbuing the idea of "disability" with a kind of normalcy that was unique for its day. Her disability became a commonplace for the children, something that was just there, a part of every day. Rosemary was slowed by her handicap, not stopped. She played tennis with Rose, crewed the sailboat for her siblings, played Ping Pong with her brothers, painted pictures, even did complex arithmetic. Rose often called Jack and Joe Jr. home from Choate to take Rosemary to tea dances. She had learned to waltz and do the fox trot, thanks to hundreds of lessons, and Rose asked her sons to ask their friends to fill her dance card. When other boys weren't available, Jack danced with her willingly and graciously, sometimes for hours. Rosemary's diaries from 1936 to 1938 are those of a prominent socialite teenager's:

> Went to luncheon in the ballroom in the White House. James Roosevelt took us in to see his father, President Roosevelt. He said, "It's about time you came. How can I put my arm around all of you? Which is the oldest? You are all so big. . . ."
> Have a fitting at 10:15 Elizabeth Arden. Appointment dress fitting again. Home for lunch. Royal tournament in the afternoon.

Rosemary kept the family grounded, serving as a gentle reminder of the hardships endured by so many people outside the Kennedy bubble of privilege. Rose believed her children's compassion for the poor and underprivileged was sparked by their sister's struggles. "As I look back I realize that these experiences have informed some of my deepest interests as a senator," said Ted, including his lifelong fight to improve healthcare.[26] "As a young child I saw the way my older sister Rosemary had, you know, mental retardation. There was concern for her. But I also saw at that time what a loving and wonderful person she was, and how she was in so many ways, uh, almost gentler and tenderer [sic] and more loving even than other brothers and sisters. . . . I knew even as a young person about the challenges that she faced. . . . And that probably made a subtle and not-so-subtle impression on me . . . and a consciousness just about some of the mysteries, you know, in terms of healthcare."[27]

Yet Rose herself struggled with her Rosemary. "Our family was the perfect family—boys brilliant, girls attractive and intelligent, money, prestige, a young father and mother of intelligence, devoted, exemplary habits and successful in the education of the children," she once wrote in a candid moment in her diaries. "But God or 'destiny' just does not allow a family to exist which has all these star-studded adornments." And therefore, she concluded, God "left me a retarded child who can contribute nothing but must receive benefits rather than bestow."

The family kept the true nature of Rosemary's condition a secret from the outside world, explaining to friends that she was quieter and shier than the rest of the rambunctious brood. It was the norm in the 1920s and 1930s to treat the retarded with shame, keeping them institutionalized or out of sight. But there was another dynamic at work in the Kennedy family that made it hard to accept Rosemary's inability to improve. As Rosemary grew older, passing from adolescence to early adulthood, she was on a trajectory opposite that of the other striving Kennedys. As long as she made small improvements and experienced small victories in her efforts to keep up, she was applauded by the family. The Kennedys were all about striving against the odds, beating back the forces arrayed against them. Jack fought through his illnesses and was celebrated by the family. Rosemary did not. Rosemary was a plodder in a family of gazelles.

The sheer velocity of the Kennedy kids may have just overwhelmed her. When you were with the Kennedys, "life speeded up," said frequent visitor Lem Billings. Rose herself, in an effort to skirt past her husband's infidelities, and other family difficulties, kept in constant motion, using distraction to deny the dark and unpleasant aspects of her family and her life. In doing so she created a kind of "Go forward rather than delve deep" ethos that still persists among family members today. She stressed *doing,* rather than developing an inner life. In one unpublished interview, Rose suggested that Rosemary's condition was a no-go area, "an accident which I don't really discuss." Reporters interviewing Ted Kennedy were always cautioned: "Don't ask him anything too reflective." Bobby Kennedy Jr. often tells reporters: "I won't answer anything personal."

Rosemary's inability to keep up with the velocity of the other Kennedys began to leave her disoriented and frustrated, especially when her sisters started dating regularly. Rose never explained to Rosemary why she was not allowed to see boys alone without her brother Joe along as a chaperone. As her condition worsened in her twenties she began to throw tantrums that often turned into violent rages. Rosemary lost her sweet disposition, and "was upset easily and unpredictably," Rose wrote in her 1974 book, *Times to Remember.* She sometimes smashed objects and struck out at those around her.

The idea of Rosemary's retardation was acceptable to the family, but her mood swings and lack of forward progress apparently were not. It is that tendency to deny the darker aspects of reality, to claim some sort of immunity from them, that has cursed the Kennedy family over the years more so than a metaphysical hex. It was exactly that denial of the darker side that led to Joe Kennedy's decision to have Rosemary lobotomized. Modern science in the 1930s was lauding the surgical procedure's ability to cure mood disorders and calm problem patients, and Joe at least partially believed he might be able to make Rosemary's condition simply go away. But there also may have been a political component to Joe's decision, which he made without consulting Rose. Joe may not have wanted the liability of a mentally unstable daughter to hamper his sons' electability.

Two surgeons in Washington who had become the leading proponents of prefrontal lobotomies agreed to operate on Rosemary in the fall of 1941. In the only interview he ever gave on the subject, Dr. James W. Watts described to author Ronald Kessler how he performed the lobotomy.[28] Rosemary was sedated but not unconscious for the procedure. "We went through the top of the head," Watts recalled. "I think she was awake. She had a mild tranquilizer. I made a surgical incision in the brain through the skull. It was near the front. It was on both sides. We just made a small incision, no more than an inch." As Watts cut, the supervising surgeon, Walter J. Freeman, asked Rosemary to recite the Lord's Prayer or to sing "God Bless America" or to count backward, according to Kessler's account. "We made an estimate on how far to cut based on how she responded," Watts said. "I would make the incisions, and Dr. Freeman would estimate how much to cut as she talked. He talked to her. He would say that's enough." When she began to become incoherent, they stopped.

Rosemary was permanently incapacitated by the lobotomy, a now discredited medical procedure that is no longer used in this country. Unable to even feed herself after the operation, she was eventually sent to a care facility in Wisconsin, where she lived apart from the family for the rest of her life. She died in 2005. Barbara Gibson, Rose's personal assistant, said Rosemary's lobotomy permanently marked nine-year-old Teddy with the fear that something similar might happen to him if he disappointed his parents.[29] Rosemary's disappearance left him forever apprehensive, Gibson believed, "never letting himself become too close to anyone, carrying anger, fear, and guilt trapped inside his troubled heart."

Because of Rosemary's illness, aiding "very special children" became a cause for generations of Kennedys. Rose took it up first, then Eunice, Ted, Jean and now Ted's son Patrick. Eunice, the sister who spent the most time with Rosemary and often visited her in Wisconsin over the years, started the Special Olympics games for disabled athletes in 1968, persuaded by Rosemary's active early years that people with disabilities could do a lot more with their bodies than they were believed to be capable of at the time. The program originated on Eunice's front lawn, where she would gather together disabled children to exercise and play games, and is now the world's largest sports program. The Special Olympics has spread to more than 150 countries, with 2.25 million athletes and their families participating, aided by 500,000 volunteers and coaches. Eunice also inspired the establishment of President John F. Kennedy's Committee on Mental Retardation as well as the National Institute for Child Health and Human Development, and was a driving force for the creation of the Kennedy Institute of Medical Ethics at Georgetown and a similar institute at Harvard University. She also was founder of Community of Caring, a program to help prevent teen pregnancy and drug and alcohol abuse that serves more than 1,200 elementary, middle and high schools in 20 states and the District of Columbia. Rose's daughter Jean founded an international nonprofit organization, Very Special Arts, to allow people with disabilities to participate in the arts. Ted's son Patrick, a recovering alcoholic and depression sufferer, has crisscrossed the country championing the rights of the mentally ill. In 2008, he successfully pushed through a bill to put insurance coverage for the mentally ill on par with coverage for other illnesses, eliminating the higher deductibles and spending limits many people with depression or alcoholism faced.

By the time of her death in 1995, Rose had achieved an acceptance of what she saw as God's will concerning Rosemary. "God has sent these children for a special reason," she wrote in her diary. "To do work he cannot do through any other child." At Rose's funeral in Boston in 1995, her grandson

John F. Kennedy Jr. quoted his grandmother on the subject of Rosemary. "Grandma said, 'My vision is a world where mental retardation will be overcome ... where we will exalt and rejoice with parents of healthy, happy youngsters." Near the end of the service, John Jr. spoke of the peace Rose had achieved because of her faith over the course of a complicated, tragedy-strewn 104 years. He once again quoted his grandmother, who was quoting in turn from one of her favorite verses of Saint Paul. "I have fought the good fight, I have finished my course. I have kept the faith."

3

A LETTER FROM JOE

I hope when you grow up you will dedicate your life to trying to work out plans to make people happy instead of making them miserable, as war does today.

—*A letter from Joseph Kennedy to his son Ted,*
September 11, 1940

On the March day in 1938 when German troops crossed into Austria and wiped their southern neighbor from the map, Joseph P. Kennedy cabled his wife, Rose, and his children back in Boston, urging them to get to London as fast as they could. "Hurry that boat up," he wrote, "terribly anxious to see all especially you." Kennedy, the new ambassador to the Court of St. James, had just taken possession of the American Embassy in London the week before. He planned to bring the family over in three waves as soon as he could: His wife would bring Kathleen, Pat, Bobby, Jean and Teddy immediately. Two months later, Joe's chief secretary, Eddie Moore, would bring Rosemary and Eunice over after Rosemary's school term ended. When Joe Jr. graduated from Harvard later that spring, and Jack finished his sophomore year there, they would come over as well. They didn't know it at the time, but they were headed right into "the lion's mouth," as one reporter put it. The resulting collision of the Kennedys with history would turn one son into a hero, plant the seeds of a new political dynasty and give birth to the "ask not" ethos of public service that was to define the Kennedys for the next 50 years. It would also cost the patriarch his political career and the life of his oldest son.

Two days after Joe's cable, Hitler made a triumphant return to his former home of Vienna, adding seven million people to the German Reich without firing a shot. Mass arrests of Jews began almost immediately, while other Jews were forced to do menial labor, such as cleaning the toilets of the barracks where German troopers were quartered. Although the Treaty of Versailles forbade the union of Germany and Austria, all the Western democracies stood by as an emboldened Hitler began a yearlong march to world war.

But Rose and the children were too giddy with anticipation to pay much mind to the storm gathering directly in their path. For the Kennedys, 1938 was to be a grand European tour, filled with glittering balls, high teas and audiences with the queen. And London was as excited about the Kennedys as the Kennedys were thrilled to be coming. For weeks before their arrival, newspapers carried dozens of stories about the ambassador's charismatic clan, accompanied by adoring pictures of the nine Kennedy kids. When Rose arrived in the city in the middle of March with Kathleen and the four youngest Kennedys, they were treated like American royalty. Londoners on the street smiled and waved at the children and the press went mad over them. "The U.S.A.'s Nine-child Envoy," one headline declared. *Life* magazine wrote glowingly about the new ambassador's reception:

> His bouncing offspring make the most politically ingratiating family since Theodore Roosevelt's. Whether or not Franklin Roosevelt thought of it beforehand, it has turned out that when he appointed Mr. Kennedy to be Ambassador to Great Britain he got eleven Ambassadors for the price of one. Amazed and delighted at the spectacle of an Ambassadorial family big enough to man a full-sized cricket team, England has taken them all, including the extremely pretty and young-looking Mrs. Kennedy, to heart.[1]

The Kennedys took up residence in a six-story, 36-room mansion given to the United States by J. Pierpont Morgan. They began a year of living like kings, with 20 servants, an elevator and a fleet of cars. Determined to make the most of their time in England, the family stepped right into the whirlwind of high British society. The social season just getting started was dubbed the "last fling before the bombs fell," and, as a result, British aristocrats served it up with unprecedented abandon. As an ambassador, Joe Kennedy was automatically made a member of all the most exclusive British clubs, including the Royal Thames Yacht Club, the Athenaeum, the Harlequin Football Club, the Queen's Club, the Monday Luncheon Club, the Sunningdale Golf Club, the Phyllis Court Club and the International Sportsmen Club.[2] The Kennedys attended the Derby Race at Epsom Downs, the Royal

Ascot Race, Wimbledon, the Henley Rowing Regatta and the Goodwood Races. They dined with King George and Queen Elizabeth at Ascot. Their older children were invited to teas, balls, dances, lunch with Lady Astor, a visit with the Duke of Marlborough and a weekend at Sir James Calder's country house. The Kennedys and their children, who as Irish Catholics had met with years of snobbery and prejudice back in Protestant Boston, had arrived like they never had at home.

"It was a wonderful time for the two of us," Rose recalled in her diaries. "[S]o much excitement, so much anticipation, so much fun."[3] Rose called a weekend spent with the royal family in April at Windsor Castle "one of the most fabulous, fascinating" events of her life. At one point during the visit, Joe turned to his wife and said, "Rose, this is a helluva long way from East Boston." She barely mentions the grim politics of the time in her diaries for 1938 and 1939, nor does she voice any concerns for the safety of her children. She was more preoccupied with the grace notes of British etiquette, later describing the embassy years as "by far the happiest in my life."[4]

Bobby and Teddy, at 12 and 6 respectively, were too young to care much about either Hitler or high society. Instead, the boys explored London to the hilt, sailing boats in Hyde Park, riding their bikes on the city's stone terraces, playing chase in Kensington Gardens. Newspaper photographers snapped little Ted in all sorts of endearing cameos: walking his dog, Sammy, at the opening of the zoo; dressed up as a Puritan; snapping the guards at Buckingham Palace with an upside-down Brownie. The boys played with the princesses Elizabeth and Margaret at tea dances, and their favorite game involved tying messages onto balloons and setting them free, hoping for a response from faraway lands. They went to day school in London, first Sloane Street and then Gibbs. "I used to meet the boys at their school and walk them home," the Kennedys' nurse, Louella Hennessy, told Kennedy historian Doris Kearns Goodwin. "We'd walk through Hyde Park and they'd kick pebbles, the way boys do. Teddy was always so bubbly and happy, always wanting to talk. If I were with him alone, he'd hop and skip to get to the outside of the sidewalk so he could act like the man protecting the woman. If they were together, Bobby was always the more serious one, always explaining in detail what had happened that day."[5] Bobby and Teddy had six months together before their older brothers arrived, and the time forever bonded them. Hennessey remembers that "the boys had always been close, but in London they were together most of their free time. I could see that they truly liked each other, which is rare between brothers. So many siblings bicker and shut one another out from their games."[6] Bobby's intensity and Ted's easygoing nature were perfect compliments. When a classmate at Gibbs asked Teddy to be his best friend, Teddy told him he already had one, Bobby.[7] Ted always said that of all his brothers and sisters, he was closest to Bobby.

No one enjoyed that last year of peace more than the three older sisters, Kick, Rosemary and Eunice. Kick had a personality that could pierce the gloom of the foggiest of London days. Full of life and playful energy, Kick was the "sunshine" of the family, said one of her friends, Dinah Bridge. "Wherever she stood, there would be warmth, fun, gaiety and charm."[8] The Kennedy sisters, following Kick's carefree, irrepressible lead, made the town theirs. Much of their time was spent preparing for their formal coming-out parties and attending the debutante balls of dozens of other young society girls. They also played tennis with Spencer Tracy, overnighted at Windsor Castle with the queen and attended the premiere of *Wuthering Heights.*

Jack and Joe Jr. joined the clan in June of 1938, and Jack immediately set about conquering the ladies of London. "Kick's male friends marveled at Jack's easy conquests," Kathleen's biographer, Lynne McTaggart, wrote. "After he'd only been in London a few weeks, a hush fell over the Ritz one lunchtime when Jack Kennedy arrived. On his arm was a staggeringly beautiful woman, dressed in a gray two-piece dress, a hat perched jauntily on one side of her head. Jack introduced her around as Honeychild Wilder, the Cotton Queen of Louisiana, who had just arrived in England to promote the cotton industry."[9]

Not all the Kennedys were oblivious to the history unfolding all around them. Joe Jr., just graduated from Harvard, found Europe thrilling exactly *because* of the crises. While Jack and Kathleen plunged readily into British society, Joe Jr. found he had a harder time of it. His "manner seemed abrasive, and his humor uncomfortably sharp-edged," according to Kathleen's biographer.[10] "Joe was much more serious and had . . . *gravitas* about him," Hugh Fraser remarked. "He was the eldest boy in the family, and I think this weighed quite a lot with the Kennedys, who were sort of hierarchical."[11] He spent his first year out of Harvard crisscrossing the continent as an informal secretary for his father, sending back dispatches on all the tensest situations he could work his way into. He surveyed the American Embassy in Paris, traveled to Prague, Warsaw, Moscow, Leningrad, Scandinavia, Berlin and The Hague. Joe Jr. became the "Crisis Hunter" in the London papers. His father began to worry for his safety, but his pride in his son's courageous high spirits quickly trumped his concern.

In histrionic, shrieking speeches that spring and summer, Hitler made his case that tens of millions of Germans had been severed from the homeland by the Treaty of Versailles at the end of World War I. He intended to bring all these people back into the German fold, by force if necessary. As he began rattling his saber over Czechoslovakia that summer, threatening to take back a portion of the country he felt rightfully belonged to Germany, Rose took the family off to a villa at Eden Roc, near Cannes in the south of France, for two months. Joe and the older boys joined her in early August, reveling in "the blue Mediterranean and the sun-drenched sands, the casualness of people in a holiday mood, luncheons, teas, dinners and golf," which Joe Kennedy Sr. later recalled.[12] But by the end of August, the State Department was insisting that Kennedy return to his post, and Joe Sr. recognized that "the holidays were clearly over."

He was back in London in late September of 1938 just in time to hear Hitler set a deadline for war. The Führer demanded that the powers of Europe, which at the time meant Britain, Italy, France and Germany, come up with a satisfactory plan for the return of the Sudetenland region of Czechoslovakia, where three million Germans lived, by September 28, or he would invade. Hitler already had mobilized 1.5 million soldiers and begun conducting menacing troop movements along the border. He secretly planned to invade the Sudetenland on October 1, regardless of whether an agreement was reached.

France was committed by treaty to help Czechoslovakia if Germany invaded, and many members of Parliament in London, most particularly Winston Churchill, were urging Britain to follow if France declared war. On August 28, Churchill ringingly denounced Hitler's mobilization, promising that, if necessary, England would defend the "title deeds of mankind."

A sense of doom settled over the city as Prime Minister Neville Chamberlain's efforts to mediate some alternative to war foundered. Londoners braced for the very real possibility of air attacks from the German Luftwaffe. Joseph Kennedy's family had been in Europe less than five months, and already he was beginning to feel that London was no place for them anymore. "All over London," Joe wrote in his memoirs, "people were being fitted for gas-masks. In the churches, in the theatres, at the sports matches, announcements were made of the depots to which they should go. A motor van slowly cruised through Grosvenor Square with a loudspeaker attachment urging people not to delay in getting their masks. It carried posters pleading for more recruits for the air protection services."[13]

In Hyde Park, where Ted and Bobby had kicked their pebbles, men began digging trenches night and day. A dark mood gripped those left in the city as hundreds of families began to pack up and leave London.

On September 26, hours before Hitler's deadline, while waiting to hear what the Führer would say at a speech at the Sportpalast in Berlin, Joe penned a note to his friend Washington correspondent Arthur Krock, saying he was feeling "very blue" because he was starting to think about sending Rose and the children back to America and "stay here alone for God knows how long. Maybe never see them again."[14]

That same day, Chamberlain delivered a speech that put the city of London on an all-out war footing. "How horrible, fantastic, incredible it is that we should be digging trenches and trying on gas masks here because of a quarrel in a far-away country between people of whom we know nothing. . . . Armed conflict between nations is a nightmare to me; but if I were convinced that any nation had made up its mind to dominate the world by fear of its force, I should feel that it must be resisted."[15]

All able-bodied Englishmen were ordered to report to the nearest labor exchange to dig trenches.[16] Schools closed so they could be used to distribute gas masks to citizens. Hospitals were emptied to make room for the 50,000 casualties expected. Kennedy had his children's things packed at the embassy and called Rose in Scotland, where she was sightseeing, to tell her to come home immediately. Joe was feeling a sense of urgency, as if the attacks might begin any moment, and he wanted his children out of harm's way. No one in the Kennedy clan wanted to leave their newly beloved home, except the baby of the family, six-year-old Teddy. Teddy "wants to go to North America to have his tonsils out because he thinks if he does he can drink all the Coca-Cola he wishes and all the ice cream," said Joe.[17]

On September 27, Joe was having lunch alone with Teddy when the prime minister's office called him to tell him a peaceful resolution was impossible. Kennedy expected a panic, and called Roosevelt's Secretary of State, Cordell Hull, and asked him to send ships immediately to evacuate all Americans.

Hitler's deadline for Czechoslovakia's acceptance of his terms for annexation was 2 P.M. on September 28, a day that was to become known as Black Wednesday. Parliament planned to meet at 2:45 in anticipation of an ultimatum from Chamberlain that would send the country into war. Joseph Kennedy crowded into the diplomatic gallery to watch Chamberlain deliver what he feared would be a historic speech. As historian Goodwin recounts it, the prime minister, a tall and lean, an aging and serious man, bent over the lectern with a pained expression on his face and slowly recounted all the steps England had taken to try to forestall war with Germany. He spoke with a world-weariness as he told the House he had directed a "last, last" appeal to Hitler. At twenty minutes to four, just as the prime minister was describing his recent conversation with the Italian dictator Benito Mussolini, an urgent message was delivered to Chamberlain from Hitler, inviting him to a meet in Munich the next morning.[18] The Italian and French leaders were also invited, but no one from Czechoslovakia or the other power player in the region, the Soviet Union, was invited. The next day Czechoslovakia paid a heavy price for a momentary peace forged in the hastily arranged summit. Hitler was allowed to annex the Sudetenland without any resistance at all. The alliance between France and Czechoslovakia was defunct, and the Soviet Union was kept out of the European realignment altogether. Yet, when Chamberlain came back to England to announce the deal, he was met by a cheering crowd of tens of thousands in front of 10 Downing Street: "My good friends this is the second time in our history that there has come back from Germany to Downing Street peace with honor," Chamberlain told the crowd. "I believe it is peace for our time." His now-famous phrase endures as one of the age's great warnings against appeasement of aggression.

Chamberlain was convinced he had been put into office to keep the peace in Europe. Forged by World War I, he was determined in his bones to avoid a repeat of that conflict. That meant almost any accommodation was justified in keeping the peace with Mussolini and Hitler, despite mounting evidence that the two had no intention of keeping any agreements. Chamberlain's policy only fed their desire for more conquests.

Chamberlain continued his desperate efforts to avoid war for another six months, aided heartily by Ambassador Kennedy. Both Kennedy and Chamberlain were convinced the war would bring "the end of civilization." Kennedy looked at the situation in Europe through the lens of a pragmatist anxious that America avoid being dragged into the "foreign entanglements" George Washington had cautioned future leaders to be wary of. Kennedy also believed that democracies and dictatorships had to figure out how to coexist, rather than destroy each other. He was pessimistic that the Western democracies could survive war intact, fearful that the political institutions and financial networks that bound America, London and Europe would collapse. Kennedy failed to read the threat that Hitler posed to the whole world. But the stereotype of Kennedy as an unrepentant appeaser or a pro-German anti-Semite is inaccurate. A review of Kennedy's papers at the JFK Library, including all the dispatches to the State Department when he was ambassador to Great Britain, and relevant newspaper clippings shows that in 1938, the ambassador was outraged by Hitler's persecution of Jews, and sought permission from the State Department to speak out at Albert Hall, but was denied.[19] Kennedy's personal intervention with the British government led to the creation of areas within the British Empire for emigration of deported Jews, including Kenya, Tanganyika, Australia and British Guiana. Kennedy also obtained increased quotas for Jewish immigration to Argentina, Brazil and Venezuela. And after Chamberlain failed to win sums of money from Germany to finance emigration, Joe Kennedy successfully intervened with German officials.

Kennedy also lodged "vigorous" protests with Germany that stopped Hitler's right-hand man, Hermann Goering, from loading boatloads of Jews onto ships and sending them to various ports around the world that didn't want them. Kennedy believed the refugees were likely to perish at sea. Instead, however, many of those who remained in Germany were eventually killed in concentration camps. The Arab chairman of the Palestine Relief Association harshly criticized Kennedy in 1939 after Kennedy said an immigration restriction of Jews into Palestine would be disastrous. In a press interview on April 21, 1939, Joseph Goebbels labeled Ambassador Kennedy "a master conspirator in a plot to add the United States to an iron ring around Germany."

Driving Joe Kennedy's antiwar attitude was not anti-Semitism or sympathy with the Nazis. It was a deep-seated desire to protect his family, a family that was then very much in the line of fire. He argued again and again that emotional investment in nationalism was a poor substitute for the deep ties of family and friends. His politics was more personal than most people remember: He was terrified that his own sons might get swept up in a deadly conflict so far from home and that the war would wreck the financial security he had so carefully built for his family. Joe Kennedy was incapable of putting the fates of his children in anybody else's hands. And his speeches of the day sound as if he believed he had the power himself to decide for or against war, that he believed he could somehow bend Roosevelt to his will. Before a huge crowd at the Boston Garden, Kennedy told the "mothers and fathers" of America: "I have said this before, but I shall say it again and again: Your boys are not going to be sent into any foreign wars."

It was Joe's passion for his family that fueled his passion for peace, at nearly any cost. He measured everything in the world against the importance of his family. "He was a man who cared more for his children than any man I've ever seen," said the children's nurse, Louella Hennessy. In one speech, Joe Kennedy said, "My wife and I have given nine hostages to fortune. . . . The kind of America they and their children will inherit is of grave concern to us all."[20] In the draft of a major speech he was scheduled to give in Scotland on August 31, 1938, just as the crisis over Czechoslovakia was unfolding, Kennedy planned to ask whether there was "any dispute or controversy existing in the world which is worth the life of your son, or of anyone else's son?"[21] The draft was immediately ordered expunged by the State Department, which also informed President Roosevelt, who had already been making speeches about the need to confront Hitler. It's hard not to wonder in that light if

Kennedy would have taken a harder line against Hitler if his family had been safely home in Boston.

Joe Kennedy made his biggest blunder as an ambassador in a speech at the Trafalgar Day dinner of the Navy League on October 19, three weeks after the Munich Agreement, when popular opinion had begun to congeal against Hitler. "The democratic and dictator countries differ ideologically, to be sure, but that should not preclude the possibility of good relations between them," he said. The State Department approved the speech at the time, but Kennedy's comment immediately unleashed a storm of criticism on the other side of the Atlantic. "For him to propose," the *New York Post* reported, "that the United States makes a friend of the man who boasts that he is out to destroy democracy, religion, and all of the principles which free Americans hold dear . . . passes understanding."

A little over a month later Nazis rampaged through the Jewish ghettoes of Germany, raping, killing and jailing thousands of Jews in an event that was to become known as Kristallnacht—the night of broken glass. Still, Rose refused to let events burst the pretty bubble around their family. When Joe went home to patch things up with Roosevelt at Christmas time that year, the rest of the Kennedys fled to Saint Moritz to ski in the new year, 1939. "Everybody got pretty good on skis including Teddy who was going along splendidly till he hurt his leg," Joe Jr. wrote to his dad. "However, he recuperated in a few days and was out showing everyone how it should be done."[22]

In March 1939, the Kennedys all decided to attend the coronation of the new pope, Pius XII, a friend of the family. At Vatican City, the pope gave the Kennedys and eight of their children a private audience. Joe Jr. was in Madrid to get a firsthand look at the prelude for World War II, the Spanish Civil War. Joe Jr. listened for news of the pope's coronation on the radio. "It must have been a wonderful sight and it certainly was a great honor. At the same time, everything was popping here," Joe Jr. wrote to his parents as Republicans and Communists were fighting in the streets. "We could see men hit right outside the house and be carried out by the Red Cross," he added. "Many civilians hit as they would be walking along the street when the shooting would begin."[23]

In Rome, the pope vividly remembered visiting the Kennedys at their home in Bronxville, New York, when he was an archbishop. He particularly remembered Teddy as a little boy, who had sat upon the prelate's lap and been curious about the large crucifix hanging from his neck. The pope gave all the children rosaries and invited Teddy back to receive first communion in the pope's private chapel the next day. On March 15, 1939, when Teddy became the first American to receive such an honor, Hitler's armies invaded

Czechoslovakia. Not satisfied with just the annexation of the predominantly German Sudetenland, Hitler made a triumphant entry into Prague by evening. By then, Chamberlain no longer believed there was any way to avoid war. He was now convinced that if England didn't act soon, Hitler would be in their backyards by year's end. Chamberlain went back to the House of Commons and announced that if Poland were attacked next, "His Majesty's Government would feel themselves bound at once to lend the Polish Government all the support in their power." World War II was less than six months away.

Jack had wrangled an extended leave of absence from Harvard by then and, in April, went on a fact-finding tour into the heart of Nazi-occupied lands in Eastern Europe. Thanks to the intervention of his father, he was able to tour Prague when it was under German occupation. The new realities of Europe were getting hard to ignore. Still, the family took one final holiday together at Cannes that summer. "It was good to get way from the bustle of London," Joe Kennedy wrote to a friend. Ted Kennedy recalled the older boys teasing him until he followed all of them, jumping off a rock 20 feet above the Mediterranean. "I was pretty scared," Ted said, "but they all seemed to be doing it."[24]

In his letter, Joe concluded, "In Cannes it was possible for me really to see my children again and have close at hand the kind of world that some men were seeking to destroy and others were too divided to preserve."

On September 1, 1939, Hitler's tanks invaded Poland in a brutal, lightning-quick "blitzkrieg." Joe Kennedy recalled it vividly in a letter. "The news . . . came with a rush, like a torrent spewing from the wires—German troops had crossed the border; German planes were bombing Polish cities and killing civilians; the Germans were using poison gas."[25] On that same day, parents placed thousands of children on trains and boats destined for rural areas of England as part of an enormous evacuation. Bobby and Teddy were fitted for gas masks and assigned an air-raid shelter just in case.[26] On their way to school they passed Londoners digging trenches and filling sandbags.[27]

On Sunday, September 3, Chamberlain once again spoke to the British people, telling them Britain was going to war. Rose, Joe Jr., Jack and Kathleen took seats in the Stranger's Gallery of the overflowing House of Commons to hear him speak. They heard Chamberlain say that the German government had never responded to Britain's ultimatum against invading Poland, and "consequently, this country is at war with Germany." Churchill, who would become the new prime minister in short order, added that day: "This is not a question of fighting for Danzig or fighting for Poland. We are fighting to save the whole world from the pestilence of Nazi tyranny and in defense of all that is most sacred to man."

Jack was spellbound by Churchill's words. Rose Kennedy's record of that day, however, was only that as she and the younger children set out to walk to the ambassador's residence in Prince's Gate, "the air-raid siren began to howl, and we ran for refuge into the nearest shelter we could find."[28]

Panic-stricken now, Ambassador Kennedy booked berths on the SS *Washington*, the first available American ship departing for New York. He originally planned to send all nine of his children home together, but 15,000 other U.S. citizens were trying to get home, too. Joe decided it was politic to stagger his family's exit, sending only Rose, Eunice, Kathleen and Bobby home on the September 9 sailing. Joe Jr. left September 14. And the rest, including Jack, left the following week. Only 19-year-old Rosemary stayed behind with Joe Sr. She remained at a convent school deep in the Hertfordshire countryside and safe from attack. When he spoke to President Roosevelt, Kennedy kept repeating, "It's the end of the world, the end of everything," according to journalists Joe Alsop and Robert Kintner.

By April, Hitler had invaded the neutral countries of Denmark and Norway despite Britain's superior navy. Less than 24 hours later, Chamberlain stepped down as prime minister and Churchill succeeded him. Hitler's forces punched through Western defenses on the continent shortly after. Within days, Belgium and Holland were occupied. By June 17, France had fallen, and Britain stood alone against Hitler's juggernaut.

A month later, Hitler issued Directive 16, calling for a full-scale air offensive against England to prepare the way for a ground invasion in September. The Battle of Britain was joined on July 10. In early September, less than a year after Joe had sent his family home, Hitler unleashed more than 400 bombers and 600 fighters on London. They began bombing day and night in a sustained attack that would become known as the Blitz. Hitler hoped his strategy would render London uninhabitable and result in "eight million going mad." For 57 nights, the bombing was unrelenting, killing tens of thousands of British civilians. More than a million homes and building were damaged or destroyed, including Buckingham Palace, the Tower of London, Westminster Abbey, St. Paul's Cathedral and the Tate Gallery.

Broadcasting from a London rooftop, journalist Edward R. Murrow sent live radio reports of the unfolding tragedy back home to Americans. "Tonight, as on every other night, the rooftop watchers are peering out across the fantastic forest of London's chimney pots. The anti-aircraft gunners stand ready . . . I have been walking tonight—there is a full moon, and the dirty-gray buildings appear white. The stars, the empty windows, are hidden.

It's a beautiful and lonesome city where men and women and children are trying to snatch a few hours sleep underground."

Antiaircraft batteries begin to let loose in the broadcast. "Those are explosions over head," Murrow intones. "Earlier this evening, we heard a number of bombs go sliding and slithering across, to fall several blocks away. Now the burst of the anti-aircraft fire. Still the nearby guns are not working. The searchlights now are feeling almost directly overhead. Now you'll here two bursts in a moment." Forlorn, staccato pops can be heard in the distance. "There they are! That hard, stony sound."

Joe Kennedy described the aftermath of one night of the Blitz in a letter to Eunice:

> Last night they dropped one in the pool at Buckingham Palace, one back of Lansdowne House: one at Marble Arch; and Piccadilly is all blocked off today . . . I don't know where it is all going to end but everything I see confirms what I thought, that it ought never to have started. The unfortunate part of this war is that poor women and children are getting by far the worst of it. I can't tell you what my state of mind would have been if any of you had been over here. I think I should have gone mad.

Writing to eight-year-old "Master Teddy Kennedy" about the raids, Joe Kennedy said:

> I don't know whether you would have very much excitement during these raids. I am sure, of course, you wouldn't be scared, but if you heard all these guns firing every night and the bombs bursting you might get a little fidgety. I'm sure you would have liked to be with me and seen the fires the German bombers started in London. It is really terrible to think about, and all those poor women and children and homeless people down in the East End of London all seeing their places destroyed. I hope when you grow up you will dedicate your life to trying to work out plans to make people happy instead of making them miserable, as war does today.[29]

That brief letter contains the first sprouts of the Kennedy legacy. It was one of more than 200 letters Joe wrote to his children, which when pieced together contain the essence of what was to become the basic Kennedy creed. Opposition to and prevention of war was unquestionably a piece of that bequest. A hatred of war has been a hallmark of all three Kennedy brothers, whether it be Jack's delicate aversion of nuclear war in the Cuban Missile Crisis, his Nuclear Test Ban Treaty, or his radical-by-today's-standards "Peace Speech" at American University. Bobby's quixotic 82-day presidential campaign in 1968 was fueled by angry passion over the conduct of the Vietnam War. Ted Kennedy counted as his "finest hour" his largely ignored speech in 2002 arguing vehemently against the launch of the Iraq War.

But more than asking his sons to fight against war, the letter asks Ted to dedicate his life to making other people's lives better. When Ted gave his eulogy for Bobby in 1968, he quoted a speech of Bobby's about their father at length:

A few years back, Robert Kennedy wrote some words about his own father and they expressed the way we in his family feel about him. He said of what his father meant to him: "What it really all adds up to is love—not love as it is described with such facility in popular magazines, but the kind of love that is affection and respect, order, encouragement, and support. Our awareness of this was an incalculable source of strength, and because real love is something unselfish and involves sacrifice and giving, we could not help but profit from it.

"Beneath it all, he has tried to engender a social conscience. There were wrongs which needed attention. There were people who were poor and who needed help. And we have a responsibility to them and to this country. Through no virtues and accomplishments of our own, we have been fortunate enough to be born in the United States under the most comfortable conditions. We, therefore, have a responsibility to others who are less well off."

That is the real core of Ted Kennedy's legacy, a commitment to the disenfranchised, to people who are not taken care of by society. Above all, the Kennedy legacy is a commitment to public service. In an interview in the late 1940s, Joe explained why he was steering his sons toward careers in public service. "The country's got plenty of businessmen," he said. "What [the nation] needs is some sound, informed, well-qualified representation in its contacts with other nations and in the handling of its own affairs. . . . We chance to be in a position in which [our sons] can be spared the necessity of supporting themselves. Spared that, why shouldn't they better try to qualify to serve their country in some needed capacity?"

Underlying Joe's advice to his sons, however, was the recognition of the coming end of his own political future. His vocal opposition to the war that Roosevelt supported meant that Roosevelt no longer trusted his ambassador, and found ways to work around him. Roosevelt began a secret correspondence with Winston Churchill to plan for the eventual entry of the United States into the war. Joe Kennedy stayed on in his post after the start of the war, but the writing on the wall was unmistakable. He sealed his fate when, in 1940, he declared: "Democracy is finished in England, it may be here (in the USA)." He resigned by the fall after 1,000 days as ambassador and returned to Boston before the presidential election. He finally came around and embraced the war effort after the attack on Pearl Harbor in 1941, but by then Roosevelt's faith in Kennedy as a trusted agent was gone. The president offered Joe several positions with the government during the course of the war, but Kennedy felt they were all beneath him, as Roosevelt probably knew he would. Joe's short career as a political being had become a casualty of precisely the thing that had brought him such success as a businessman: his unshakable belief that he could fix any problem and bend any man to his will. His ambitions had also fallen victim to his love for his family.

Tragically, Joe's fears about the personal cost of the war would prove dead-on. Interrupting law school, Joe Jr. enlisted as a naval air cadet in 1941, talking his father into giving his blessing by persuading him that his service would help his father's image. "I think that Jack is not doing anything, and, with your stand on the war, the people will wonder what the devil I am doing back at school, when everyone else is working for national defense."[30] With Joe Jr. in the military, Jack felt pressure to enlist, too. He also felt a son's obligation to fight a war his father hadn't fought in or supported. The Army and Navy turned Jack down because of his health problems, but he strengthened his bad back through a tough regimen of exercise and applied to the naval reserve. His father arranged an exam by a friendly physician, and Jack became an ensign in September 1941. Jack's father didn't mind Jack being close to combat in the war, but he tried to keep his heir apparent, Joe, as far away as possible. Jack actually outranked Joe because of their father's maneuvering to keep Joe safe, and the oldest son resented it. The last time the two brothers were together was to pose for a photograph in their naval uniforms, Jack an officer and Joe a seaman second class.

And because of Jack's proximity to conflict, he was the brother who got to test his courage in war first. When the Allies began island-hopping toward Japan through the South Pacific in early 1943, small PT boats were sent out in clusters from island bases to attack Japanese subs and ships. Lieutenant Kennedy became skipper of a small attack boat, *PT 109*, in the Solomon Islands. During a patrol in Blackett Strait on a starless black night, a Japanese destroyer plowed right through Kennedy's boat at 40 knots, cutting it in half. Jack, who had been on the Harvard swimming team, rescued several of the injured men who were thrown into the water, pulling them back to the floating wreckage of the boat. Clenching a life jacket strap in his teeth, Kennedy towed one badly burned crewman three miles to a small island. A few days later, Jack led the surviving crewmembers on a second harrowing swim to another island, where they survived on coconuts for six days. Natives in a canoe found them there and reported their position to a nearby U.S. base, and Jack and his crew were rescued. For saving the lives of several of his crewmen on *PT 109*, Kennedy was awarded the Navy and Marine Corps medal. But he never felt he deserved the honors. When asked by interviewers how he became a war hero, he always answered in humble way. "It was involuntary," he said. "They sank my boat."

Because of his position in the family, Joe Jr. took the news of Jack's heroism poorly. The competition between the two brothers had carried into the war, and Joe felt he needed to try to best his younger brother's feat. An officer on Joe's base in Jacksonville, Florida, noticed a change in Joe. "When news came out about brother John's PT-boat activities, I think it inspired him to try harder," said Chief Degman. "I don't think anyone was more intent on seeking out the enemy and meeting him than Joe Kennedy."[31] Joe came home on leave for Joe Sr.'s fifty-fifth birthday shortly after the rescue, and it was Jack's deed that received the hero's salute, not Joe. A family friend, Boston police commissioner Joseph Timilty, shared a bedroom with Joe Jr. during the weekend celebration, and said he found Joe crying uncontrollably in his room. He remembers Joe clenching and unclenching his fists, saying, "By God, I'll show them." The competition between Joe and Jack had never abated, and now, thanks in large part to Joe Sr.'s public relations connections glorifying Jack's feat, including a lengthy *New Yorker* article by John Hershey, Joe Jr. could no longer claim to be the family star.

Less than a year later, Joe was flying bombing missions during D-Day, June 6, 1944. Disobeying orders, he flew so close to German fortifications that his plane was strafed.[32] His crew began to complain about Joe's recklessness. Still, he was promoted to lieutenant and transferred to Bombing Squadron 110. On June 12, Joe wrote to his mother and father that it looked like he would be home in about ten days.[33] But when his crew left, Joe volunteered to take over another for a boy who was ill. "I thought I might as well stay over. There are a great many more possibilities now than in the past, and I think it is silly to miss them," he wrote. Still, he thought he'd be home by the first of August. Joe Jr. soon extended his tour of duty by volunteering for ten extra bombing missions. He completed them, and volunteered for more. "I now have 39 missions, and will probably have fifty by the time I leave. It is far more than anyone else on the base, but it doesn't prove a hell of a lot. Don't worry about me. I don't think I am in as much danger now as I was (knock on wood), and with any luck I should be home by the end of July or the first of August."

On July 7, 1944, Robert wrote to Joe, telling him to hurry home. "The fatted calf is getting fatter and fatter, so don't wait too long as we are all longing to see you."[34] On August 9, 1944, writing that it looked like the war might be ending soon, Joe Sr. told his son: "don't force your luck too much."

By then, Joe's outfit had already been rotated back to the States, and the Kennedy family anxiously awaited his homecoming. Joe's gear was packed and ready to ship out when he heard about a secret new mission, "Aphrodite," in need of volunteers.

Aphrodite's target: the launching sites of the "buzz bomb," a frightening new German V–1 rocket that could fly 350 miles an hour from Germany and hit London with an enormous explosive charge. "These pilotless things," as Joe called them, were the first intercontinental ballistic missiles, and the Allies feared they would change the balance of the war if not nipped in the bud. Three hundred were launched against England in the last year of the war, causing enormous damage.

Joe's plane, *Zootsuit Black,* was loaded with ten tons of explosives. The idea was that Joe and his crew would set the aircraft to crash into its target, and they would parachute out of it at the last possible moment. Joe told a friend he thought he had a 50–50 chance of survival, but was also given to believe that if the mission succeeded he would get the Navy's highest honor, the Navy Cross. Joe figured those were good enough odds. Just hours before, Joe's electronics officer Earl Olsen asked him to postpone the flight because of some electrical problems he felt heightened the risk unnecessarily. Joe refused to delay. "I think I'm gonna fly it," he said.

Franklin Delano Roosevelt's son Elliott was flying photoreconnaissance that night, taking pictures of the mission. He heard two sudden explosions and saw Joe's plane disintegrate in the air. Pieces scattered over a mile-wide area, and no body parts were ever found. The cause of the crash was never determined, but an investigation pointed to electrical malfunction. It was almost exactly a year since Jack had rescued his crewmembers at sea. The sibling rivalry had proven fatal.

The whole family—including Jack, who was on weekend leave from Chelsea Naval Hospital—was home at Hyannis Port when the news came. Two priests knocked on the door and asked to speak to Joe Kennedy. "We sat with the priests in a smaller room off the living room," recalled Rose Kennedy, "and from what they told us we realized there could be no hope, that our son was dead." Joe and Rose sat awhile, holding each other and hiding their tears. "Then he came out to the sun porch," Teddy recalled, and said, "'Children, your brother Joe has been lost. He died flying a volunteer mission.' His voice cracked and as tears came to his eyes he said in a muffled voice, 'I want you all to be particularly good to your Mother.'"[35] And then Joe went up to his room and shut the door. Joe never drank much, but on that day, a friend said, he took a bottle of scotch and drank the whole thing.

Joe had been the central figure in Teddy's life, and his disappearance was incomprehensible to the boy at the time. It was almost as if he had lost a parent or his guardian angel. In Europe Joe and Ted had been especially close. Joe had read to Teddy at dinnertime, romped on the beach with him, shared the Sunday morning comics, took him riding along Rotten Row in Hyde Park in London. There had been no rivalry between the two because they were so far apart in age.

Bobby suffered the most outwardly of the brothers after the death, and Jack's reaction was delayed for a long time as he sought to make some sense of it. Years and years later, when Jack was writing notes for a letter to Ernest Hemingway, he tried to put his finger on the complicated motivations behind his brother's final act of courage. A hero's courage, he wrote, probably came from "pride—his sense of individuality—his desire to maintain his reputation for manliness which may be more important to him than office—the desire to maintain his reputation among his colleagues as a man of courage, his conscience, his personal standards of ethics—morality—his need to maintain his own respect for himself which may be more important than his regard of others—his desire to win or maintain the opinion of friends and constituents."[36]

★ ★ ★

The ambassador never really got over young Joe's death. "All my plans for my own future were all tied up with young Joe, and that has gone smash," Kennedy wrote to his friend Arthur Houghton.[37] To another friend, Bunny Green, he explained, "When the young bury the old, time heals the pain and sorrow; but when the process is reversed the sorrow remains."[38] His worst fears about the war had come true. "For a fellow who didn't want the war to touch your country or mine," he wrote to Lord Beaverbrook. "I have had a rather bad dose." Not longer after, Kick's fiancé, Billy Harrinton, was killed in battle, by a sniper's bullet, shortly after the two had announced their engagement. "I have had brought home to me what I saw for all the mothers and fathers of the world. . . . As I sit here and write you this letter with the natural cynicism that you and I share about a great many things, I wonder if this war will do anything for the world."[39] Joe deepened his investment in his family after his oldest son was gone and his political career was over, forever transferring his ambitions for Joe to his remaining sons. "My work is my sons," he told a golfing partner once.[40] He told people around him that he was a caterpillar, and his sons would be butterflies. At the heart of his ambitions for Jack, Bobby and Ted, however, lingered a bitter rivalry with Roosevelt, whom he now blamed for the death of his first-born. Joe once accosted Harry Truman in Boston in 1944 after Truman had become Roosevelt's running mate for his fourth term. "Harry," he said, "what are you doing campaigning for that crippled son of a bitch that killed my son Joe?"[41] Joe intended to have his revenge against Roosevelt and the war by erecting a political dynasty he hoped would eclipse the greatest American political dynasty of the age. And he set about building that dynasty one remaining son at a time.

ACT II
JACK, BOBBY AND TEDDY

4

THE SWEET-AND-SOUR BROTHER ACT

Yes, this candidate . . . has a patina of that other life, the second American life, the long electric night with the fires of neon leading down the highway to the murmur of jazz.

—Norman Mailer

He looked like a little boy dressed up in his father's clothes. The collar of his white shirt gaped two sizes too large around his neck and his gray jacket and trousers hung slackly on him. His chestnut hair was an unruly thatch. His voice was high-pitched and scratchy, and he raced through his talk, barely pausing to take a breath. It was clear from his darting eyes that he did not enjoy crowds, preferring, he often admitted, to be off reading a book or painting a picture. The 28-year-old boy-man had little confidence in himself and no interest in the backslapping, handshaking and small talk—the meat and potatoes of Boston politics—that came afterward. "Jack Kennedy more closely resembled a high-school senior chosen as Boys' State representative . . . than a young man on the threshold of his political career," said local historian Leo Damore of John Fitzgerald Kennedy's debut as a politician at the Hyannis Port Rotary Club in September 1945.[1] Such was the birth of the Kennedy dynasty.

"To be perfectly truthful," Speaker of the House Tip O'Neill once recalled, "this pasty-faced-looking kid didn't look any more like a Boston politician that was going to go to Congress than the man on the moon."[2]

"The first time I saw him," said Ben Bradlee, "he was this very skinny, not very well pulled-together kid. You know, he looked a little disorganized. He didn't have good clothes particularly." None of that mattered much, given the money behind his candidacy and his much-publicized war heroism. Nineteen forty-six was a great year for veterans. Jack's speech that day in September was titled "England and Germany: Victor and Vanquished," and the crowd was eager to hear a first-hand account of the war. Jack spoke sincerely and seriously, hardly ever departing from his written text, and hardly ever smiling. Except once. "Stumbling over a word, he flashed a quick, self-deprecating grin that, a member of the audience remembered, 'could light up the room,'" said Damore. (Norman Mailer once remarked that when Kennedy smiled, his teeth "were clearly visible at a distance of fifty yards."[3]) That day in September, the Kennedy smile won over its first audience.

A year before the speech, the ambassador had already begun to transform his hopes for his son Joe into a legacy project for the entire family. According to one version of the family story, just a few days after Joe Jr.'s death in 1944 the patriarch announced dramatically that Jack would be the central character in this new drama. Joe was dead, the father said, and it was therefore Jack's responsibility to run for political office. Jack told his father he didn't want to do it, that he didn't feel like he had the ability Joe Jr. had. Joe didn't necessarily disagree with him—he'd always felt that Jack didn't have the "sociability and dynamism" needed for politics—but he told him he had to do it anyway.[4] "Sometimes we all do things we don't like to do," Jack later told a friend.[5] "I was drafted" to go into politics, he told reporter Bob Considine. "My father wanted his eldest son in politics. 'Wanted' isn't the right word. He demanded it. You know my father."

When Joe Jr. was alive, there had been no well-defined expectations of Jack as the second son, so anything he accomplished made that much more of a splash, as had been the case with his heroism aboard *PT 109*. Now he was the lightning rod for *all* his father's expectations. His competition in the family, however, was a revered ghost rather than a flesh-and-blood brother he could occasionally get the better of. Jack could never compete with the hallowed memory of Joe's unfulfilled promise, just as Ted later could never hope to match the sacred memories of Jack and Bobby. Early death made them all invulnerable, and for many, many years, unfulfilled promise would be a central motif of the Kennedy legacy. "I'm shadow boxing in a match the shadow is always going to win," Jack told Lem Billings.[6]

Right after Joe's death, Jack Kennedy was the family member who displayed the least emotion. Partly that was due to the stoicism he'd been taught—"Kennedys don't cry"—but it was also because of the mixed feelings he was experiencing. His had been a love/hate relationship with an older, stronger substitute parent, and now his role in the family had changed forever. Joe had provided a kind of insulation from his father's will, allowing Jack wiggle room to create more of his own quirky personality than Joe had. Jack felt exposed after Joe was gone. For all their competitions, Jack had depended on his brother as a kind of shield. Once when asked by a reporter about Joe's death, he was quoted as cavalierly saying "It was a matter of statistics. His number was up." But there was more to it than that. "He was very close to my brother Joe, and it was a devastating loss to him personally, and he saw the enormous impact that it had on my father," Ted Kennedy told journalist David Talbot. "He was a very different person when he came back from the war. I think this burned inside of him."[7] In the months after Joe's death, Jack put together a memorial book of family reminiscences, *As We Remember Joe,* 50 copies of which were privately printed. "It was Jack who disappeared every evening from five to seven-thirty," Eunice recalled, "and wrote letters and made calls, and collected information, and wrote the book while the rest of us were still playing games."[8] No one else spent so much time memorializing the lost brother, and Jack's father couldn't even look at the book for very long because of his grief. But the book was well done, with an essay by Jack as an introduction that included the line "His worldly success was so assured and inevitable that his death seems to have cut into the natural order of things."[9]

The book became the vehicle by which Joe began thinking about his second son in a new light, as a possible surrogate for Joe Jr. Without intentionally doing so, Jack had inched his father a half-step out of his grief.

With Bobby and Teddy, Jack gladly took up the big-brother role Joe had filled so willingly. "I was in school when Jack came down there as a PT-boat instructor," Ted Kennedy remembered, "and he used to smuggle me aboard a PT boat and take me for rides. We used to chew tobacco and spit and have a great time. He taught me to ride a bicycle, throw a forward pass and sail against the wind."[10] But living out Joe's professional life as his father had already dictated it was a different matter. Jack thought he might be headed for a career in journalism, or a quiet academic life, or even the carefree life of a dilettante. His trust fund meant he really didn't need to worry about making a living. But he'd also begun to realize that the charm and social skills that had made him so popular in Europe were something that might serve him to larger ends. He'd launched a newspaper career after his discharge from the Navy, but it had lasted only from May to August 1945, after which he told a friend that reporting was too passive. "Reporters and writers have to stay up in the stands, and be observers. I'd rather be an activist, down on the field."[11]

Though his father claimed he gave Jack the order to run for office, Jack was already 28 at the time and could have resisted if politics had had no personal appeal whatsoever. Blaming his father for the choice in interviews gave him an out if he failed along the way. He later remembered the birth of his political career differently than his father had, however. "We all liked politics, but Joe seemed a natural to run for office. Obviously, you can't have a whole mess of Kennedys asking for votes. So when Joe was denied his chance, I wanted to run and was glad I could."[12] His friend Lem Billings seconded that view of history in an interview: "Knowing his abilities, interests and background, I firmly believe that he would have entered politics even had he had three older brothers like Joe." Two of Jack's closest aides said later that Jack "was drawn into politics by the same motive that drew Dwight Eisenhower and other World War II veterans, with somewhat the same reluctance, into the political arena—the realization that whether you really liked it or not, this was the place where you personally could do the most to prevent another war."[13]

This explanation of Jack's willingness to take on his brother's mantle makes sense as a motivator. Joe's death instilled in Jack a cynicism about the war that now echoed his father's. In a letter to a teacher at Choate, he wrote, "This war makes less sense to me now than it ever made and that was little enough—and I should really like—as my life's goal—in some way and at some time to do something to help prevent another."[14] Some time between his brother's death and his first political speech at the Hyannis Port Rotary Club, for a mix of reasons that included ambition, power, excitement, guilt, the desperate need to please his father and the grand hope of preventing another war, Jack Kennedy had begun to embrace his brother's legacy as his own.

In a pattern that would continue for 50 years, the entire family went to work for their candidate. Twenty-year-old Bobby, fresh from a tour of duty in the Navy aboard a U.S. destroyer named after his brother Joe, asked to be sent to the toughest place to campaign. He was dispatched to East Cambridge, which was a stronghold of one of Jack's nine rival candidates in the 1946 Democratic primary for Congress in Boston's Eighth District. His job, which he worked at harder than anyone else in the campaign, was to reduce the vote against Jack from five to one to four.[15] After long days of knocking on doors, he often joined the neighborhood softball games as if he were one of the kids. Then he went around with Jack at night meeting everyone "from Irish bartenders to Negro members of the VFW." Working under Billings, Bobby "campaigned as if his life depended on it."[16]

Teddy, a 14-year-old ninth-grader at Milton Academy, joined the campaign as an office boy, messenger and coffee-and-tea fetcher, often accompanying his grandfather Honey Fitz on expeditions around town. During those trips, Honey Fitz plied Teddy with stories of how he had run for office in his day, riding the train from Boston to Old Orchard Beach, Maine, where so many Bostonians vacationed. "He'd walk through twelve cars," Teddy remembered, "shaking hands and trading stories, and by the time they reached Maine, Grampa knew almost everyone. Then he'd get right back on the train and come back to Boston with a new group of travelers who were returning home, and he'd do the same thing all over again."[17] Joe Sr. may have been a businessman all his life, but politics was the Kennedy family business.

Jack's father presided over the campaign's every detail but stayed behind the scenes so as not to dilute Jack's appeal to veterans and other supporters of the war. He had 100,000 reprints of the *Reader's Digest* version of John Hersey's *PT 109* article printed up and sent one to every registered voter. He got newsreel photographers to shoot Jack campaigning and persuaded Boston area theaters to show the footage a few nights before the election. He also became Jack's most important adviser. Many nights after Jack gave a speech—and he gave 450 of them during the campaign—the candidate would go over to see his father for a post mortem. Jack was often frustrated that his delivery had put people to sleep, and Joe would reassure him that people who had been there had called to say it was a fine speech. Asking his son constructively what he might change to make it better next time, Joe worked with Jack mutually and painstakingly over time to improve his pacing.[18] Slowly, Jack tweaked his delivery so that his basic charisma began to shine through.

Eunice and Pat coordinated the volunteers who hosted house parties, bringing the campaign directly to voters in their neighborhoods. The sisters actually provided the cookies, silver, flowers, coffee, cups and saucers for the elaborate soirees, overseeing every detail.[19] Rose Kennedy joined the campaign late, giving it a last-minute injection of glamour by warming Jack's audiences up with stories about her family, Jack's youth and visits with the king and queen of England. The mayor's daughter was the most natural campaigner in the family, and Jack was enormously moved by his mother's efforts on his behalf. Once Rose was involved, with her polished manners and sophisticated clothes, suddenly "everybody wanted to be in the high society with the Kennedys."[20]

Campaign workers advised Jack to emphasize his family connections on the stump. A longtime Boston pol, Patsy Mulkern, described a typical campaign day: "We'd start Jack out in the morning early, what they call street

work . . . meet the city worker, meet the cabby, meet the waitress, wander in
and say, 'My name is John Kennedy, I'm running for Congress.' Some would
say, 'I knew your grandfather Honey Fitz,' and another would come up and
say, 'I knew your grandfather PJ,' or 'I knew your mother, Rose Fitzgerald.' He
didn't have to talk nothing," the old Boston pol recalled. "They might ask him
about his war record, but nothin' 'bout issues."[21] Mulkern and others say Jack
was a tireless campaigner, rarely sleeping more than five hours a night, climbing enthusiastically up through the three-decker buses despite his bad back.
"He kept goin'," said Mulkern. "Never ate much. Great frappe drinker. He had
the biggest rallies ever held in the North End . . . rallies, house parties,
dances. . . . Every girl you met thought she was going to be Mrs. Kennedy."

Toward the end of the campaign, the whole family worked together to
host a huge formal reception at the Commodore Hotel in Cambridge, with
engraved invitations sent to women voters by the "Ambassador and Rose."
The plan was ridiculed by some of Boston's old politicos, as well as some of
Jack's staff members, who thought the party a kind of pretentious dress-up
ball that would leave the Kennedys a laughingstock if it didn't draw a crowd.
But Ethel took the idea and ran with it. She felt the campaign had tapped
into a desire among Boston's Irish for a leader who showed them the heights
to which they might climb. "There was a basic dignity in Jack Kennedy," said
Dave Powers, an Irish immigrant who served as Jack's campaign manager
for Charleston, Massachusetts, "a pride in his bearing that appealed to the
very Irishman who was beginning to feel a little embarrassed about the sen-
timental, corny style of the typical Irish politician. As the Irish themselves
were becoming more middle-class, they wanted a leader to reflect their upward mobility."[22]

The reception was held three days before the Democratic primary,
which meant its success or failure could be the last thing people remembered about Jack's campaign. By all accounts, it was a glorious success. One
reporter called it "a demonstration unparalleled in the history of Congressional fights in this district." At least 1,500 women came in their finest
clothes, though many of the evening gowns that night were rented. The receiving line was a block long, and hundreds of women unable to get into the
ballroom right away piled into the streets, hoping to get a glimpse of Jack.
The ball may have marked the moment when the Kennedys realized they
could market themselves as a middle-class fantasy of American royalty. The
campaign offered not just a candidate but a kind of pop culture aristocracy
that average Bostonians could join for a day. The Kennedy model suggested
powerfully that the upper class really was within their reach, just as it had
been for the Kennedys. The illustrious family had captured Boston's social-

climbing imagination. Jack and his campaign for Congress, and later the campaign for the Senate and then the presidency, was the American dream in motion, involving all those who participated in a contagious optimism about their improving future.

On June 18, Kennedy won more than 40 percent of the ballots cast in the primary, a stunning victory that landed him on the front page of the *New York Times*. When Jack entered campaign headquarters that night, his supporters erupted. Honey Fitz leapt up on a table and danced a jig. Tears in his eyes, he led the crowd in a chorus of "Sweet Adeline." The ambassador told a friend that night, "I would have given you odds of five thousand to one that this couldn't have happened."[23] Jack choked up as he thanked everyone, fighting back his own tears.[24]

Jack was elected to the House in a landslide that November over token Republican opposition. "It cost Old Joe a million dollars to buy Jack a seat in the House," insisted columnist Robert S. Allen.[25] It was more like $300,000, but that far exceeded the expenditures of all the other candidates combined. The success was more than Jack's, it was the entire family's, and it went a long way toward beginning to heal their wounds over Joe's death. Joe was never far from Jack's thoughts, and in many ways the campaign served as a memorial for his brother's dreams. When Joe Jr. had been at Harvard speculating about his future political career, he had promised his roommate, Ted Reardon, a job on his first office staff. It was Jack Kennedy who hired Reardon as his chief aide in Washington, a tip of the hat to his brother's memory.[26] On Armistice Day, just a few days after his victory, Jack gave a speech to the Veterans of Foreign Wars. When he came to the line "No greater love has a man than he who gives his life for his brother," he broke down crying and never finished his speech.[27]

★ ★ ★

On his first day in Congress, John Fitzgerald Kennedy showed up in tennis shoes, an open-collared shirt and no jacket.[28] And he was late. House doorkeeper Monroe Melletio, mistaking Jack for one of the congressional pages, announced that all page boys had to wear blue uniforms.[29] Jack just smiled at the reactions his youthful appearance provoked. "Well how do you like that?" he announced half seriously as he arrived at his office one morning. "Some people got into the elevator and asked me for the fourth floor!"[30]

Jack escorted Ted around Washington shortly after he took office to show him the sights. "He showed me the White House, the Supreme Court, the Library of Congress, and finally the Capitol and the House and Senate office buildings," Ted recalled. "Jack had the same knack as Grampa for bringing history alive. But the thing that seared in my memory and that has influenced the rest of my life is what my brother said to me at the end of our day of touring. 'It's good that you're interested in seeing these buildings, Teddy. But I hope you also take an interest what goes on inside them.'"

It's debatable, though, whether Jack Kennedy took much of an interest himself. Kennedy found that the daily grind of legislating bored him. He didn't have the patience for the homework and the detail of it, as his brother Ted later would. He could certainly gather publicity for a speech on nearly any subject—under his father's tutelage, he had become an engaging speaker—but fellow congressmen complained that he knew little about the subjects of his speeches. Sam Rayburn, the Speaker of the House, privately referred to Jack as a "sickly little fellow" and a "cipher."[31] Rayburn thought telegenic Jack got all the media attention that colleagues who worked harder should have gotten. He regarded Jack as a lazy congressman who voted pretty much as he pleased, without any regard for the Democratic leadership. "We are just worms here," a friend recalls Jack as saying. The House "totally failed to fascinate him. It never really grabbed him," said another friend. "I think his father may have made one mistake, which was to give him an air travel credit card. So that he was on the plane to Palm Beach every Friday night during the winter, and of course, up on the Cape in the summer. He seemed to me to stay pretty much on the periphery of House life."[32] Senators complained about Bobby for the same kind of detachment, but they never complained about Teddy's absorption of granular policy detail. Jack did have an organized mind and a colossal memory, as did Bobby, colleagues said. But both were already looking beyond Congress the day they got there.

Jack's most important hire as a freshman congressman had to be Theodore Sorensen, who became his "intellectual blood bank" and history-making speechwriter. More important, perhaps, Sorensen became Jack's social conscience, something he had never really developed on his own. "And he sure didn't get his social conscience from his father," observed one Kennedy insider. Unlike Ted, Jack never developed any principled consistency behind his politics. "Some people have their liberalism 'made' by the time they reach their late twenties," he told James MacGregor Burns. "I didn't. I was caught in crosscurrents and eddies. It was only later that I got into the stream of things."[33] Sorensen, through the music of his speeches and the solid Nebraska liberalism he brought to the job, was a key figure in the formation of what would become the Kennedy liberalism, which defined the model Democratic party for a generation or more. Sorensen was the one with the commitment to progressive ideals; in his early years, Jack never had much of an ideology other than getting ahead in the game. A critic at *The New Republic* once called his ideology "popularism"—giving people what they wanted but shunning any set of overarching liberal principles. It was Sorensen who began pushing Kennedy toward the progressiveness he later came to symbolize. Sorensen's influence also began edging Jack ever so slightly away from his father's dominance by encouraging him to take stands more liberal than Joe's. Sorensen's trusted friendship and counsel helped Jack begin to become his own man.

Despite his lack of real engagement in the House, Jack's combination of boyish good looks, intelligence, drive and his freshness, in contrast to the ward heelers of old, generated positive press coverage in Massachusetts and an increasing popularity. His name was often mentioned in connection with the governor's race, or the Senate, or even higher office. Jack, whose interest in foreign policy had been stoked by his travels in Europe, leaned more toward the Senate than the sewers-and-drains politics of state office. But a politician every bit as charismatic as Jack stood in the way. Henry Cabot Lodge was a polished, debonair "Brahmin" from an old and prominent Boston family, just the kind of family that had snubbed Joe Kennedy for so much of his life. Lodge had dominated Massachusetts politics for two decades. For the Kennedy family, this was a grudge match. Lodge's grandfather, the legendary isolationist and vehement conservative, had beaten John's grandfather Honey Fitz in 1916 to win the state's first popular election of a U.S. senator. Lodge himself would reappear as Richard Nixon's running mate in 1960. And Ted would end up facing Lodge's son, George, in the 1962 Senate race. Joe was eager for the challenge, telling Jack "When you've beaten him, you've beaten the best. Why try for something else?"[34] He also told his son that when he defeated Lodge, "I will work out the plans to elect you President."

Joe believed Jack's extraordinary personal qualities, rather than his lackluster record of lawmaking, was what they ought to emphasize in his political climb. When Jack decided to take on Lodge for the Senate in 1952, Joe Kennedy was convinced the election would turn on personality more than issues. And Joe believed the best way to transmit Jack's abundance of personality to voters was through a brand-new political tool: television.

★　★　★

Not long after the campaign launched, Joe Kennedy gathered together the brain trust in an apartment he'd let at 84 Beacon Street—right in the thick of Boston. The former Hollywood producer sat smack in front of the television set as his son's wavering image spoke to the eight men there. Joe Kennedy had already put himself in charge of expenditures, advertising, campaign policy decisions, hiring and daily strategy sessions; now he wanted to review Jack's television performances. The speechwriter was there, the adman, Sargent Shriver—the savvy political hand who was soon to marry Eunice—and a host of "yes men." When the speech was done, Joe Kennedy asked what they all thought of it. After a few moments of uncertain silence, the men gave "mealy-mouthed" answers, generally agreeing among themselves that the speech wasn't too bad. All of a sudden, Joe Kennedy "got ferocious."

"I tell ya, that TV program was the worst goddamn thing I ever saw— a disgrace!" Joe bellowed. "Everybody in this room should have the guts and intelligence to know that it was a fiasco! And I never want to see my son on TV, making such an ass of himself as he made tonight. And I'll tell you (pointing his finger at the speechwriter) that was the lousiest writing I've ever seen on any show. And I've been in show business for thirty years. It stunk!"[35]

He told his brain trust that his son was too stiff and too arrogant. "Get the hell out of here," commanded the producer-turned-director. He wanted to start from scratch, to teach Jack to appear more informal, more common man. "We'll meet again tomorrow morning at ten, and I want a whole new TV program. 'Cause we're wrecking this boy. We've got the most precious political asset in the world, and you stupids just don't know how to use it."

Shriver said that, half an hour later, Jack called and his dad told him, "Boy, Jack, you were great, Triffic."

Shriver believed Joseph Kennedy's experience making Hollywood movies was the key to the 1952 election for Jack. The congressional election had been won on the streets; the Senate race would be won on TV. "For one reason, [Joe] had a fantastic knack for knowing what the public was inter-ested in," Shriver said. "That's how he made money, too. . . . He was spooky brilliant at it. . . . He figured that TV was going to be the greatest thing in the history of politics. He set out studying TV, and how Jack could utilize it most effectively. . . . The whole strategy of that campaign came from him—the whole, bloody damn thing."[36]

"I have heard so much about the so-called charisma of the Kennedys, whatever it is," said Rose. "When I first saw Jack on TV, I could see the same kind of appeal . . . my husband sensed it, too, he said TV would be a better medium for Jack than billboards or newspaper ads."[37]

Jack appeared on the newly minted *Meet the Press*, he competed on quiz shows, and he enlisted his sister Pat, who was working in television in New York, to create a "public service type" telecast of 10 to 15 minutes with Jack "interviewing important people down in Washington about their jobs, etc., and about problems of the day."[38] On October 15, 1952, more than 45,000 women across Massachusetts invited friends and neighbors over to watch *Coffee with the Kennedys* on WNAC-TV, starring Jack, Rose, Pat and Eunice. Jack answered phoned-in questions in between Rose's soliloquies on the intricacies of raising nine kids. Rose sometimes pulled out her famous index cards to share with the audience. In one clip from the show, several young women on the set are dressed up in the popular poodle skirts of the day, with the name John F. Kennedy embroidered in cursive across their skirt fronts. "What is there about Kennedy," an Eisenhower supporter would later lament, "that makes every Catholic girl in Boston between eighteen and twenty-eight thinks it's a holy crusade to get him elected?"[39]

Joe Kennedy knew star power and he knew how to use it. At one point near the end of the election, when Jack was physically and emotionally exhausted, campaign strategists spliced together his film clips from earlier in the campaign so that he looked healthy in a "live" 15-minute television broadcast.[40] With Jack Kennedy's emergence as a national politician, "America's politics would now be also America's favorite movie, America's first soap opera, America's bestseller," as Norman Mailer described it in his essay "Superman Comes to the Supermarket." Kennedy aides Kenneth O'Donnell and Dave Powers believed that "voters in that election were not interested in issues. Kennedy won on personality—apparently he was the new kind of political figure that people were looking for that year, dignified and gentlemanly and well-educated and intelligent, without an air of superior condescension that other cultured politicians, such as Lodge and Adlai Stevenson, too often displayed before audiences."[41] That new kind of political figure would come to dominate politics in the future as celebrity and personality often trumped knowledge and hard work. But to dismiss Jack Kennedy's appeal as all style over substance is to deny an important function of politics in the United States. Politicians serve as custodians of American hopes, values and dreams, political scientist Tom Cronin points out. Jack Kennedy had begun to stir a subconscious longing among Americans for not just another lawmaker but a political prince of their own to rival the real princes of Europe. And the Kennedys knew it. The success of the high tea of 1946 was repeated 33 times during Jack Kennedy's Senate campaign, drawing some 75,000 people, mostly women. "Kennedy's career is a curious reversal of the law of the log cabin," observed one reporter. "That family behaved like royalty at rallies. Whoever heard of a reception line in politics, as though to meet the king and queen. They fancy themselves in that role, and it was all they could do to keep those old gals who came to the affairs from curtsying. They had every tendency to drop one knee."[42] The first stones of Camelot were being laid.

★ ★ ★

In Jack's first congressional race, Joe had operated mostly in the background; with the stakes higher, he was in the background, foreground and middle ground. And his hard-driving personality—bawling out Jack in front of the staff, knocking over tables in fights with aides, firing people left and right—was turning the operation into chaos. At a meeting in late May of 1952, Joe flew into a rage over Mark Dalton's management of the campaign. "We've got to hit the Jews," Joe insisted. "We've got to attack labor unions! The lapel buttons were all wrong!"[43] At the end of the tirade, Dalton walked out the door and never came back.

Ken O'Donnell called up Bobby in a panic to tell him the campaign was "a shambles." O'Donnell thought Bobby could serve as a buffer between Joe and the rest of the campaign workers and salvage the race. Bobby, all of 26, wasn't so sure. "I'll just screw it up," he told O'Donnell. A frequent captive of his own morose moods, Bobby had launched himself into the workaday world with a gnawing lack of self-assurance none of his other brothers had been bothered by. When Jack went off to Congress, Bobby went off to Harvard, where he had lacked much of a goal for his college education. With the blowtorch on Jack, the blowtorch was off Bobby, and he drifted through school as a result. "I didn't go to class very much, to tell you the truth. I used to talk and argue a lot, mostly about sports and politics." He told his parents, "I'm certainly not hitting the honors like my older brothers." Harold Ulen, the swimming coach at Harvard, recalled Bobby as being "heavy in the water. . . . He would sink quite easily." Jack he remembered for his "float ability." The coach saw this as an apt metaphor for the difference between the two brothers. "Jack's sensibility was buoyantly literary; Bobby's was heavily moral, however inchoate. Bobby sought responsibility as compulsively as Jack tried to evade it."[44] The differences would actually help the two brothers immensely as a working team in years to come.

When Bobby graduated in 1948, Joe worried to an old friend that his brothers' shadows were a burden. "He is just starting off, and he has the difficulty of trying to follow two brilliant brothers, Joe and Jack. That in itself is quite a handicap, and he is making a good battle against it."[45] However, Bobby married the gregarious Ethel, and she built up his self-confidence. Jack and Bobby had taken an overseas trip together while Jack was a congressman, and Jack had come to better appreciate his brother's depths. They had talked hours on end during the trip, exchanging ideas and philosophies and cementing a tighter bond than Jack and Joe had ever had. When Jack personally told him he needed him on the campaign, Bobby finally agreed. In doing so, he found the purpose he had lacked

Bobby's dedication, work ethic and willingness to take on the patri-arch—forcing Joe back beneath the surface of the campaign, where he had been so effective before—would turn the campaign around overnight. After Bobby arrived, workers started referring to "before the revolution" and "after the revolution." As he had in the Congressional race, Bobby worked harder than anyone else, arriving at the Boston headquarters at 8:30 every morning to unlock the door and going to bed at midnight. He found an enormous ca-pacity, like his father, for getting things done. He created a shadow organiza-tion to the regular Democratic party machinery so that he didn't have to spend all his time sucking up to the old party bosses. If elder statesmen wan-dered into headquarters wanting to chat, Bobby asked them to get to work or get out, and his reputation as "Ruthless Bobby" was born. One night Dave Powers suggested to Bobby that he was becoming unpopular among the party bigwigs. "I don't care if anybody around here likes me, as long as they like Jack," he answered.[46] Bobby did the dirty work of the campaign. He cracked heads while Jack charmed crowds. Stewart Alsop called it a "sweet-and-sour brother act . . . Jack uses his charm and waves the carrot and then Bobby wades in with the big stick."[47]

And it worked.

The 1952 Kennedy campaign "was the most methodical, the most scien-tific, the most thoroughly detailed, the most intricate, the most disciplined and smoothly working statewide campaign in Massachusetts history," jour-nalist Ralph Martin observed.[48]

The night before the election, the three brothers were together for a final rally in the Mattapan neighborhood of south Boston. Teddy mostly missed his brother's Senate campaign because he had signed up for a stint in the Army to do penance for a cheating incident at Harvard. Worried about losing his eligibility for football because of low grades in Spanish, he had paid an-other student to take an exam for him, and got caught. He was immediately suspended but offered the chance to come back at a later time. His father for-gave him rather quickly, Rose remembers, and even hired the man who had taken the test for him.[49] Teddy's solution to his dilemma was to follow his brothers' footsteps into the military. "I was told I had to do something if I wanted to come back into Harvard," Ted recalled. "It seemed that if I went into the Army then for two years, if I had a good record, it would . . . strengthen the case of trying to come back."[50] The experience would awaken Teddy's own social conscience and replant at least one of his feet in the real world, far from the life of private schools, tennis tournaments, sailing and parties he'd grown up in. Like Joe, Jack and Bobby, he slept in a barrack with men from diverse backgrounds and none of the privileges Ted had always taken for granted. Military service was a great equalizer in the Kennedy brothers' generation, creating a widespread camaraderie among men of the era. It was a camaraderie and sense of larger purpose that many of the soldiers said they missed when they came back home. But when Ted did get back to Massachusetts, he was ready to work. "He really loved the pace of campaigning," James King told Burton Hersh. "You'd go to one fire station in Springfield, and then he had to go to all the others. So you'd have fourteen hours of visiting fire stations that day. I remember once we got stalled in a traffic jam and he jumped out and started going from car to car shaking hands and attaching bumper stickers to every car they'd let him."[51] He found 50 or 60 willing drivers. "He loved campaigning, you couldn't hold him down."

At that final rally, when it was John's turn to speak, he walked up to the microphone and said, "Ladies and gentlemen, everything that has been said and everything that could have been said in this campaign has been said." The crowd roared. "Instead of that, the brothers Kennedy are going to sing a song." He said to the bandleader, "Do you know 'They're Breaking Up that Old Gang of Mine?'" The other brothers got up and they all started singing. John Seigenthaler remembers thinking "This was the first time I ever realized that Bob Kennedy couldn't carry a tune in a bucket. . . . But Teddy and Jack carried him, and they did very well. When they got through . . . they had everybody in the hall singing with them, literally turning it into a great rally." The campaign's final image was a testament to the fraternal loyalty that had given John the edge over a candidate who otherwise was his equal.

John Kennedy beat three-term senator Henry Cabot Lodge by 70,000 votes even though a Republican, Dwight D. Eisenhower, won Massachusetts and the presidency. Lodge wouldn't concede until 7:34 A.M. the day after the election, but when Lodge's telegram congratulating John was read at headquarters, the exhausted staffers burst into cheers, applause, whistles and whoops of joy. Jack slowly made his way to the platform to speak, and when he did, he started out by expressing special thanks to his brother Bobby. "I don't think Jack had been aware that Bobby had all this tremendous organizing ability," said Lem Billings. "But during the campaign Bobby had proved himself again and again, forging a blood partnership that would last until the two of them died."[52]

Ted Kennedy bet a friend named Carey $500 that Jack would be president one day.[53] Joe Kennedy kept the bet in a sealed envelope.

5

THE KENNEDY GENERATION

*I'd never done anything political, patriotic or unselfish because nobody
ever asked me to. Kennedy asked.*

—*A volunteer for the Peace Corps, 1962*[1]

One spring day in 1959, a Pontiac Bonneville convertible cruised past
student Steny Hoyer on the University of Maryland campus in College Park,
carrying someone who looked vaguely familiar, like a lesser-known movie
star or semifamous athlete. Hoyer impulsively followed the car to the student
center. The featured speaker at the spring convocation was the young Massachusetts senator who'd *almost* been picked as Adlai Stevenson's running mate
in 1956, a "triumphant defeat" that had brought Jack Kennedy a wealth of
national exposure. In 1957, Kennedy had been invited to give 144 talks,
nearly one every other day.[2] By early 1958, he was receiving a 100 requests a
week to speak. When Hoyer sat down to listen to him in College Park on
April 27, 1959, Kennedy had been roaming the country giving such talks for
three years. He'd become not just an adequate public speaker but an idealistic, inspiring one. His talking tours were weaving a broad quilt of grassroots
support for a 1960 presidential bid.

Speaking to a crowd of over 5,000 that day in Maryland, Kennedy suggested the country was headed into a new era of activist government. He
urged graduating students to seriously consider entering politics, where they
might work to truly solve the problems of the nation. He told them government was the solution, not the problem. He told them they just might change
the world with the force of their idealism and energy.

Kennedy's ideas for many such campaign speeches had been inspired in part by Arthur Schlesinger, who had written a memo called "The Shape of National Politics to Come," arguing that the country's political life ran in cycles, and a more complacent period in American history was drawing to a close. Schlesinger had predicted that an epoch of "affirmation, progressivism and forward movement" was ready to break out.[3] He argued that "a revival of a new sense of the public interest will be central to the period." Schlesinger's memo crystallized ideas about public service that Kennedy had already been thinking about as he sought an identity for his presidential bid, and he took Schlesinger's ideas and ran with them. Kennedy told the Maryland students he foresaw the need for a new time of self-sacrifice to win the cold war, just as his generation had helped win World War II when he was young. "I am sick as an American of reading these studies . . . which show that the image of America as a vital, forceful society, as it once was under Franklin Delano Roosevelt, has begun to fade," Kennedy said often during his talks. "I believe it incumbent upon this generation of Americans to meet the same rendezvous with destiny of which Franklin Roosevelt spoke in 1936. This country has to do better. This country has to move again."

Kennedy's talk was not long. He subscribed to that old preacher's doctrine that "few souls are saved after the first 20 minutes." He had a typewritten text at hand but seldom looked at it or tried to follow it. He often shortened, interpolated or embellished his speeches to fit the temper of the occasion. He was good at reading crowds. When he got down to the substance, he preached a hard gospel. He did not flatter or talk down to the students. When he told them there were tough times ahead and the sooner they faced it the better, when he said that they all must prepare for harder work and stricter self-discipline, he was initially met with a look of puzzled uneasiness. But as the speech went on, the impact of his facts and figures, of his earnestness and vitality, was clearly felt. More than anything, Kennedy made public life sound attractive, like a worthy endeavor. He asked the students to stretch their capabilities and enlarge their concerns. At the end of his speech there was an instant of tense silence, then a rising ovation. It was not that Kennedy had changed the students, "but most of us have, beneath our outer optimism, a troubled feeling that we have failed to live up to the greatness of our heritage," wrote one reporter. "It is this chord which Kennedy strikes and brings to life."[4]

Hoyer listened spellbound. The next week, he switched his major from public relations to politics. "It was just like that," Hoyer says. "Just like that."

An unfocused, mediocre student until then, suddenly he started getting A's. He went on to Georgetown law school because of Kennedy's speech. He threw himself into his local Democratic association in Prince George's County and began interning for Senator Daniel Brewster (D-MD) alongside Nancy Pelosi, who said Kennedy similarly inspired her. Just months after graduating in 1966, Hoyer was elected to the Maryland State Senate from Prince George's County. He was 27.

Hoyer has never left politics. Today, a bust of John F. Kennedy and several photographs and paintings of the Kennedy brothers adorn his office in the Capitol, where he now presides as majority leader of the House of Representatives. Thousands of other current Washington politicos were similarly inspired. "We were all at an age where we were susceptible to having heroes," said Hoyer. "When you're 19, 20, 21 years of age. And it was a time when Kennedy just inspired young people. His energy and his rhetoric and his looks. He was compelling, particularly for young people, who tend not to be as cynical as older people." Jack Kennedy still stands out in a lineup of presidents because he didn't have gray hair. He was a kind of mirror in which young people saw their own light reflected back at them. Kennedy's grace and poise amplified their expectations of themselves, what they might achieve, who they could be. He confirmed a belief after World War II that America was "exceptional," with a special mission to play in the world. "JFK inspired me the way he inspired a whole generation of people," said Bob Shrum, who also spent a lifetime in politics because of Jack and Bobby, and later wrote speeches for Ted. "The call to purpose, the sense of idealism. The sense that you could actually make a difference, and that government had to be there for people who couldn't necessarily fend for themselves."

In anticipation of someday writing his memoirs, John Kennedy periodically dictated notes for a book that was never published.[5] In the fall of 1960, during the height of the presidential campaign, Kennedy reflected on his philosophy of politics as public service:

> I hope all Americans, men and women, regardless of what may be their chosen profession, will consider giving some of their life to the field of politics. Winston Churchill once said: "Democracy is the worst form of government except for all of the other systems that have been tried." It is certainly the most demanding; it requires more from us all than any other system. Particularly in these days when the watch fires of the enemy camp burn bright, I think all of us must be willing to give some of ourselves to the most exacting discipline of self-government. The magic of politics is not the panoply of office. The magic of politics is participating on all levels of national life in an affirmative way, of playing a small role in determining whether, in Mr. [William] Faulkner's words, "freedom will not only endure, but also prevail."

★ ★ ★

For Christmas 1959, Jack's brothers and sisters bought him a secret weapon—a two-engine airplane fitted out in "executive style" with a desk and sleeping quarters. It cost $339,500, and it revolutionized presidential campaigns. The chartered plane, which Jack named the *Caroline* after his daughter, gave Kennedy a "margin of mobility" early on that no other candidate could match. He logged 110,000 miles on it in a little over a year, hopscotching from town to town and state to state until he'd visited all 50 states. Chartered planes became a staple of campaigns soon after, but Jack's was the first.

The plane came with a personal stewardess, Janet Des Rosiers, who happened to be the former secretary and secret mistress of Jack's father, Joe. Des Rosiers said in an interview that "one of my functions as a stewardess, which could not have pleased Jackie very much, were the neck and shoulder massages I gave Jack every day."[6] It often raised a few eyebrows when Jack and Janet disappeared behind a curtain for an hour and a half, but Des Rosiers claimed the massages worked out Jack's kinks and knots after the long days of campaigning. The plane allowed Jack to rest and unwind in between stops, she said. He often slept on it overnight when the team was traveling longer distances, so that he could emerge each day rested and ready. And it allowed Jack to campaign at breakneck speed.

The day started at dawn and often lasted 18 hours, a kaleidoscope of faces, speeches and scenery changes. Jack attended picnics, receptions, state fairs and band performances. He would give town hall talks, make speeches, take questions, meet with local officials, jump in a car for a ride at breakneck speed over winding country roads to an interview by the local radio station, give more talks, make more speeches, then move on to the next town. "Each day there are a hundred local dignitaries to be met and talked with, each day a thousand hands to be shaken. And always there is the shuffling presence of the multitude, the eager clamor of autograph seekers," wrote Beverly Smith, Washington editor for the *Saturday Evening Post*. "There is a sense of history in watching a competitor playing it boldly, all out, for the top stakes. Kennedy moves through the grind and rush of the day with a casual, jaunty air. He makes it look easy. He never seems in a hurry, and his high-spirited combination of earnestness and good humor seems as fresh at night as in the early morning." Kennedy liked and enjoyed people, and they knew it. Presidential scholar Tom Cronin says his candidacy appealed to the wellsprings of hope, compassion and decency in Americans. His crowds began to grow and his presence on the campaign trail became something incandescent. He had stage presence—and political sex appeal. Young girls would run alongside Jack's open-air car, jump up and down when he drove by and scream or climb right onto the car. Some would bounce, some would leap, some would teeter. After each town, reporters would count up the score at the last stop: "15 jumpers, 5 bouncers, 85 leapers. This burg is mostly leapers."

And, like his earlier campaigns, it wasn't just Jack on the stump. Two brothers, three sisters, three brothers-in-law and sisters-in-law and scads of Kennedy cousins were out on the campaign trail as well. The Kennedy family had "quickly developed into an entire political party," Hubert Humphrey, Jack's toughest competitor for the Democratic nomination in 1960, said he "felt like an independent merchant competing against a chain store. They're all over the state. They all look alike and sound alike so that if Teddy or Eunice talk to a crowd, wearing a raccoon coat and a stocking cap, people think they're listening to Jack. I get reports that Jack is appearing in three or four different places at the same time."[7] Humphrey had a geographic advantage in Wisconsin since his home state of Minnesota was next door, but the celebrity of the Kennedy family obliterated it. "Muriel and I and our 'plain folks' entourage were no match for the glamour of Jackie Kennedy and the other Kennedy women, for Peter Lawford and Sargent Shriver, for Frank Sinatra singing their commercial, 'High Hopes.' Jack Kennedy brought family and Hollywood to Wisconsin," said Humphrey. "The people loved it and the press ate it up."[8]

It was Bobby, of course, who first prodded Jack in 1958 to start thinking about specifics if he wanted to run for president in 1960. "All right, Jack, what are you doing about the campaign? I mean, have you done anything about the campaign yet? What sort of organization have you arranged? And where are we going? I don't hear anything about what you're doing and what you're saying about the campaign." Jack leaned over to a friend and said, "How would you like to hear that raspy voice in your ear for the next six months?"[9] But he soon made Bobby his campaign manager, and he and Stephen Smith, the 32-year-old husband of Jack's sister Jean, set up campaign headquarters in a nine-room office in Washington just weeks before the speech in Maryland. On the walls were detailed maps showing areas where Jack was likely to be weak or strong. Kennedy hired Lou Harris as a full-time pollster and began using opinion polls more effectively than any candidate had before, setting his campaign schedule and issues by them. Bobby quickly became the tactician as Jack evolved into the strategist. Jack paid attention to policy and speeches, Bobby to organization and staff. Bobby did the details, Jack the ideas. The brothers didn't see each other much since Bobby stayed put in Washington, but they talked by phone every night. Bobby was the more aggressive, more decisive communicator with staff. Jack would ask someone to do something, Bobby would order it. The mantra among harried staffers became "Little Brother is watching you."

Rose Kennedy, as usual, was one of Jack's most effective campaigners. She worked the crowds in the first primary state of New Hampshire with a strong maternal antiwar message. "Jack knows the sorrow, the grief, the tears and the heartbreaking grief and loneliness that come to a family when a mother has lost her eldest son and a young bride has lost her bridegroom. So I know Jack will never get us into war," Rose told receptive audiences.[10]

Jack won New Hampshire in a walk.

Bobby recommended against campaigning in the next primary, Wisconsin, since it bordered Humphrey's home state, but Jack's father insisted he go, "otherwise they'll say you're yellow." Jack's father had returned to his stealth role in the national election, making sure his $400 million fortune was put to good use in donations to churches, newspapers and charities all along Jack's path. Ted Sorensen said of the campaign, "The Ambassador was never present, but his presence was never absent."

The first strategy session was held next to the swimming pool at Joe Kennedy's Palm Beach estate on April 1, 1959, and Ted Kennedy was not present. "He was too young to play much of a role in the election," said Ben Bradlee. "He didn't know politicians across the country, which might have been helpful. He didn't have that experience yet." Though he didn't play a strategic role, Ted became something of a powerhouse campaigner for Jack. His talent lay in dreaming up innovative ways to win over crowds. Schlesinger called Kennedy's team "brilliant improvisers," not "systematic calculators." They ran their campaign with a lot of imagination. During the Wisconsin primary, Ted was told he could speak to a crowd of 10,000 at a ski-jumping contest if he made the 180-foot jump himself. He warned his host that he had never made a ski jump and would not likely be making his first one then. "But I went to the top of that 180-foot jump," Kennedy told Tom O'Hara of the *New York Herald Tribune*. "The first man went down. And disappeared. I knew he arrived safely because in the distance I could hear the faint sound of applause. The two others went down and disappeared. Then the announcer called: 'And now at the top of the jump is Ted Kennedy, brother of Sen. John F. Kennedy. Maybe if we give him a round of applause he will make his first jump.' I wanted to get off the jump, take off my skis or even go down the side. But if I did, I was afraid my brother would hear of it. And if he heard of it, I knew I would be back in Washington licking stamps and addressing envelopes for the rest of the campaign."[11] Kennedy would later tell friends that he had never been so deeply terrified as when he pushed his skis over the edge and jumped.[12] Once he was airborne, he straightened his skis as much as he could, and, 75 feet later, came crashing down into the snow, sliding into a row of spectators. Afterward, an anti-Kennedy politician said Ted had more guts than brains. He meant it as a compliment.

Bob Healy of the *Boston Globe* watched Ted campaign one morning at dawn. "He bounces around at 5:30 in the morning the way most men do after the third martini of the evening. Ted was sticking signs on the insides of car windows in a parking lot. A dog inside one of the cars nearly took his arm off but he kept on sticking signs."[13] Ted spent seven weeks campaigning in Wisconsin, interrupted only once—by the birth of his daughter Kara Anne Kennedy on February 27, 1960. Soon after, Jackie summoned Ted's wife, Joan, to the campaign trail, insisting she wear some of Jackie's clothes rather than her own. Joan, the former model, a a good sport about Jackie's tutelage on fashion and political hostessing, and they formed a tight bond during the campaign. Over a period of two weeks, each of the Kennedy sisters and wives attended nine house parties a day. Jack called Bobby's wife Ethel "Miss Perpetual Motion of 1960."

Jack won Wisconsin by more than 7,000 votes, surprising everyone except perhaps Joe. The House had bored Jack, but chasing after the country's biggest prize found him at his best. He may have been better at trying to win the presidency than he was at being president. Reporters never saw a hint of the impatience that had marked his legislative efforts. "Was Jack ever bored? He showed no trace of it," wrote Beverly Smith Jr., Washington editor of the *Saturday Evening Post*, after shadowing him for weeks. "His active mind and acute perceptions are at work. He is picking up local color and references for his own remarks later on. He is sensing the mood of the crowd. He is appraising and remembering each of the persons introduced. For these people, if they are not delegates themselves, will help choose the delegates for the National Convention."[14] With only 16 state primaries then, it was more important to win over state party leaders, though winning primaries was a sure way to impress them. By making direct contact with thousands of such officials, Kennedy was creating a loyalty that would later surprise other more seasoned candidates who were late getting in the field. Once again, Kennedy and his team drew a blueprint for the modern campaign by competing early and hard in many of the states that held caucuses, outhustling Humphrey and other major-league competitors like Senator Stuart Symington, Senator Lyndon Johnson, and two-time presidential candidate Adlai Stevenson.

When Joe, Jack, Bobby and Ted Sorensen were together plotting strategy, Ted Kennedy was often the odd man out. As campaign manager for Jack's 1958 reelection, he had helped win his brother a landslide, gaining

Jack considerable credibility as a rising Democratic star. But Ted was still considered the baby of the family by his brothers. In 1959, reporters joked, "Jack and Bobby run the show, while Ted's in charge of hiding Joe." At that stage in his career, Ted was more the eager mascot of the Kennedy team, willing to do somersaults, jump through hoops and risk his neck for his brother and the cause. He never minded doing the dirty work but he longed to be taken more seriously as well. "Teddy wanted to be one of the group," said Sorensen. "There was a big difference in years. And he took a lot of razzing and kidding and chastening. I'm sure he was not brought into the inner circle, in the early days. But he paid his dues."

At one point in the campaign for West Virginia, where John Kennedy's faith was his biggest stumbling block because of deep-seated prejudice against Catholics, Jack spoke so often and so loudly that he lost his voice. In Clarksburg, he wrote Dave Powers a note, saying: "Get Ted." Ted was summoned from a coal mine and took the stage in his brother's place. "We're all on the platform, and there's a great crowd," said Powers. "Oh what a great speech Ted made that day. He was goin' like mad. Ted had copied all the flourish and rapid-fire of his brother's speech, and even his phrases. 'Do you want a man who will give this country leadership? Do you want a man with vigor and vision?'"[15] Ted told the crowd a parable about two brothers who went fishing. One brother caught all the fish and the other caught nothing. The next morning, the one who caught nothing decided to fish alone. He fished for hours without catching anything and, finally, a fish stuck its head out of the water and asked, "Where's your brother?" Teddy then announced, "Well, here's my brother." With that, Jack Kennedy took the microphone to whisper, "I'd just like to tell my brother that you can't be elected President until you are thirty-five years of age."

Though he was advised to sidestep the religion issue, Jack decided in West Virginia to tackle it head-on. On the very first day of campaigning, speaking on the steps of the Charleston post office, he told a crowd of 300 to 400 people, "I am a Catholic, but the fact that I was born a Catholic, does that mean that I can't be the President of the United States? I'm able to serve in Congress, and my brother was able to give his life, but we can't be president?"[16] He made speech after speech in the same vein. The campaign aired a TV documentary that showcased his devotion to the country as a war hero, father and Pulitzer Prize–winning author of *Profiles in Courage*. "Over and over again," according to journalist Theodore White, "there was this handsome, open-faced candidate on the TV screen, showing himself, proving that a Catholic wears no horns."[17] A few weeks later, after it was clear that Kennedy had pulled off an improbable win in West Virginia, Jack told Ben

Bradlee on the campaign plane, "How the hell can they stop me now!"[18] When Bobby was congratulated on the campaign victory, he quipped: "I couldn't have done it without my brother."[19]

Kennedy added big wins in Nebraska, Maryland, Indiana and Oregon, and the *New York Times* wrote that the country had heard "the unmistakable sound of a bandwagon calliope."[20] As the campaign moved across the country, John put Teddy in charge of the Rocky Mountain states. "But all they gave me was a two-page memorandum with about ten different names on it, plus a speech my brother made in Montana in 1957," said Ted. "The rest was up to me. Luckily I learned how to fly a plane when I went to law school." Ted made it up as he went along, traveling to the tiniest of towns, drumming up publicity for his brother. Former senator Al Simpson remembers when Ted walked into Svilar's bar and lounge in Hudson, Wyoming, population 400, where Simpson was working at the time. "Then he went down to Frontier Days, to Cheyenne, because there's a lot of people there in late July." Kennedy talked somebody into letting him ride a bull in the Cheyenne rodeo, which is still known across the West as the Grandaddy of Them All. With a fairly Republican crowd egging him on, he rode seven seconds before he was bucked off, a respectable feat for a novice, Simpson remembers. Ted also rode a bronco named Skyrocket in Miles City, Montana, during the general election campaign, after which Jack called to say he was arranging to have a sharpshooter shoot a cigarette out of Ted's mouth the next week.[21]

Flying to central Utah during another campaign jaunt, Ted's pilot ran into fog and set the plane down on a highway about 15 miles away from their destination of Price.[22] Ted found a car parked on the side of the road and tried to hotwire it. As he leaned under the steering wheel, a trapper wearing two revolvers came up and demanded, "What are you doing with my car?" Ted's companion, Oscar McConkie, knew the man and talked him into giving them a ride to Price. Seems McConkie's father was a judge and had once given the trapper a break.

Ted was trying to prove himself to his brothers. He peppered Bobby with memos during the campaign suggesting subjects for Jack's talks and people he should contact. He helped build an organization out west. "Brother Teddy has largely been the man who goes after the grass-roots vote, and has seen more factory gates at dawn than many factory workers," said Jack.[23] He never said it to Teddy, but Jack told others his brother "accomplished wonders." Dave Powers, one of Jack's closest friends and a political mentor, said, "What I loved about Bobby and Teddy was that in the history of American politics, I never saw brothers as dedicated to the success of Jack as Bobby and Teddy were."[24]

Ted made seven trips to Wyoming, and they paid off at the Democratic convention in Los Angeles. Johnson and Stevenson were plotting ways to step in if Kennedy's support crumbled, so the Kennedy team hoped to sew up the nomination on the first ballot to avoid the unpredictability of party deal-making. They needed 761 votes and came into the convention with 550. In an echo of Rose's card file, Bobby kept four-inch by six-inch blue cards on the 4,509 delegates in a file known as the box.[25] The cards included their vital stats, hobbies, habits and children's names. When it came to pressuring them for votes, Bobby knew just which buttons to push. "We held a review on the states every morning to determine our gains and losses," Ted said, "and we knew where we stood to within a vote and a half."[26] The evening before the roll call, Bobby felt that his count was so close it would come down to the last state. He asked Ted to visit Wyoming's Democratic National Committee member, Tracy McCraken. Ted asked Tracy, "If it comes down to where Wyoming can make the difference, would you be willing to commit all fifteen in your delegation?" McCraken didn't think five votes would make much of a difference (ten were already committed to Kennedy). So he said sure, why not.

The day of the roll call, Bobby worked the floor relentlessly, making sure his vote count was accurate and keeping the Kennedy commitments solid. Ted stayed with the Wyoming delegation as the vote began. He was there right in the middle of the picture, smiling broadly, as television cameras captured the moment when Wyoming put Jack over the top. McCraken kept his word and announced the news to the country: "Wyoming casts all 15 votes for the next President of the United States."

Ted Kennedy stayed out West for the general election campaign, but the scale of the campaign shifted, making his grassroots political skills less important. Jack Kennedy would sprint through 47 states in ten weeks carrying the slogan "to get the country moving again." But in 1960, the candidates were also beginning to realize the power of television to reach large audiences without any rallies, parades, handshaking or bands. "This is the beginning of a whole new concept," said a young Roger Ailes as he stage-managed Richard Nixon's 1968 presidential campaign. "This is the way they'll be elected forevermore. The next guys up will have to be performers."[27]

The three television networks offered both candidates free TV exposure in prime time for four debates. The first televised debate between Nixon and Kennedy on September 25 reached 60–70 million people, and the two-podium format set a standard for such encounters that still reigns today. Kennedy was carefully coached on how to present himself on television. He wore a dark suit and very little makeup while Nixon had on a gray suit that didn't contrast with the background very well. Nixon was recovering from the flu at the time and had lost weight, so he appeared less vigorous than Kennedy onstage. He shifted his eyes when the camera was on him, leaving an impression of nervousness. The heavy theatrical makeup Nixon wore to hide his jowls and heavy beard caused him to sweat under the lights, while Kennedy looked forceful and cool. After the debate, Kennedy was treated like a rock star, and the wall between traditional political power and modern media celebrity dissolved forever. Enormous, wildly enthusiastic crowds met him everywhere he went. He had the momentum and never looked back.

In the waning days of the campaign, 10,000 people gathered in the middle of the night to hear John Kennedy speak at the University of Michigan. Kennedy finally arrived at 2 A.M. after an exhausting 18-hour day and delivered some extemporaneous remarks from the steps of the Student Union. Earlier in the evening, he'd faced off with Richard Nixon in their third and last debate. Nixon had made a remark that stayed with Kennedy. The Republican nominee said he did not mean to suggest that the Democratic party was a "war party," but he observed that three Democratic presidents had led the country into war in the last century. For most of the campaign, Nixon had been attacking Kennedy and the Democrats for not being tough enough on Communists, and suddenly he'd turned the tables and accused the Democrats of being warmongers. Nixon's words likely were still rattling around in Kennedy's head when he decided off the cuff to challenge the students in Ann Arbor to do something constructive for the world when they graduated. Remembering some ideas about public service that had been floating around the campaign for a few weeks, he exhorted them to rise up and form an army of peace.

"How many of you [who] are going to be doctors are willing to spend your days in Ghana? Technicians and engineers, how many of you are willing to work in the Foreign Service, and spend your lives traveling around the world? On your willingness to do that . . . will depend the answer whether we as a free society can compete."

The students answered with a standing ovation.

Kennedy had stirred something. The proposal encapsulated the entire thrust of his campaign and its call for a public service awakening. Shortly after, students Alan and Judy Guskin wrote a letter to the editor of the *Michigan*

Daily, Tom Hayden, who would later become the leader of Students for a Democratic Society and eventually marry Jane Fonda. The letter asked people to
help them push for Kennedy's idea of a global army of peace. In response, 250
students, accompanied by a few professors, organized Americans Committed
to World Responsibility. They answered Kennedy's challenge with petitions,
and students volunteered for the fledging group in droves. After nearly 1,000
signed up, the organizers got in touch with Kennedy's campaign. When the
candidate heard about their surge of interest, he decided to formally propose
the idea as one of his campaign promises. On November 2, 1960, at the Cow
Palace in San Francisco, Kennedy pledged that, if he was elected, he would form
a Peace Corps to tap the talents of young American volunteers who "could work
modern miracles for peace in dozens of underdeveloped countries." As evidence that the country was in the mood for such an idealistic undertaking, he
cited the response of the Michigan students.

Nixon derided the idea as a form of draft evasion. Eisenhower called it
"Kennedy's Kiddie Korps." But media response was overwhelmingly positive.
In his inaugural address, Kennedy called on Americans to do something for
their country, and the Peace Corps became his concrete answer to those
moved to answer that call. The Peace Corps was one of the first programs
launched during his administration, and the two students who had written
the letter to the *Michigan Daily* became two of its first volunteers. Kennedy's
spontaneous desire that night in Ann Arbor to cast himself as a man of peace,
not war, turned into his most representative—and perhaps most enduring—
legacy. In his book *Of Kennedys and Kings,* Kennedy aide Harris Wofford
wrote, "Nothing symbolized the passing of the generational torch in 1960 the
way the Peace Corps did, and no light from that confident period shines
brighter today."

★ ★ ★

Historians believe the Peace Corps idea won Kennedy thousands of crucial
votes and helped mobilize students and other newly registered voters in the
final weeks of the campaign. Then Bobby padded the margin just a bit more
when he helped get civil rights leader the Reverend Dr. Martin Luther King,
out of jail, planting the very first seeds of another legacy all three brothers
would eventually pursue: civil rights.

King had been sentenced to four months of hard labor for a minor traffic
offense by a segregationist judge in Georgia. King's wife, Coretta, worriedly
called Harris Wofford, who had been assigned to work on civil rights aspects
of the campaign with Sargent Shriver. "They are going to kill him. I know
they are going to kill him," Coretta told Wofford. King was being held in the

DeKalb County jail, a rural Southern prison notorious for mistreating black prisoners. The future Pennsylvania senator reassured her but thought Kennedy ought to call Coretta himself. Wofford believed such a call would send two messages to Georgia officials: "Don't mess with King in jail because the eyes of the nation are watching you" and, "He's got to be released." Wofford and Shriver didn't try to run the idea through the regular campaign channels, namely Bobby, because they knew they'd get shot down. So Shriver went directly to Jack, who responded, "That's a good idea. Why not? Do you have her number? Get her on the phone."[29] Shriver had the number, and within minutes Kennedy was talking to Coretta. The future president expressed his concern, sympathized with how extremely difficult the situation was and promised to do all he could to help.[29]

Bobby was furious when he found out. "You bomb-throwers probably lost the election," he told Wofford and Shriver. By aligning Kennedy with black activism, Bobby thought they had probably alienated a host of white Southern voters. Ted remembered going into a room after the call and listening as Jack and Bobby talked and talked and talked. Bobby stalked out and got on a plane to New York. For some reason, Bobby began to transfer his fury from the staff to the judge who started it all. The injustice of the sentence "burned me up," he recalled later. He felt the judge was "screwing up my brother's campaign and making our country look ridiculous before the world." So Bobby decided to call the judge and give him a piece of his mind. When he landed in New York, he went straight to a phone booth. Bobby made it clear to the judge that it was not a political phone call, but a call from a lawyer who believes in the right of all defendants to make bond. He said that if the judge were a decent American, he would let King out by sundown.[30] Feeling pressure from many directions, the judge thanked him for the call and did just that. As a result of the two phone calls, Daddy King—a Baptist minister and lifelong Republican because Abraham Lincoln had been a Republican—decided to hold a press conference. He announced that Senator Kennedy had called his daughter-in-law and helped get his son out of jail. I got a "suitcase full of votes—my whole church" for Kennedy, he added. Kennedy and Kennedy had struck their first two small blows for civil rights. The calls had been made more out of political expediency rather than moral rightness, but they were the start of a commitment among the brothers that would grow into one of their primary legacies, a legacy that would come to full fruition in Ted Kennedy's 45-year dedication to civil rights.

Kennedy headquarters distributed 2 million pamphlets recounting Jack's intervention in the King case. Campaign workers dubbed the pamphlet, which was printed on light blue paper, "the blue bomb."

Two days later, the entire Kennedy clan gathered at Hyannis Port to await returns. Bobby set up an election command post in his breakfast room. Ninety assistants in key precincts all over the country called vote tallies into him. When the results started coming in, Hawaii was the first state to go for Kennedy. A great hurrah went up at the Kennedy compound, and Ted stood up and said, "And you fellows all thought I was doing nothing else in Hawaii but lying on the beach!"[31] By midnight the race was still up in the air. At 2 A.M., Boss Daley called from Illinois to promise that he'd carry the state for Jack. Later, gangster Sam Giancana claimed he had stolen enough votes to guarantee Jack's victory in Illinois, a boast that was impossible to prove. But Jack would have won the election even without Illinois.

Jack went to bed at about 4:30 A.M. before the results were final, but Bobby stayed up into the small hours of the morning, running up a $10,000 phone bill keeping tabs on the count. Joe was the last one to go to sleep, however, and only after he was sure his son's victory was assured. It was Caroline who woke her father with the news the next morning, jumping onto his bed and pulling the blankets off him. "Good morning, Mr. President," she exclaimed.

John Kennedy was elected by 115,000 votes out of 71 million, about one vote per precinct. The small margin shocked the Kennedys, whose polling had predicted a victory between 53 and 57 percent. But statistical breakdowns would later show that Kennedy's Catholicism was still an issue for many voters, even though they wouldn't say so to pollsters. For the first time, a president had won with a minority of Protestant voters. Ten out of the 13 states out West, where Teddy had campaigned, ended up going for Nixon.

In the end, many observers, including President Eisenhower, thought Kennedy had eked out his slim victory at the last minute with the two phone calls to Georgia.

6

LET US BEGIN

A golden age of poetry and power
Of which this noonday's the beginning hour.

> —Closing lines of the poem Robert Frost
> penned for the Kennedy inaugural
> but never read

Four inches of snow had fallen in Georgetown over the weekend, and the morning was ice cold. Jack was serving bacon and eggs for breakfast at the house on N Street. Bobby arrived with his best friend, John Seigenthaler, a former reporter for the *Nashville Tennessean* who had edited Bobby's book on the Mafia, *The War Within*. Seigenthaler had come along for moral support because Bobby had decided the night before that he was going to turn down the job of attorney general in his brother's administration. He had made the decision after soliciting the opinions of a number of old Washington hands, all of whom had recommended against taking the job. *It'd look like nepotism*, they warned. *Jack's popularity would take an immediate hit. You're too young and inexperienced. You've never practiced law, how can you be the nation's preeminent lawyer? The president already has a vice president.* It wasn't just their advice that made up his mind, though. Bobby told friends he was "tired of chasing bad guys." He'd made a raft of enemies with his sharp elbows during the campaign and earlier, as chief counsel fighting labor racketeering for the Senate Select Committee on Improper Activities in the Labor or Management Field from 1957 to 1959. And now he was telling people he wanted to travel around the world, or write a book, or become a college president, or run for governor of Massachusetts.[1] The night before, he'd called Jack up to say he didn't want the job, and Jack had told him to come by in the morning to discuss it. Bobby turned to a friend after the call and said, "This will kill my father."

In Joe Kennedy's mind, Jack's presidential victory belonged to the entire family, and he wanted both Bobby and Ted to reap some of the spoils. He had decided Ted would fill Jack's Senate seat, and he insisted Bobby be attorney general. The brothers had won the election together; there was no reason why they ought not to run the country together now. "Why should the president appoint people whose qualifications he doesn't know first hand," Joe asked, "and not appoint people whose qualifications he does know first hand—simply because they are relatives?"[2]

As Bobby recounted the story later, he, Jack and Teddy had all been dead set against the idea from the start. Jack sent several people to try to talk his dad out of it, including Senator George Smathers and Clark Clifford. "He wouldn't hear of anything else," Bobby said. "He felt that Jack should have somebody that . . . had been close for a long period of time, and he wanted me in this job. I was against it and we had some rather strong arguments out here, all the family—a couple of my sisters, Jack and Teddy and my father." If he took the job, Bobby foresaw a clash of the titans in the White House between his strong-willed brother and him. "It would be impossible with the two of us sitting around an office looking at each other all day," Bobby said. "You know, it was like the campaign . . . he had his role in the campaign and I had my role and we would meet and discuss when a crisis came up . . . but he never involved himself in what I was doing—the running of the campaign—and I was not directly associated with what he was doing . . . we had to have our own areas—I had to be apart from what he was doing so I wasn't working directly for his and getting orders from his as to what I should do that day. That wouldn't be possible. So I would never consider working over at the White House."[3]

When Bobby sat down to eat in the small breakfast nook, Jack began commenting on the merits of his Cabinet appointments. Finally Bobby stopped him. "Now, Johnny, can we talk about my situation?"[4]

Jack began making his case, which was really his father's case, Seigenthaler recalls. "I need to know that when problems arise, I'm going to have to have someone who's going to tell me the unvarnished truth, no matter what he thinks," Jack said, addressing Seigenthaler more than Bobby. "I don't want somebody who is going to be fainthearted. I want somebody who is going to be strong; who will join with me in taking risks . . . and who would deal with the problem honestly. . . . We're going to have to change the climate in this country. And if my administration does the things I want it to do, I'm going to have to be able to have someone as Attorney General to carry these things out, on whom I can rely completely."[5]

The president added that he really needed someone who would "never screw him."

Jack and Bobby kept talking for 40 minutes. Bobby listed all the reasons why he had to turn the job down, and his brother told him all the reasons why he had to take it. Finally, Jack summed up his position by appealing to Bobby's unshakable sense of loyalty. "If I can ask Dean Rusk to give up a career; if I can ask Adlai Stevenson to make a sacrifice he does not want to make; if I can ask Bob McNamara to give up a job as head of that company— these people I don't even know . . . certainly I can expect my own brother to give me that same sort of contribution. And I need you in this government."[6]

Bobby, so determined the night before, told Jack he thought he should think about it.

Jack pushed back his chair and left the kitchen. Seigenthaler and Bobby sat there, not sure if he was coming back. After a few minutes, Seigenthaler figured that Jack had terminated the conversation.

"Let's go, Bob," he said.

"No wait. I've got some points I want to make."

"There's no point to make," Seigenthaler replied.

Jack walked back in, saying "So that's it. . . . General, let's go." He had cut off all argument by announcing his brother's new title.

For all his prior reluctance, Bobby came around fast to Jack's point of view that morning, probably because the whole scene was faked. If the Kennedys made it look like Bobby was dragged into the job by his ear, perhaps charges of an overly ambitious family trying to make the U.S. government its own private court would dissipate. In his book *Unfinished Life*, Robert Dallek points out that Bobby had written a letter the day before his conversation with Jack that said "I made up my mind today and Jack and I take the plunge tomorrow." Seigenthaler had been brought along not for moral support but to get the story of Bobby's reluctance, and Jack's insistence, on the record. The brothers play-acted the whole scene.

Jack told Ben Bradlee that he had actually wanted to announce the appointment at 2 A.M. some morning. He would open the door, look up and down the street, and if no one was there, he would whisper, "It's Bobby." Instead, the announcement came at about noon that same day on the front steps of Jack's narrow brick townhouse. "Well, let's go out and announce it," Bobby said to Jack. "Let's grab our balls and go." Jack told him to brush his hair, to which Bobby said "it was the first time the president had ever told the attorney general to comb his hair before they made an announcement." As they went through the door, Jack also warned him not to smile too much "or they'll think we're happy about the appointment."[7]

Reaction in the press was mixed, which is probably the best the brothers could have hoped for. Once Bobby proved his worth to the country, Jack believed, the cries of dynasty building and nepotism would die down forever. Or at least until Ted ran for the Senate. When Ted heard about Bobby's appointment, he wasn't quite sure what his place would be in the family firmament. "Any room in the Department for a guy who graduated in the top half of the bottom quarter of his Class . . . congratulations," he wrote to Bobby.[8] At 28, Ted was never considered for a position in the administration. He would have to wait two years for his chance to play a role.

It was 22 degrees on the day of the inauguration. Eight inches of snow had shut down Washington the night before, stranding 10,000 cars across the city, including one containing Teddy and his father. Rose saw Jack at Mass at St. Michael's early the next morning, sitting by himself, lost in thought. Rose wore the same gown for the inauguration she had worn when she was presented at the Court of St. James 20 years earlier, and the brothers all wore top hats. An 18-mile-an-hour wind whipped against the portico as Jack gave his inaugural address from the Capitol. The youngest president in history was a snapshot of the nation's belief in its own virility: He delivered his speech without a coat. Observers gathered on the lawn below could see his breath as he spoke. A physician noticed that he was sweating, and wondered if he'd had a double dose of the cortisone that he relied on to make it though the day.[9]

At a deliberate pace, the new president rolled out the cadences of what would become known as one of America's great speeches, often punctuating each half of his parallel phrases with a forceful down-thrust of his fist. At times he would point a finger out at the crowd as he pumped his clenched hand up and down, like a baton, as if he were keeping beat to the music of his words. His voice would rise and fall dramatically to the rhythm of his antitheses and alliteration. The crowd was rapt. It was five minutes before anyone thought to applaud.

The speech's most memorable lines came at the end, and embodied the entire speech and all that came before, in the campaign, and would come after, in the presidency—a two-sentence legacy.

> And so, my fellow Americans: ask not what you your country can do for you—
> ask what you can do for your country. My fellow citizens of the world: ask not

what America will do for you, but what together we can do for the freedom of man.

The poet Robert Frost was too blinded by the sun to read his tribute poem to Jack afterward, so he recited "The Gift Outright" from memory instead.

It took three buses, marked *Kennedy Family*, to deliver the entire, joyous clan to the reviewing stand for the parade up Pennsylvania Avenue. A million people had bundled up in their snowsuits, wool coats, fur hats, mufflers, hoods, scarves, boots and galoshes to see the new president and his 31-year-old wife make the drive to the White House. The tanned leading man and his model first lady looked impossibly young and glamorous as they glided by in their convertible. With a face-splitting smile, Joe Kennedy told his friends simply, it was "a great day." As the president drove past the reviewing stand in his open limousine, his father rose up out of his seat and doffed his silk high hat to his son. The president looked up and took off his own hat and tipped it to his father. They'd done it. Later, family members would remember the moment as the weekend's most moving. Eunice quoted poet Laurie Lee to her father: "Any man's child is his second chance."[10]

That night on one of the inaugural party buses, Clare Booth Luce remembers Teddy robustly singing Irish ballads. She thought to herself, "He looks like a Greek god!"[11] Ambassador Herve Alphand of France saw Ted "dancing madly on the platform" later after drinking "more than is customary." And sometime during the long inaugural weekend of balls and parties and unbridled exuberance, John Kennedy gave Ted a small cigarette box, engraved with the words "And the Last Shall Be First."

For their first Cabinet meeting, Jack told Bobby to go in a different door so it didn't look like they had arrived together. In the early days of the new administration, the president meant to keep Bobby at arm's length to damp down the cronyism complaints. The president's private secretary, Evelyn Lincoln, required Bobby to make appointments to see the president just like everyone else. But that was for show as well. Bobby slipped into the back door of the office whenever he wanted to see Jack. "He didn't come through the front, where the press would spot him," said Washington correspondent Esther Tufty.[12] History has painted Bobby as the No. 2 man in the White House, but speechwriter Ted Sorensen doesn't remember it that way. Bobby was very busy with the Justice Department, whose charge included the fight against organized crime and the enforcement of civil rights. Sorensen said Bobby wasn't in on every major decision, and Jack kept him off the National Security Council, which made most of the administration's foreign policy decisions. And Bobby wasn't briefed on the ill-fated Bay of Pigs invasion of Cuba until the week before it launched.

★ ★ ★

With the kind of boldness he had promised during the campaign, Jack set the Cuban invasion in motion less than 90 days after he had taken office. The plan had been concocted by the Eisenhower administration, but it was John Kennedy who pulled the trigger. At a secret Guatemalan base, CIA agents had trained and armed a brigade of 1,500 Cuban exiles for an attempt to overthrow Communist firebrand Fidel Castro. The Bay of Pigs, however, was one of Castro's favorite locations, a place he went on weekends to fish and knew well. It was also miles and miles from the mountains, where the exiles might have disappeared to begin an insurgency. Castro quickly directed troops to surround the exiles and push them back into the sea. His fighter planes blew up supply ships and strafed the beaches, leaving the U.S.-backed invaders dying in the surf. "The United States sponsored the attack because it cannot forgive us for achieving a Socialist revolution under their noses," Castro boasted triumphantly after his victory.[13]

In the hours and days after the landing went disastrously wrong, many people in Kennedy's inner circle were counseling a full U.S. invasion to rescue the exiles. But Kennedy, who didn't want the landing to have the telltale footprint of a large-scale American invasion, refused to order the U.S. planes and ships just offshore to rescue the survivors.

As the Bay of Pigs was coming to an end, the president said, "It's a hell of a way to learn things." He asked Ted Sorensen: "How could I have been so far off base? All my life I've known better than to depend on the experts. How could I have been so stupid, to let them go ahead?"[14] He took full responsibility for the failed attack, noting at a press conference that "victory has a thousand fathers, but defeat is an orphan." After the Bay of Pigs, Kennedy vowed to involve Bobby in all critical foreign policy, intelligence and defense decisions so he could get the "unvarnished truth." "I made a mistake of putting Bobby in the Justice Department," he said. "Bobby should be in CIA."[15]

Arthur Schlesinger and Ted Sorensen, in the two best-known books on the Kennedy presidency, argued that the Bay of Pigs made Kennedy a better and wiser president. Robert Kennedy also believed that the Bay of Pigs "made the President a different man."[16] But once Bobby got involved in foreign policy, efforts to eliminate Castro never really stopped. Instead they became covert, in the form of Operation Mongoose, which Bobby personally oversaw. During the next year, the CIA did everything in its power to try to

get even with Castro, short of an invasion. "My idea is to stir things up on island with espionage, sabotage, general disorder, run & operated by the
Cubans themselves," Bobby wrote in a November 1961 memo.[17] Jack may
have begun to learn something about the limits of American power, but
Bobby wanted revenge for his brother. As a newcomer to foreign policy,
Bobby Kennedy was an easy target for the "military-CIA-paramilitary type
answers" that dominated discussions about Castro, said Chester Bowles, the
one top adviser who had opposed the invasion plan. Bobby invited Green
Berets to come and do training exercises at Hyannis Port. The CIA's techni-
cal services division planned activities like putting chemicals in Castro's
shoes that would cause his beard to fall out, damaging his macho image.
They planned to spray drugs into his broadcasting studio so he would sound
incoherent on the air. There was even a secret plan to treat Castro's cigars
with poison.

The fear of being soft, the resolve never to be seen as a coward, was still
very much a part of the Kennedy presidency after the Bay of Pigs. Jack and
Bobby both treated the competition with Castro as *mano a mano*. Critics
began to sense a disconnect between Jack Kennedy's rhetoric and his actions
when it came to Cuba. Though the president clearly felt the execution of the
invasion was bungled, it's not entirely clear he ever concluded that the idea of
the invasion, of overthrowing Castro, was a mistake. The lesson of the Bay of
Pigs was only half learned. It would take the Cuban Missile Crisis for Bobby
and Jack to arrive at a new understanding of the courage that both men
treasured.

After the Bay of Pigs, John Kennedy's presidency really became a joint presidency between John and Bobby. Bobby installed a special direct phone line
so he and Jack could talk several times a day. They'd often huddle for hours
in the Oval Office or take extensive walks together in the Rose Garden. Jack
came to rely on Bobby's advice more than anyone else's. "It was almost like a
single organism, or the two cylinders of a two-cylinder engine," said Bobby's
associate John Nolan.[18] A White House official, Richard Goodwin, came to
believe that Bobby's sometimes harsh style "reflected the president's own
concealed emotions, privately communicated in some earlier intimate conversation. . . . [There] was an inner hardness, often volatile anger, beneath
the outwardly amiable, thoughtful, carefully controlled demeanor of Jack
Kennedy."[19] Bobby was the critical, moralizing superego to Jack's ego. At this
stage, Ted was probably the instinctive, impulsive id in the Kennedy brain
trust, though certainly Jack's womanizing made him a candidate for that

classification as well. Having a ruder, rougher version of himself in the White House allowed Jack to skate above the fray, maintaining his outward grace and charm as Bobby did the dirty work. The good-cop, bad-cop nature of the friendship expressed itself in full force in times of crisis, when Jack was trying to make a decision. Just as he had in the campaign, Bobby often dressed down other aides and shouted orders during crisis management. "Bobby would sit there chewing gum, his tie loose, his feet up on the desk, daring anyone to contradict him," recalled Thomas Parrott, the official White House note taker at Operation Mongoose meetings. "He was a little bastard, but he was the president's brother, the anointed guy, and you had to listen to him. Everyone felt that he would tell Big Brother if you didn't go along with what he was proposing."[20] Norman Mailer once described Jack as a realist disguised as a romantic and Bobby as a romantic disguised as a realist.

By October 1962, Bobby may have begun to grow weary of all the secret plots and shadow wars, however. Harris Wofford, a special assistant to the president at the time, believes Bobby's attitude and approach to his role shifted dramatically after May 1962. That's when J. Edgar Hoover sent the attorney general a memo admitting the FBI was using underworld crime figures Sam Giancana and John Rosselli as a link to criminals in Cuba who might help with the CIA's clandestine campaign against Castro. Giancana had been a primary target of the McClellan committee probes when Bobby was counsel. As attorney general, Bobby had also singled out Giancana in a stepped-up drive against organized crime. Hoover also told Bobby that a woman the president had an ongoing relationship with was a close associate of Giancana. Judith Campbell Exner later published a book, *My Story,* claiming simultaneous affairs with John Kennedy and Sam Giancana. Whatever the truth of her assertions, which have never been verified, the information about her mob connections must have sent Bobby's moral compass spinning. Bobby and Jack had also ordered wiretaps on the Reverend Dr. Martin Luther King.

Wofford believes the CIA, Mafia, assassination and sex entanglement had a profound effect on Bobby's puritan soul. He may have felt his brother's administration was slipping into a moral quagmire and wanted desperately to right the ship. He got the chance with the Cuban Missile Crisis.

The major difference between the handling of the Bay of Pigs and the handling of the October showdown was the strength of Bobby's voice. When the president learned in October 1962 that the Soviet Union was stationing nuclear missiles in Cuba within striking distance of the United States, many aides close to the president advised Kennedy to launch preemptive air strikes before the missiles became operational. But the failure to overthrow Fidel Castro in the Bay of Pigs had made John Kennedy twice shy about using military force. Over the course of 13 tense days, when Russia and America came closer to nuclear war than they ever had, Robert Kennedy argued passionately that a first strike against Cuba contradicted American values. He told his brother it would be perceived as a Pearl Harbor in reverse. "I said we were fighting for something more than just survival and that all our heritage and our ideals would be repugnant to such a sneak military attack," Bobby reported later. "For 175 years, we have not been that kind of country," he argued.[21] For the first five days of the crisis, Bobby insisted the advisers spent more time on "this moral question" than anything else.

Because of his clear views on right and wrong, Bobby served as Jack's— and the country's—conscience during the crisis. In an article written early in Bobby's tenure as attorney general, *Life* magazine's Paul O'Neil wrote: "He is motivated—in his concern for his friends and allies, in his almost emotional refusal to be swayed by wealth and social position, and in his pugnacity as well—by a stern and literal belief in concepts of good and evil which most humans abandon after childhood, and by a sense of duty to family and country which overrides his own considerable ambition. . . . Though he clings to attitudes the world considers impractical in the extreme, he practices them with a calculating pragmatism."[22] Bobby may have been the most passionate opponent to an offensive attack because he was intimately aware of all the clandestine efforts by the CIA that had provoked Castro. The Soviets had claimed the missiles were being stationed for purely defensive reasons, to deter the United States from its constant efforts to undermine Castro's regime. Bobby knew the Russians had a point, that the United States had actually started the fight. Bobby knew the missiles were not an act of sheer aggression, and therefore the Russians might be open to some sort of bargain.

The president decided to follow his conscience, namely Bobby, instead of his generals. Rather than attack preemptively, President Kennedy blockaded Cuba and gave Castro a deadline for withdrawing the missiles. Bobby delivered a secret message to the Russian ambassador that promised the United States would dismantle nuclear missiles in Turkey if Russia dismantled the Cuban missiles, a trade that was not made public until after Bobby's death. With Sorensen's help Bobby drafted the president's message to Khrushchev that ended the showdown. Douglas Dillon, the secretary of the treasury who had favored an air strike, had been persuaded—and impressed—by Bobby's "intense but quiet passion." He felt the moment was "a real turning point in history."[23]

The crisis became the basis for new agreements on nuclear weapons and the template for détente for the rest of the cold war. Never again would the two countries go to the brink as they had during the Cuban Missile Crisis. It also allowed Jack Kennedy to regain some of the moral authority he had squandered in the Bay of Pigs. When the president delivered his "Peace Speech" at American University on June 10, 1963, he had come to see an urgent need to beat swords into plowshares, to channel America's competitive drive and conflict with Russia into new, nondestructive avenues, such as a competition to reach the moon. Immediately after the speech, the Soviet Union entered into high-level discussions that led to the first nuclear arms control accord. The Test Ban Treaty of 1963 eliminated all aboveground and underwater nuclear weapons tests and laid the foundation for the Nuclear Non-Proliferation Treaty signed in 1968 by President Lyndon Johnson. President Nixon later pushed that treaty through Congress, and nearly 200 countries have signed it, voluntarily forgoing nuclear weapons. "It may sound corny," President Kennedy said in 1963, "but I am thinking not so much of our world but the world Caroline will live in."[24]

The shift toward détente and arms control has become a key part of the Kennedy legacy. The restraint the Kennedy administration showed, thanks largely to Bobby, had a ripple effect for decades to come. In the Soviet Union, after the crisis the Kennedys would always be regarded as a family that understood the costs of war. Ted Kennedy would come to be seen in Russia as a leading fighter for nuclear disarmament, sometimes to the dismay of American presidents. Ted pursued better relations with the U.S.S.R. for decades, holding several personal talks on arms control with Soviet leaders. In a meeting with Leonid Brezhnev in 1974, he picked up where his brother had left off with the atmospheric test ban, pushing for a ban on all nuclear tests, which is what John had really wanted. Ted had a draft treaty with him in his pocket to show Brezhnev. It was translated and read to the Soviet leader, who was enthusiastic. "If you were President of the United States now," Brezhnev said when the reading was finished, "I would ask you to sit over here in front of this fireplace. We would light a fire, and we would have some vodka and both of us would sign it and celebrate a great step toward halting nuclear expansion."[25]

During the Reagan years, when the president was trying to build up the U.S. arsenal of nuclear weapons, Ted Kennedy offered a congressional resolution calling for a freeze of nuclear weapons at existing levels, and then a reduction. Nuclear freeze rallies began attracting huge crowds in the United States and Europe. More than 100,000 people attended a rally in New York City. Ted Kennedy wrote a book on the movement. Though the resolution eventually failed, Ted Kennedy argued that the freeze movement "had an impact in terms of the American people's understanding of what mutually assured destruction was really all about. . . . I think we were able to have some impact in people's thinking that they could not really be winners in terms of the arms race."[26]

Two days after Ted introduced the resolution, the Reagan administration announced a new arms control effort, which later became known as the Strategic Arms Reduction Treaty (START). In those talks, Reagan proposed a dramatic reduction in strategic forces in two phases. Later, Kennedy became a crucial back channel to Soviet leader Mikhail Gorbachev for Reagan as the talks progressed. During a meeting in 1986, the Soviet leader told Kennedy he had prepared for their conversation by watching a film on President Kennedy, and said he would never forget John-John saluting his father's coffin.[27] He asked how John Jr. was doing, and told Ted that it was important to keep their communication going. The Strategic Arms Reduction Treaty (START) treaty was finally signed on July 31, 1991, five months before the collapse of the Soviet Union, and Kennedy helped ensure its approval in Congress. It has more than halved the world's arsenal of nuclear weapons.

In 1996, after years of advocacy by Ted, John Kennedy's dream of a comprehensive treaty banning nuclear tests in all environments was signed by 71 nations. The United States was one of the signatories, but Congress has not ratified the treaty yet. Ted Kennedy still considered his work unfinished, and saw nuclear arms control as one of the country's most important challenges. During the presidency of George W. Bush, Ted fought against efforts to manufacture "mini-nukes" and "bunker-buster" nuclear weapons. And in 2006, Kennedy wrote: "Terrorism is our newest enemy, but the spread of nuclear weapons remains our greatest threat."

The Cuban Missile Crisis and the pursuit of arms control and détente are what history recognizes as John's main legacy, but other aspects of his presidency have resounded for decades, both negatively and positively. For large numbers of Americans, his inaugural address was more meaningful than even his presidency.

"It's almost a cliché to say it, but I was stunned by the inaugural address. As I think lots of people were," said political strategist Bob Shrum. Rose said the speech reminded her of the words of St. Luke "which I had recited to him so often. 'Those to whom much is given, much is expected.'"[28] In the years to come, the other Kennedy brothers would follow the speech like a road map as they sought to complete their brother's unfinished dreams.

One of the most moving parts of the address was the galvanizing call to public service and volunteerism. More than anything, the speech was a rallying cry to a new generation to get *involved*: "The energy, the faith, the devotion which we bring to this endeavor will light our country and all who serve it—and the glow from that fire can truly light the world."

Over the years, Ted Kennedy watched over the government's commitment to John's call to service and expanded on it via AmeriCorps, Points of Light, VISTA and the Corporation for National Service. In 2008, Ted Kennedy introduced a bill in Congress, with cosponsor Orrin Hatch, to dramatically scale up the national service idea first launched by his brother John. He has hopes of enlisting more than 200,000 people in a comprehensive national service program.

Another major piece of JFK's legacy, also announced in the inaugural address, was the idealism and optimism he inspired with his New Frontier imagery: "We stand at the edge of a New Frontier—the frontier of unfulfilled hopes and dreams."

JFK became emblematic of a much-imitated form of leadership celebrating aspiration and challenge. Leaders such as Bill Clinton, Gary Hart, Ronald Reagan and Barack Obama all attempted to echo JFK's approach. Presidential scholar Tom Cronin believes John Kennedy "was more than anything else a motivator, a morale builder and a renewer of spirit."[29] Friend and biographer Arthur Schlesinger Jr. said, "The energies he released, the standards he set, the purposes he inspired, the goals he established would guide the land he loved for years to come."[30] Perhaps the most concrete example of that ability to lift up the country's sights was the space program Kennedy set in motion. "I believe that this nation should commit itself to achieving the goal, before this decade is out, of landing a man on the Moon and returning him safely to the Earth," Kennedy said in a speech given on September 12, 1962, at Rice University Stadium in Houston, Texas. In JFK's memory, the country would do just that, landing Neil Armstrong and Buzz Aldrin in the Sea of Tranquility on July 20, 1969, just seven years and nine days after Kennedy's challenge.

John and Bobby Kennedy also midwived a revolution in equal rights that continues to unfold via the civil rights movement, the fight for the rights of the disabled, and the modern battle for women's rights.

> Let the word go forth from this time and place, to friend and foe alike, that the torch has been passed to a new generation of Americans . . . unwilling to witness or permit the slow undoing of those human rights to which this Nation has always been committed, and to which we are committed today at home and around the world.

Kennedy was slow to rise to the cause of civil rights as president, but by his third year he and Bobby had become ardent champions of enforcing desegregation in the South. Later, President Johnson, with the help of Ted and Bobby Kennedy in the Senate, passed the Civil Rights Act and the Voting

Rights Act. Ted Kennedy personally took on the issue of the discriminatory poll tax, and succeeded in eliminating it. He made sure over the course of 46 years that the Civil Rights Act was renewed, strengthened, and its provisions enforced equitably.

A strong involvement in Latin America—for better and sometimes worse—was a piece of the Kennedy legacy as well.

> To our sister republics south of our border, we offer a special pledge—to convert our good words into good deeds—in a new alliance for progress—to assist free men and free governments in casting off the chains of poverty.

Both Bobby and Ted made the Alliance for Progress a special focus of their legislative efforts after Jack's death, and visited Latin America often to speak out on human rights issues. When Augusto Pinochet led a coup that toppled Salvador Allende's regime, Ted Kennedy successfully introduced an amendment denying all military aid to Chile. In late summer of 2008, Chilean president Michelle Bachelet presented Ted with the Order of the Merit of Chile—her country's highest civilian award—for his long commitment to democracy in the country.

One of the more controversial legacies of the Kennedy years was the mounting military involvement in Vietnam, a direct consequence of Jack Kennedy's promise to protect democracy around the globe.

> Let every nation know, whether it wishes us well or ill, that we shall pay any price, bear any burden, meet any hardship, support any friend, oppose any foe, in order to assure the survival and the success of liberty.

It was Kennedy's "New Frontiersmen," a collection of academic scholars, Ivy League grads and other East Coast intellectuals, who pushed Lyndon Johnson into committing half a million troops to Vietnam and ordering massive bombing strikes. Johnson's most frequent defense of the escalation after his presidency was to ask how could he have done otherwise, when "all the Kennedy men"—the "Best and the Brightest," were telling him the buildup was absolutely necessary.[31] He told Doris Kearns Goodwin that if he hadn't deepened the commitment to Vietnam, "there would be Robert Kennedy out in front leading the fight against me, telling everyone that I had betrayed John Kennedy's commitment to South Vietnam. That I had let a democracy fall into the hands of the Communists. That I was a coward. An unmanly man."[32]

As a result of Vietnam, and the paucity of Kennedy's legislative accomplishments in his early years, Kennedy's record as president has always been regarded by historians as a mixed one at best. Yet in polls he continues to maintain his reputation as one of the country's great presidents. Historians generally regard his first two years as cautious and unremarkable. But by his third year he was taking bold action on civil rights, the Test Ban Treaty, détente, and an antipoverty program. "His legacy lies less in what he achieved than what he began," writes Cronin.

> All this will not be finished in the first 100 days. Nor will it be finished in the first 1,000 days, nor in the life of this Administration, nor even perhaps in our lifetime on this planet. But let us begin.

Kennedy's unfinished presidency "left us with tantalizing 'might have beens,'" writes historian Robert Dallek. Yet for those willing to look, there is an answer to those might-have-beens in the legislative records compiled by Bobby and Ted. It would fall to them to build a political legacy to match their brother's words.

7

TED'S TURN

We few, we happy few, we band of brothers;
For he today that sheds his blood with me shall be my brother.

—*William Shakespeare*, Henry V

Ted went to visit the president-elect in his Senate office shortly after Thanksgiving, 1960, to ask for a job. Something in foreign policy might be interesting, he suggested earnestly. But the president/big brother advised instead that Ted should get serious about running for Jack's now-empty Senate seat, and he should get started on it right away. "Teddy, you ought to get out and get around," Jack said. "I'll understand, I'll hear whether you are really making a mark up there. I will tell you whether this [a White House job] is something that you ought to seriously consider."[1] At the president's insistence, an old college friend, Benjamin A. Smith, was appointed by the Massachusetts governor to keep the seat warm until the special election scheduled for November 1962. By then, Ted would be constitutionally old enough to run.

That night after their meeting, at his brother's insistence, Ted boarded a flight for Africa to tag along on a Senate Foreign Relations Subcommittee tour of African countries. If Ted was going to be a senator, he'd need some experience. Ted served as Jack's surrogate during a tour of nine countries in 15 days, often overshadowing the fact-finding senators because he was the president's brother. He took a similar trip to Italy that spring, and Latin America the following summer. Like his brothers had before him, he wrote a series of articles about his travels. Among his headlines in the *Boston Globe*: "Latin America to Go Red? Crisis is On." "Why So Many Students of Latin Area Are Turning Left," and "Can't Feed a Hungry Peasant with Words About Democracy." Later that same year, he would tour Israel and the Berlin Wall.

The question of whether Ted would run for the Senate was far from resolved in the early months of 1961. In the new White House, there were serious worries about a negative impact on Jack. Two of the president's top advisers, Kenneth O'Donnell and Lawrence O'Brien, cautioned that Massachusetts voters would recoil at the audacity of the Kennedys. And they thought Ted could easily lose, which might be taken as a midterm vote of no confidence in the president. Jack's advisers were also worried about the relations with the new Speaker of the House, John McCormack, who happened to be the father of Ted's likely primary opponent, Massachusetts attorney general Eddie McCormick. Have him run for a lesser post, such as attorney general, they counseled. Bobby was probably the least enthusiastic member of the president's inner circle.

When word got out that Ted was serious about the race, regardless of White House misgivings, journalists were savage. "Teddy's bid for the Senate, at 30 years of age, with the connivance of the President, is widely regarded as an affront and a presumption," wrote James Reston of the *New York Times*. "One Kennedy is a triumph, two Kennedys at the same time are a miracle, but three could easily be regarded as an invasion." Academia was outraged, too. Pro-Kennedy intellectuals like Archibald MacLeish, Samuel Eliot Morison and Harvard's Mark De Wolfe Howe joined together to castigate his candidacy as "preposterous." Reporters canvassing votes in Massachusetts often heard cries of "Too many Kennedys."

"But Teddy had to do *something*," a sister responded to the press. After a long talk one night with Jack about all the pros and cons, Ted made the decision. He'd gotten a taste of campaigning, and found that the thrill suited him, perhaps better than it suited his brothers. As his mother put it, "He naturally wants to do what the other boys did."[2] "It's Ted's turn now," Joe Kennedy told Bobby and Jack. "Whatever he wants, I'm going to see that he gets it."

★ ★ ★

First things first. Ted felt that since he hadn't held a job in his life, he ought to put himself to work. In February 1961, he signed on as 1 of 26 assistant district attorneys employed by the Suffolk County, New York, District Attorney; his salary was a dollar a year. What surprised everyone at the office wasn't that he was positioning himself for a higher office, but that he worked so hard prosecuting his cases. He was willing to take whatever cases came his way, including those his colleagues didn't want, and pursue them to the hilt. Kennedy said he enjoyed the work, and managed to win a few convictions that held up in appeals court. "Teddy's the hardest worker I've got," the D.A., Garrett Byrne, reported after just a few months.

After the office closed at 4 P.M., he did just what his brother John had done in the year before he ran for public office: He started making speeches. Get a "sense of the state," John advised. Ted used his trips to Africa, Latin America, Israel and Germany as fodder for his talks, which invariably opened with the story about two brothers who went fishing together. One had expensive gear, and one a hook and some worms. When the brother with worms seemed to be catching all the fish, the other brother decided to try his pole and the worms the next morning, when his brother took the day off. Still no luck. Just as he was about to give up, a fish jumped out of the pond and asked, "Where's your brother?" After inevitably getting a laugh, he'd say, "I hope none of you wonderful people is going to ask me, 'Where's my brother?'"

In December 1961, before Ted had officially launched his bid, Joe Kennedy suffered a debilitating stroke on the sixteenth hole at Palm Beach Country Club. He was raced by ambulance to St. Mary's Hospital, where he plunged into a deep coma. The president, Bobby, Ted and the rest of the family descended on Palm Beach, taking turns in an all-night vigil at his bedside. Last rites were said, and everyone prepared for the worst. The furnace that had driven the Kennedy men for so long looked as if it were about it go out.

Ted spent the night on a deathwatch across the hall from his father. But late the next afternoon, while Ted was holding his hand, Joe's eyelids flickered to life. Ted immediately called Jack, who came to the hospital with Jackie and White House Press Secretary Pierre Salinger. Bobby came soon after. Joe couldn't speak, but showed signs that he recognized his sons.

Joe would live on that way, half alive, for nine more years. His fierce blue eyes still burned bright; he was aware of his surroundings, could still read magazines held in front of his face and occasionally muttered an epithet, but otherwise he was a ghost. Just as Jack, Bobby and Ted were reaching the pinnacle of power in America, their Moses had gone dark. "The father so desperately wanted to speak, and he couldn't," Ted Sorensen remembered. "Tears rolled out of his eyes. No one knows how much he understood; but he couldn't communicate in any way. . . . Kind of blue in the face. We could see emotion in the eyes, we thought, but we wanted to think so."[3]

Bobby and Ted would come back to Hyannis Port every weekend in the coming months to see their father, and Jack would fly in often by helicopter. The ambassador was alert enough to refuse to wear his leg braces when his sons came to visit, and would always be waiting out on the porch when Jack landed.[4] The boys still talked to their father, read him stories, sang him songs, sought his unattainable approval. But they were playing to a silent audience now.

And Joe would still visit the White House on occasion in a wheelchair. A family friend, Kay Halle, remembers telling the patriarch at tea, "What other father, in all of American history, could ever say that, here's one son who's President of the United States; another who's Attorney General; and another, who's going to be a Unites States Senator? And the old man started laughing, or doing the equivalent of a laugh."[5] Four years earlier, on September 7, 1957, in a remark to the *Saturday Evening Post,* Joe Kennedy had predicted exactly such a scenario.

Doctors had given Joe only a year or two to live, so Ted's campaign took on the air of a win-one-for-the-Gipper crusade. The lastborn was in an urgent race not so much to beat his opponent, but to show his father his ultimate worthiness. Once Ted launched his campaign on March 14, 1962, the Kennedy team simply outhustled McCormack. Jack officially stayed on the sidelines, just as Joe had with his campaigns, but he watched every twist and turn and ordered some of his aides into the fray. Sixteen hours a day, Ted would shake hands, make speeches, hold court on street corners, and do television interviews. Kennedy's team bought more TV spots, polls and flyers than McCormack, and had far more volunteers. Teddy was most effective out in the streets. He was a "corner guy." He liked standing on a street corner talking to people. "Jack didn't really like adulation, open flattery embarrassed him," said McCormack, "but Teddy was already a . . . freewheeler, a swinger, he liked to be with people, good with the glad hand, the big smile, the slap on the back."[6]

Out of a fondness for his grandfather, Teddy went retro, campaigning with bands and banners and oratory, just the way Honey Fitz had. He was consciously attempting to evoke memories of the grand old days of torchlight parades and street corner rallies, when his grandfather had brought the crowds to a froth with his honey-sweet speechifying and the singing of "Sweet Adeline." Ted knew his audience and his town. "Bostonians like the feeling of being steeped in history," he once wrote. "They give special deference to the old—the ancient buildings, the small shops, the restaurants with the large overhead fans where their grandfathers ate, the old characters who stand around the Court House." Ted used history as a campaign weapon because history, and his family's history, was wrapped into the city's sinews.

Journalist Stewart Alsop remembers one of Teddy's nighttime rallies at a big square in South Boston.[7] Searchlights played the clouds as faint music started up in the distance. A buzz of anticipation spread through the crowd, and young girls twittered about how handsome the candidate was. The music grew, and then Ted, with a jaw-splitting grin, marched in at the head of the band. When Alsop first saw him, he thought Teddy was "decidedly better-looking than his brothers, with the precisely balanced features of the old Arrow-collar ads. He looks like a boy, but he looks like a boy who can take care of himself." After his grand entrance, Ted leapt up onto the roof of a station wagon as a loudspeaker below amplified the noise of the crowd back at them, ratcheting up their exuberance. Then Ted began his speech in the old style, sans microphone, "a sustained shout," Alsop called it. He reminded everyone, "My grandfather owned a saloon not a hundred yards from here," and his voice took on a bit of the Irish lilt, as it did whenever he was in an Irish section of town. And then he wound up a stem-winder and let fly. "I hope there are no Republicans in the crowd, because they are not going to like what I'm going to say!" he vowed. The speech itself was a thoroughly partisan harangue, delivered to a thoroughly partisan crowd. The neighborhood had come out to enjoy itself, and Teddy made sure it did. After the speech and the handshakes, a reporter tallied the returns. "He's the greatest." "Just wonderful." "We're with him all the way." "Isn't he cute?" In conclusion, Alsop wrote, "Teddy Kennedy was designed by his maker to be a politician."

The cheating incident at Harvard hadn't come up yet, but the campaign decided it was better to get it out early so that it became a nonissue by the end of the campaign. President Kennedy asked *Boston Globe* reporter Robert Healy to come see him, and explained how Ted had been expelled for asking someone to take a Spanish exam for him. Jack wanted Healy to bury the incident in a profile, but Healy argued that every other newspaper would have it in the lead. "We're having more fucking trouble with this than we did with the Bay of Pigs," the president told McGeorge Bundy, his national security adviser. "Yes," Bundy nodded, "and with about the same results."[8]

Healy wrote his story, which appeared on the front page of the *Globe*, with a full mea culpa from Ted. "What I did was wrong" and "I have regretted it ever since. The unhappiness I caused my family and friends, even though 11 years ago, has been a bitter experience for me, but it also has been a valuable lesson."[9] Given Ted's youth at the time, the incident didn't bother Massachusetts Democrats much. Polls taken soon after showed Teddy pulling away.

Early in August 1962, McCormack asked for what every lagging politician asks for: a debate. Confident in his own debating skills, Ted agreed. They met at South Boston High School, McCormack's alma mater, on August 27, and the crowd was decidedly pro-McCormack. Ted's people wanted it that way, so their candidate would appear on TV as the brave underdog in an area of town known for its crooked deals and corrupt office holders. McCormack planned an aggressive attack on the upstart candidate, while Kennedy had been ordered by his brother to remain unruffled, senatorial, informed. "Now listen," Jack reportedly said, "you forget any personal attack on Eddie McCormack. You're going to need all the supporters that McCormack has right after the primary. Let McCormack attack you as much as he wants. You're running for United States Senator. Stay on the issues and leave the personal attacks out."[10]

In his opening remarks, McCormack began blasting away. "I ask my opponent 'What are your qualifications?' You graduated from law school three years ago. You never worked for a living. You have never run or held elective office. You are not running on qualifications. You are running on a slogan: 'You Can Do More for Massachusetts' . . . and I say 'Do more, how?' Because of experience? Because of maturity of judgment? Because of qualifications? I say no! This is the most insulting slogan I have seen in Massachusetts politics, because this slogan means: Vote for this man because he has influence, he has connections, he has relations." He finished with a jab right at the family's heart. "The office of United States Senator should be merited, not inherited." As McCormack sat down, applause broke out across the packed hall.

Kennedy was not allowed a response, as the next part of the debate consisted of questions put to the candidates by a panel of journalists. McCormack was relentless during the questions, too, savaging Kennedy for a recent trip abroad. In East Germany, McCormack said, Kennedy had "caused embarrassment" by recognizing the East German government; in London, he "Caused a taxi strike"; in Panama, the ambassador reportedly told Kennedy, "It will take me five months to undo what you have done in two days."

Kennedy, who is known to have a temper when provoked, stayed calm and collected, as his game plan dictated, even though one aide said later he had to strain to hold himself back.[11] When he finally got the chance to respond to McCormack's attacks in his closing arguments, he maintained his equanimity. Rising up from his stool, he took the high ground. "The great problems of this election are the questions of peace and whether Massachusetts will move forward or not. We should not have talk about personalities or families. I feel we should be talking about the people's destiny in Massachusetts."

McCormack had saved his most biting attack until the closing remarks. "I ask . . . if his name was Edward Moore, with his qualifications, with your qualifications, Teddy," he said, jabbing his finger at Kennedy's face, "if it was Edward Moore, your candidacy would be a joke, but nobody's laughing because his name is not Edward Moore. It's Edward Moore Kennedy, and I say it makes no difference what your name is, in a democracy you stand on your own two feet." Ted sat blank-faced, as if he'd just been right-crossed. But he did not take the bait. The hall, packed with McCormack supporters, once again burst into applause.

The two contenders left the stage without shaking hands, and Ted told an aide he had wanted to punch McCormack in the mouth for that Edward Moore line.[12] The McCormack camp was ecstatic afterward, fully confident they had dealt Kennedy a knockout punch. The men in the White House shared the view that rhetorically, Eddie had mopped the stage with Ted. But the next day, the reaction from those who watched on television was just the opposite. On television, McCormack's attacks came across as slicing and vicious. Visually, Ted had come across as the temperate good guy. The *impression* viewers got was of an old, smarmy political tribe from Southie ganging up on a fresh-faced prince. And Ted's pronounced jaw line played well on TV.

McCormack dropped his attacks completely in the second debate, but it was already over. On primary day, Ted got 559,303 votes to McCormack's 247,403. Edward Moore Kennedy may have run on his family name, but it was Ted's own vitality and likability that won the election for him.

The Cuban Missile Crisis distracted Jack and Bobby from the general campaign, but they sent Ted Sorensen out to carefully counsel their brother to stay away from Cuba in his speeches lest he provoke a nuclear war. Ted managed to get through the fall without incident, and went on to beat George Cabot Lodge, grandson of Honey Fitz's old nemesis, 1,162,611 to 877,669.

The president, who had been doubtful about Teddy running, was so delighted with the victory that he told a Harrisburg, Pennsylvania, audience, "I will introduce myself. I am Teddy Kennedy's brother."[13]

★ ★ ★

On his first day in the Senate, Ted told reporters he planned to stay "out of the limelight, out of the headlines and out of the swimming pool."[14] He managed to keep the first two vows, but broke the last within weeks. After working hours he would often visit Jack at the White House, where the brothers would retreat to the sanctity of the White House swimming pool. It was a place no one else in the White House was allowed. Secret Service men have since reported that the brothers were sometimes joined in the pool by two secretarial assistants, whom the Service nicknamed Fiddle and Faddle. Jackie once blithely informed a French journalist that Fiddle and Faddle were "my husband's lovers."

In the Senate, however, Ted did not follow his brother's lead. Unlike John, Ted was a rule follower, not a rule breaker. He deferred to the system. He was at heart a joiner, someone who wanted to fit in. His position as the ninth child had educated him in the ways of deference and respect for his elders, a quality the clubby, gray-haired Senate relished in its junior members. "He started by impressing his elders in the 60s as someone who worked hard and didn't speak a lot," said Walter Mondale, who started his career in the Senate just after Kennedy did. "He would simply go and listen, even to committees he wasn't on." One journalist described him as a model child—he "just soaked things in as he went along." Kennedy told reporters: "There is a great deal to learn. . . . I fully appreciate the wisdom of saying freshmen should be seen and not heard."[15] Where fellow senators had expected brashness and presumption, they found humility.

He focused on Massachusetts rather than national issues in his first months. In no time he was announcing federal grants and loans for home-state projects. The attentiveness of his constituent services would soon be revered back home, as would the effectiveness of his staff, which was led by Milton Gwirtzman, a graduate of Harvard College and Yale Law School. Ted didn't get much help from his brother the president, however. Ben Bradlee remembers seeing John "roaring with laughter" while talking to Ted at a dinner dance. "Some pipeline I have into the White House," the new senator told Bradlee. "I tell him a thousand men are out of work in Fall River; four hundred men out of work in Fitchburg. And when the Army gets that new rifle, there's another six hundred men out of work in Springfield. And do you know what he says to me? 'Tough shit.'"[16] Still, Jack's experience in the Senate was a secret weapon for Ted, even if his influence wasn't. The president advised his sibling to pay courtesy calls on senior senators and urged Ted to bone up on the three biggest issues of the time: civil rights, nuclear arms control and Vietnam. In time, Ted saw that he could make his own name on those issues. But the new senator held off making his maiden speech for more than a year as he learned to navigate the folkways of the upper chamber. When he did speak, civil rights was his cause.

In the White House, the president was criticized for his slow pace addressing civil rights. John Kennedy was determined to maintain control of the pace of civil rights changes, hoping to keep dissent off the streets and in the courts. He was also worried about alienating segregationist voters right before a midterm election. But Bobby was ahead of Jack. In April 1961, just months after the inauguration, Attorney General Robert Kennedy used a court order to open the public schools in Prince Edward County, Virginia, to black children. In a speech three weeks later, he made the moral case for civil rights, comparing racial segregation to organized crime and stating "On this generation of Americans falls the full burden of proving to the world that we really mean it when we say that all men are created free and equal before the law."[17]

As attorney general, Bobby Kennedy sent 500 marshals to ensure that James Meredith could enroll at the University of Mississippi, and he pushed Jack to go on radio and television to ask Mississippi residents to support the federal integration order. But things got out of hand. Nearly 200 of the marshals were injured and 2 were killed. In response, John Kennedy federalized the Mississippi National Guard and sent federal troops to the university.

Just as he had done in the Cuban Missile Crisis, Bobby began pushing his brother toward a decisive politics of right and wrong. Bobby had seen the necessity of a strong stand against segregation before Jack had, probably because he had fewer constituencies to please. But in May 1963, police turned fire hoses and police dogs on black children who were demonstrating for the right to use snack bars; the sight turned Jack's stomach. The following month, 161 civil rights incidents were recorded across the United States. On June 11, President Kennedy assumed control of the Alabama National Guard to force Governor George C. Wallace to admit two black students to the University of Alabama. Wallace had pledged "Segregation Now! Segregation tomorrow! Segregation forever!" That night, the president went on television to promise the country a comprehensive civil rights bill. He spoke for 18 minutes, concluding his address extemporaneously.

> If an American, because his skin is dark, cannot eat lunch in a restaurant open to the public, if he cannot send his children to the best public schools available, if he cannot vote for the public officials who represent him—then who among us would be content to have the color of his skin change? Who among us would then be content with the counsels of patience and delay? . . . The fires of frustration and discord are burning in every city, North and South, where legal remedies are not at hand.

Black America responded with thunderous approval. "For the first time, it was full of passion," said NAACP chairman Roy Wilkins. "It electrified us." Eight days later, Kennedy formally asked Congress to outlaw discrimination in hotels, restaurants and stores and sought the desegregation of public education.

But the bill went nowhere.

The president had never learned to grease the wheels of power in Washington. In his first two and a half years, John Kennedy had expected the Hill to follow his lead by sheer dint of his brilliance. Jack and Bobby displayed some of their father's arrogance when it came to the political machinations of Washington. By the start of 1963, a third of the president's legislative program was still in subcommittee. In eight years as a senator, he'd never had the patience to learn the fine art of horse-trading for votes or how to backscratch in a town filled with backscratchers. He hadn't returned many of the favors people had done for him over the years. "When I was in Congress, I thought all the power was down at the other end of Pennsylvania Avenue, at the White House," Kennedy told reporter Jim Deakin of the *St. Louis Post-Dispatch*. "Now I'm down here, and am amazed at all the power those bastards have."

On August 28, more than 250,000 people marched on Washington to demand action from Congress on civil rights. Ted Kennedy, fully committed to the issue now, was eager to join in, but the president told him no. Jack was still worried about the official amount of White House involvement in the black activist movement and how much it might alienate voters in the next election. From the Truman Balcony of the White House, the president watched the throng collect in front of the Lincoln Memorial, and he could even hear the Reverend Dr. Martin Luther King deliver his "I Have a Dream" speech in the far distance. It was a turning point in American history. Ted desperately wanted to participate in the moment somehow, so he spent the day receiving delegations of civil rights demonstrators in his office.

In a speech three weeks later in Yugoslavia, Ted condemned racial discrimination in no uncertain terms. "In a sense, my nation has asked to be judged in this area, because of the leadership we have taken in the cause of freedom and democracy around the world." He told his audience he was sure the country would end discrimination for African Americans, saying "Neither I, nor the President of the United States, would hold the positions we do, if America had not taken down the signs that said 'No Irish need apply.'"[18]

In his first year in the Senate, Ted closely hewed to his brothers' lead on most issues. He was also usually the one Jack asked to come by when the president wanted a break. "At the end of a long day, [Bobby] was often too demanding, too involved in issues," Arthur Schlesinger said.[19] And too much of a moralist. "Teddy made the president laugh." Bob Shrum told *New York Times* journalist Adam Clymer that on one of those nights at the White House, the president took Ted out on the Truman Balcony and told him that one day, he, too, might be standing there as president. "By the time I arrived in the Senate and he was President, the sense of great age difference had almost disappeared," Ted told Jack's speechwriter, Ted Sorensen. When he was in the Senate and Jack was in the White House, the two "were enormously close as brothers," Ted said, maybe closer than they'd ever been.[20] In the late summer of 1963, as Jack's New Frontier promises began to bear fruit, and the president, attorney general and senator presented a united front on civil rights, the three Kennedy sons stood astride the most powerful city in the most powerful country in the world. They were at the height of their power, three righteous brother-kings.

★　★　★

Just over two months later, Ted was presiding over the Senate when press liaison officer William Langham Riedel burst onto the floor, rushing from senator to senator. Langham spotted Ted at the front of the chamber, where he was looking down at his desk, busy with a portfolio of correspondence. "I ran up to the rostrum and leaned over the desk. 'Senator Kennedy,' I said, 'your brother the President has been shot.'"

Kennedy's only question to Riedel: "How did you know?"[21]

"It's on the ticker. Just came in on the ticker."[22]

Kennedy collapsed back into his chair "as if he had been hit by whiplash." Riedel said he looked utterly stunned. The legendary Kennedy stoicism kicked in after a moment, and Kennedy methodically assembled his papers, picked them up, got back on his feet and, without saying a word, walked out. He charged into Vice President Johnson's office and grabbed his phone, but could not get through to Bobby. He finally was able to call the White House, but Bobby was on the line to Dallas.

Running red lights, Milton Gwirtzman drove Ted home so he could make sure his wife was okay. She was out at a beauty salon getting ready for their fifth anniversary party that night, so Kennedy and Gwirtzman jumped back into the car and went straight to the White House. The radio was on, and broadcasters were saying the president was still alive. But when Kennedy got to the West Wing, he could tell from the looks on everyone's faces that the reports weren't true. Ted finally reached Bobby. "He's dead," said Bobby. "You'd better call your mother and our sisters." Eunice joined Ted at the White House, and they all decided on the phone with Bobby that Bobby would look after Jackie, and Ted and Eunice would go to Hyannis Port to be with Rose and Joe. Suddenly, Ted remembered Caroline and John-John up in the nursery. He ran upstairs to find them in the competent care of their governess, Louella Hennessy, who had also been Ted's governess. He kissed her and called her "Lulu." "His face was so white and drawn," she said later. "He was so shocked he could barely speak. . . . I got the feeling that if he said any more he would break down and cry." He hugged Caroline and John-John silently, and then left the room. He and Eunice boarded a helicopter for the Cape.

Rose asked Ted to break the news to his father. She'd been out walking on the beach after she'd heard, unable to bring herself to tell her husband what had happened. Joe Kennedy was upstairs, lying down in his bedroom reading a magazine when Ted and Eunice walked in. The ailing patriarch was already suspicious and gestured toward the television. Ted went over to plug the cord in, but then tore the wires right out of the set. Eunice took her father's hand and kissed him. "Daddy, Daddy, there's been an accident. But Jack's okay, Daddy. Jack was in an accident."[23] Eunice couldn't bring herself to tell her father the awful truth either, but then, in an instant, she did. "Jack's dead. He's dead. But he's in heaven. He's in heaven. Oh God, Daddy. Jack's okay, isn't he, Daddy?"

Ted fell on his knees, burying his face in his hands.

"Dad, Jack was shot," Teddy said.

"He's dead, Daddy," Eunice said again. "He's dead."

Rose came into the room to find Joe beating his hand against the sheet.[24]

"I can still see that dress," Ben Bradlee said, 45 years later. "She came in and that dress was covered with blood." Bradlee had gone to Bethesda Naval Hospital to be with the family the night after the shooting, and Jackie arrived in the same pink cashmere outfit she'd had on during the shooting in Dallas. "I do not want to remove this," she told one of Jack's aides, General Godfrey McHugh. "I want them to see what they've done to him."

Two days later, the assassin, Lee Harvey Oswald, was shot to death in front of a Dallas police station by Jack Ruby, a nightclub owner.

The next day, six gray horses pulled the caisson carrying the president's flag-draped coffin from the White House to St. Matthew's Cathedral. A riderless horse followed. Jackie walked behind, Bobby on her right and Ted on her left. World leaders shuffled after them bareheaded. Teddy wore the formal pants his brother had worn for his inauguration, and a pair of his gloves.[25] His rental suit had arrived with items missing, so Jackie's maid had let out the president's pants that morning, and pressed Jack's gloves. Jack's hat wouldn't fit Teddy's head, though, so Charles de Gaulle, Haile Selassie, Prince Philip and all the others removed their own hats out of respect.

The Kennedy family had always found solace in Catholic ritual, and now the country did as well. At St. Michael's, Bishop Philip Hannon read biblical passages Jackie had chosen. "Your old men shall dream dreams. Your young men shall see visions. And where there is no vision the people perish." The bishop also repeated some of the uplifting sections of Jack's inaugural address, but they sounded too much like broken hallelujahs. It was after the funeral, when the coffin was placed back on the caisson outside the church, that Jackie whispered to her son: "John, you can salute Daddy now and say goodbye to him." John-John raised his right hand in a crooked salute to his father as tens of millions watched on black-and-white TVs.

At Arlington Cemetery, 50 Air Force F-105s barreled across the sky, followed soon after by Air Force One, which dipped its wings in salute. In the trees of Arlington, birds twittered wildly in response. As the ceremony came to a close, Jackie walked to her husband's grave holding a lit taper. She bent forward and ignited the flame that still burns there uninterrupted. She then turned to Bobby and passed the taper to him. He touched it to the flame, too, and then passed it on to Ted.

ACT III
BOBBY AND TED

8

BROTHERS IN ARMS

Each time a man stands up for an ideal, or acts to improve the lot of others, or strikes out against injustice, he sends forth a tiny ripple of hope, and crossing each other from a million different centers of energy and daring, those ripples build a current which can sweep down the mightiest walls of oppression.

—Bobby Kennedy, Cape Town, South Africa, 1967

The night of the funeral, the extended Kennedy family gathered bravely upstairs in the White House for John-John's third birthday party. After cake and ice cream for the children, and strong drinks for the adults, Jackie suggested they all sing some of Jack's favorite songs. Teddy started belting out "Heart of My Heart," the tune the three brothers had all sung together on the last night of Jack's campaign for the Senate 11 years earlier.[1]

We were rough and ready guys,
But oh, how we could harmonize.

Bobby, however, could not find it in himself to sing. He left the room and spent the rest of the night in seclusion. But Ted was not one to be alone with his grief. Instead, he invited friends and White House staffers over to his house after the birthday party for a boisterous Irish wake. The youngest brother led everyone in Irish songs as they all laughed and talked and cried and drank. At the end of the night, after everyone had gone, Ted went back to Arlington to visit his brother's grave.[2]

The two brothers continued to mourn in their own distinct ways in the coming months. Bobby brooded—questioning everything and withdrawing into melancholia. Ted chose motion, activity and velocity. For hours at a time, Bobby would sit staring out the window at Hickory Hill. He refused to say the words "November twenty-second" or "Dallas." He questioned his faith and his own culpability in Jack's death. Behind closed doors, friends could hear him sob and ask, "Why, God?"[3] He could bear no reminders of Dallas or of the day, turning pictures of Jack against the wall in his house, in his relatives' houses, in his friends' houses.

Ted, on the other hand, tried to emblazon and perpetuate Jack's name and works everywhere—parks, boulevards and airports. He attended every memorial and tribute he could schedule, smothering his grief in activity. He helped unveil the letters "JFK" on the renamed New York airport.[4] He took a nine-nation tour of Europe to raise money for the JFK Library and Museum. He tried to conquer his pain with endless talk and fellowship, hoping to continue the happy/sad Irish wake he'd begun the night of the funeral for as long as he humanly could, maybe for the rest of his life. He also threw himself into his family, devoting hours on end to his children and Jack's children at Hyannis Port. Bobby's way was solitary; Teddy's, collective.

Jackie coped by becoming the valiant guardian of her husband's memory. Five days after the assassination, the new widow asked author Theodore H. White, who had written a Pulitzer Prize–winning book on the 1960 election, to come to Hyannis Port for an exclusive interview. She had something she wanted *Life* magazine to know about her husband. "At night, before we'd go to sleep, Jack liked to play some records, and the song he loved most came at the very end of this record," Jackie told White. The record was the soundtrack album for the Broadway musical *Camelot,* and the tune Jackie referred to was a reprise of the title song, sung by Richard Burton. "The lines he loved to hear were: 'Don't let it be forgot, that once there was a spot, for one brief shining moment that was known as Camelot." History belongs to heroes, Jackie told White, and heroes must not be forgotten. Because of White's article, the imagery of King Arthur's court, of heroes, legends, and a fairy-tale White House, became forever a piece of the Kennedy legacy, just as Jackie meant it to be. "So the epitaph on the Kennedy administration became Camelot," White wrote later, "a magic moment in American history when gallant men danced with beautiful women, when great deeds were done, when artists, writers and poets met at the White House, and the barbarians beyond the walls were held back."[5]

The ancient Arthurian story Jackie liked to invoke, however, is a complicated one, involving adultery, an illegitimate son, warring friends and secret, bloody deeds. More than anyone, Bobby knew the dark side of Camelot. He and John had an "acquaintance with the night" during the three years of the Kennedy presidency, and those secrets gnawed at him in his grief. They would begin to change not only who Bobby was but his politics as well. When President Johnson learned about the CIA's assassination plots against Castro, he said to a *Time* magazine reporter that the Kennedy administration "had been operating a damned Murder, Inc. in the Caribbean."[6] As Bobby knew, his words weren't far from the truth. The violence of Jack's death had left Bobby with a metaphysical revulsion to violence done in the name of politics, especially the violence he himself had instigated as attorney general. In conversations with intimates, Bobby questioned whether he had, indirectly, played some role in his brother's death. Oswald was a pro-Castro zealot who had spent time in Russia. Had Bobby's pursuit of Castro through Operation Mongoose inspired some sort of retaliatory assassin? Had his efforts to destroy the Mafia, including Sam Giancana, who had worked with the CIA to undermine Castro, led them to kill the president? Or had his crackdown on Jimmy Hoffa and the Teamsters' ties to crime figures come back to haunt him? "I thought they'd get one of us but . . . I thought it would be me," he told J. Edgar Hoover. Instead of zealously investigating his brother's death, Bobby wanted no part of it. He said he was satisfied with the Warren Commission's official finding that Oswald had acted alone, but not because he felt the investigation had been thorough—he never even read the report. It was because, emotionally, he could not bear to pick that scab any more, or he didn't want Jack's sexual liaisons and questionable ties to mobsters made public. When the New Orleans district attorney James Garrison claimed he had found evidence of a conspiracy involving the CIA and the mob, Bobby asked his friend and future press secretary Frank Mankiewicz whether he thought there was anything to it. Mankiewicz started to give his opinion, but Bobby stopped him. "Well, I don't think I wanted to know."[7]

Ted, who wasn't privy to all of Bobby's dark secrets, arranged for his own team of investigators to check the various conspiracy stories. He testified about their findings to a closed session of the Senate Select Committee on Intelligence Activities, saying he had found no evidence to contradict the Warren report.[8] There is no evidence that Ted and Bobby ever discussed the report with each other.

Ted, instead, found his way out of mourning by trying to carry forward his brother's agenda on the Hill. He had stayed in the Senate shadows while his brother was alive, but Jack's unfinished agenda was now his, and taking a backseat to his fellow senators was no longer the best way for Ted to serve the family. The tragedy emboldened the youngest brother. On April 4, 1964, he rose from his brother's old desk in the last row and announced his plans to speak in favor of his brother's civil rights bill, which had been filibustered to death 11 times. "Mr. President, it is with some hesitation that I rise to speak on the pending legislation before the Senate," Ted began. "A freshman Senator should be seen, not heard; should learn, and not teach." He had planned to devote his maiden speech to problems of employment and industry in Massachusetts, but that approach would no longer suffice. "I could not follow this debate for the last four weeks—I could not see this issue envelop the emotions and the conscience of the nation—without changing my mind. To limit myself to local issues in the face of this great national question would be to demean the seat in which I sit." As he would time and again for the next 50 years, he cited his own family's experience with prejudice to argue the case for civil rights. "In 1780, a Catholic in Massachusetts was not allowed to vote or hold public office. In 1840, an Irishman could not get a job above that of common laborer." Kennedy paused and looked off to one side, as if looking for a reason not to go on. Then he quoted Lyndon Johnson's words five days after the assassination. "No memorial oration or eulogy could more eloquently honor President Kennedy's memory than the earliest possible passage of the civil rights bill for which he fought for so long." The 33-year-old senator's voice broke, and the chamber fell quiet. He started again, haltingly. "My brother was the first President of the United States . . . to state publicly that segregation was morally wrong. . . . His heart and soul are in this bill." Ted had to stop again. "If his life and death both had a meaning," he said, his voice so low it was barely audible, "it was that we should not hate but love one another, we should use our powers not to create conditions of oppression that lead to violence, but conditions of freedom that lead to peace."[9]

In the gallery above, Ted's wife Joan wept. Several senators on the floor were seen with tears in their eyes as well. The next day, the *Washington Post* called it "the most moving moment of the current civil rights debate." Ted's first speech, in essence, had been an echo of his father's letter to him as a child. I hope when you grow up you will dedicate your life to trying to work out plans to make people happy instead of making them miserable, as war does today.

After one of the longest filibusters in Senate history, Lyndon Johnson used all the powers of his office and many of the skills he'd learned as master of the Senate to pressure and persuade Republican leaders that the time had finally arrived for civil rights legislation. It was really Johnson, evoking Jack's memory, who won the day for the Kennedys. More than two months after Ted's speech, on June 19, the Senate ended the filibuster and approved the bill, 73–27.

The historic vote went late into the evening, delaying Ted's departure for the Democrats' nominating convention in Springfield, MA. The election Ted had won in 1962 only allowed him to fill out the remaining two years of Jack's Senate term. In 1964 Ted launched his campaign for a new six-year term. Thousands of supporters were already waiting for Kennedy and Senator Birch Bayh of Indiana, the keynote speaker, at the Coliseum on the West Springfield fairgrounds. Ted arranged to speak to the crowd on a phone line from Washington 15 minutes before the vote. He promised to be with them as soon as possible, and told them he looked forward to accepting their nomination. He finished his brief address by saying, "And I ask you not to get so impatient that you decide to nominate Joan instead."[10]

Ted couldn't fly to Massachusetts on the *Caroline* because Bob wanted to fly to Hyannis Port that weekend, and the older brother always got preference in the Kennedy family. Ted borrowed the plane of a family friend instead, and the twin-engine, six-seat Aero Commander had been standing by for hours at Washington's National Airport. As the Senate vote dragged on, though, the weather in western Massachusetts began to deteriorate. The pilot, Ed Zimni, began to worry.

Just before they boarded, Ted's administrative assistant, Ed Moss, joked that, to cap off the night, "You should make some kind of spectacular entrance at the convention."

"What do you want me to do," Ted responded, "crack up the airplane?"[11]

Even with time tight, Ted insisted on a visit to Jack's grave on the night *his* bill had passed. He knelt at the eternal flame in silence for several minutes as Moss waited in the car. It was 8:35 P.M. before the small plane finally left Washington for the hour and twenty-minute trip. By that time fog had enveloped the area around Springfield, and visibility had plummeted to zero. Still, Ted pressured Zimni not to divert the plane to another airport, saying "Damn it, we're late already."

Feeling the pressure of time, Zimni found a hole in the fog three miles from the runway and plunged through. Everyone in the plane could immediately see they were too low. "I could see the trees," Ted said later. "We seemed to be riding along the tops of them. It was like a toboggan ride. I knew we were going to crash."[12] Zimni pulled back hard on the stick, but it was too late. The plane tangled in the treetops and plunged into an approaching apple orchard. When it struck the ground, the craft somersaulted through the orchard, spraying white blossoms, and the cabin roof came off. Seventy yards later, the crumpled plane came to rest against a tree. Senator Bayh saw Ted sprawled on the floor of the plane and thought he was dead. Bayh hurriedly pushed his wife Marvella out through a broken rear window, and she helped pull him out through the same opening. He got 50 yards from the plane, smelled the leaking fuel and realized that Ted might not be dead. He went back and found Kennedy halfway out the window, unable to move his legs, but conscious. Bayh told Kennedy to grab him around the neck, and he somehow pulled Ted's limp body out of the plane. If Bayh hadn't pulled Kennedy out, it's likely Ted wouldn't have received medical attention in time. Bayh probably saved his life.

Bayh and his wife flagged down a car on a nearby road with a flashlight from the plane. State troopers and an ambulance arrived, and Kennedy and Bayh were rushed to Cooley-Dickinson Hospital in Northampton. Zimni was dead on the scene, and Moss died seven hours later. Doctors were not sure Ted would last the night. He was in a state of shock and bleeding internally. One lung had collapsed and three vertebrae on his lower spine were crushed. If the fracture had been a quarter inch deeper, damaging the spinal cord, he would have been paralyzed for life.

Bobby raced from Hyannis Port in a state police cruiser, arriving at the hospital at 4 A.M. By morning, 20 Kennedys were at the hospital.[13] It hadn't been five months since Jack had died, and the family was in the grip of another deathwatch. A reporter asked Bobby the next day, "Is it ever going to end for you people?" Bobby shrugged his shoulders. "I guess the only reason we've survived is that there are too many of us. There are more of us than there is trouble."[14] It was a week before doctors knew for sure that Ted would live, and Bobby was by Ted's side when he finally regained consciousness. His first words to his brother were a joke about Bobby's reputation for cutthroat politics. "Is it true that you are ruthless?" Ted asked.[15]

Nearly everyone around Ted and Bobby expected each of them to *be* Jack, to personify all he had been and had come to represent. Bobby often wore Jack's old tweed jacket in honor of his fallen brother, and seemed to assume some of Jack's identity, continually quoting him, imitating his gestures, smoking his cigars. Tragically, Ted would carry on Jack's physical legacy. He was the one who would endure back pain for the rest of his days. Doctors recommended the same surgery Jack had undergone to fuse the vertebrae in his back. But there was still enough life left in Joe Kennedy, who was visiting Ted, to protest the operation that had been so crippling for Jack.

"Naaaaaa, naaaaa, naaaa," Joe spat, stunning Ted's doctors. Joe shook his head violently and made his feelings clear. Though Joe couldn't speak, Ted understood him completely and eventually refused to have the surgery. In its place, doctors prescribed complete immobility, placing Ted in a contraption called a Stryker frame for five months. He was rotated "like a human rotisserie" several times a day, barely able to move his hands and feet.[16] The constant motion he'd kept up after Jack's death came to a sudden, extended halt.

But Ted didn't let his body's state of suspension stop his mind. He summoned professors from MIT and Harvard to conduct seminars in his hospital room. He began reading biographies of Roosevelt and the Adams family, and Winston Churchill's history of World War II.[17] Jack had written a book while he was recuperating from back surgery, so Ted wrote a book, *The Fruitful Bough,* a privately printed volume of reminiscences about his father. Like Jack, he painted seascapes when he couldn't sleep. Every evening he read a bedtime story to his children over the phone.[18]

Back in Washington, Bobby Kennedy's political future was falling apart, thanks to Lyndon Johnson. Johnson held a deep grudge against the family even as he set about fulfilling Jack's legacy. Only Ted would engineer any sort of working relationship with the president. Ted had gone out of his way to defer to and accommodate him as vice president, and Johnson repaid the favor by visiting Ted in the hospital. But Bobby was a different story. Johnson had begged Bobby to stay on as attorney general, telling him he needed him more than Jack did, but Jack had warned Bobby that Johnson was an inveterate liar, prone to charm people with hyperbole that wasn't genuinely meant. Bobby stayed halfheartedly, but it soon became apparent he really didn't have much of a portfolio. He had been told shortly after the assassination that Johnson had said Jack's death was "divine retribution" for all the shady dealings of his administration, and Bobby could never forgive him for that. Johnson ruptured the relationship permanently when he refused to consider Bobby as his running mate in the 1964 election. The president had decided by the summer that if there were a Kennedy in his next administration, he would always be looking over his shoulder, judging his own performance by an impossible yardstick. He began to try to distance himself from the Kennedys and the power of their myth.

At the Democratic convention that summer, Johnson scheduled a televised tribute to the fallen president for the latest slot in the convention lineup, after the vote among the delegates, so there would be no surprise nomination of Bobby. Johnson knew he had to act as guardian of JFK's unfinished legacy to win the election, but he also knew it was Bobby who was the heir apparent to that legacy in the minds of most Americans. If Johnson hadn't been president, the crowd surely would have nominated Bobby, he believed. The reception Bobby got when he took the stage to introduce the film *A Thousand Days* seemed to confirm Johnson's fears. The applause on the floor turned into a deafening roar when Bobby began to speak. He raised and lowered his hands to quiet the crowd, and the applause only grew. After some time, Bobby bit his lip to keep from crying, but the cheering went on for 22 minutes, swelling and subsiding and swelling again like rolling waves. "It just went on and on," said John Seigenthaler. "I had to leave. I walked away . . . and I just fell apart." Bobby spoke briefly and emotionally about Jack, concluding with lines from the third act of Shakespeare's *Romeo and Juliet* that Jackie had suggested:

> *When he shall die*
> *Take him and cut him out in little stars,*
> *And he will make the face of heaven so fine*
> *That all the world will be in love with night,*
> *And pay no worship to the garish sun.*

The audience was utterly silent as they watched tears run down Bobby's face. Nobody had seen a Kennedy cry in public before.

★ ★ ★

When Bobby emerged from his grief, Harris Wofford says, he emerged a different person. After Johnson passed him over, he resigned as attorney general and moved to New York to run for the Senate. He was determined to reenter politics under his own power, in his own right. He now was head of the family. He insisted people call him Bob, instead of Bobby, which had been the name preferred by Jack. "I sensed something was going on with this guy," remembered civil rights activist Jack Newfield. "What I realized when I got to know him was that he had never thought [about] what he believed until his brother was murdered . . . then he stayed home reading Camus and Emerson."[19] In other words, Bob had so internalized Jack's priorities as his priorities, he wasn't even sure what his own belief set consisted of, or if he even had one. But after Jack's death, Bob shed his former persona as a ruthless enforcer of Jack's will and let his own deeply felt compassion rise to the surface. As he campaigned for the Senate, he turned more to populist causes, now that Jack was no longer his cause. He grew his hair longer. "Before John Kennedy was shot, Bob was cold and tough," said journalist Larry Newman, who covered Kennedy for the *Standard Times* in Massachusetts. "But when John was shot, you could almost see the compassion that had been missing from Bob's life just sort of begin to move out of him."[20]

"In the next few years a new perception of Robert Kennedy grew in me, as he ran for the Senate from New York, as he became the senator for the young and the poor, the black and the brown, the sick and the old, as he started on the hard climb to the presidency," Wofford said.[21] Columnist Anthony Lewis agreed: "Most people acquire certainties as they grow older; he lost his. He changed—he grew—more than anyone I have ever known."[22]

★ ★ ★

Bob and Ted both won their campaigns, but Bob won by a smaller margin than his bedridden brother, thanks to Joan's energetic barnstorming all over Massachusetts on her husband's behalf during his convalescence. Shortly after the election, the new senator from New York visited the reelected senator from Massachusetts in his hospital room. A photographer asked the brother senators to pose for a picture. "Step back a little, you're casting a shadow on Ted," the photographer said to Bob. Ted smiled and said, "It'll be the same in Washington."[23]

Ted's first day back in Congress after his crash was also Bob's first day on the job, and young senators riding Johnson's coattails surrounded them. Ted was 32; Bob, 38; Walter Mondale of Minnesota, 36; Fred Harris of Oklahoma, 34; and Joe Tydings of Maryland, 36. "We had what I called High Tide," said Mondale. "The progressives finally got a working margin in the Senate and the House, and we had an extraordinary community of youthful senators. And Ted was one of our leaders because he had seniority. He'd been there two years ahead of us and he was full of vinegar."

To his infinite pleasure, Ted was now showing his big brother the ropes of the Senate. Bob would consult Ted on everything: pushing a bill, writing a statement, making a speech. They'd talk every morning and every night. "You know how to handle these fellows," Bob would say to Ted. "You're the likable one . . . What should I do now?"[24]

Mondale doesn't remember much difference in their roll call votes. "I never saw them separate on an issue. Bob probably came first in the pecking order," he noticed, but politically they were like twins. "You see, in terms of our general philosophy, my brother and I started off the same," said Ted. "Much of the input from the family was the same. Our exposure and development as human beings was very similar. And so we moved in similar, or maybe parallel, directions. Bob was interested in education; I got interested in health. He got involved in the problems of the Middle East; I spent more time on the problems of the Far East. But we had the same general parameters of interest and concern."[25]

Ted was the better nuts-and-bolts operator, but Bob had more passion for causes. Ted enjoyed the game of bartering and persuasion; Bob just wanted to get things done. As far back as 1965, he was talking about setting a record for longevity in the Senate, while Bob was restless to move on the day he got there. Ted did what his brother asked him to do, but he also began to carve out a path of his own. He took on the discriminatory poll tax when Johnson wouldn't and won kudos from his fellow senators when he led the debate on the issue. He failed to win enough votes to have the ban included in the Voting Rights Act that Johnson was pushing, but the Supreme Court declared the tax unconstitutional a year later, vindicating Kennedy's efforts. He later said fighting the poll tax was the first step of the defining goal of his career: expanding and protecting civil rights.

Ted's first major personal victory in the Senate came from fulfilling a dream of John Kennedy's to give all those who wanted to immigrate to America an equal chance to come. The quotas in place in 1965 favored Northern Europeans, and John Kennedy had argued strenuously that the immigration laws of the country should show *no* racial preferences, that Asians, Africans and Greeks should be treated the same as Britons, Germans and Irish. Echoing his brother's speeches on the issue, Ted pushed the bill through the Senate Judiciary Committee and brought it to the floor for a vote.

In the closing debate, the brother senators dramatically displayed their different approaches. A Southern senator, Spessard Holland of Florida, was against the bill because he was loath to equate Europeans with Africans.[26] Ted took the high ground, replying that the bill reaffirmed American principles of equal opportunity for everyone. He kept his argument abstract and broad, and respectful. Holland argued back that blacks in America didn't even know where they came from in Africa, and Robert exploded at him. He attacked Holland personally, asking sarcastically if he knew that blacks had been brought from Africa in slavery.[27] The brothers won the day and the bill passed 76–18, but Ted had preserved his relationship with Holland for another day; Bob had made an enemy for life. Senators generally liked Ted better because of such tactics, but they tended to treat Bob with more respect, like a future president. "There was always this *Camelot*," said Mondale. "Reclaiming what was taken from them and taken from the nation. I think Ted planned to help Bob become president right away. I don't think it was ever far out of their minds."

The Immigration Act itself literally changed the complexion of the country, from 85 percent white to one that is one-third minority today, and on track for a nonwhite majority in 2042. In the 1950s, 53 percent of all immigrants were Europeans; by 1990, just 16 percent were. Nothing is more responsible for the country's current diversity than the Immigration Act.

Ted also found the cause of his life while Bob was in the Senate with him. After a three-hour visit to one of the first community health care centers in the country at Columbia Point in Boston, Ted became convinced that the best way to improve the nation's health was to bring health care into neighborhoods. At the time the Columbia Point center was built, the nearest hospital for the indigent took five hours to reach, which meant a great many people living in poverty never bothered. Within just a few months of his visit, Kennedy won $51 million to build 30 other community health clinics across the country. Since 1966, Kennedy succeeded in expanding that number to 1,200 centers, providing care to more than 9 million people. He has fought off repeated attempts to cut funding for the centers. He continues to pursue this cause, and now, in an effort to provide health care for some of the 40 million uninsured Americans, Kennedy is pushing for expansion of the health center system to nearly double its current capacity—to serve 30 million people—by the year 2015.

Back in 1966, on the first anniversary of the opening of the Columbia Point center, Kennedy returned to congratulate the staff on what they started. "You have not only assured the best health care for your families and neighbors," Kennedy told them, "but you also have begun a minor revolution in American medicine."[28]

In 1966, Ted was acting locally to improve lives, while Bob was thinking globally. Bob visited South Africa in a journey that completed his personal and political evolution. South Africa is also where he gave his greatest speech. Bob had accepted an invitation from the University of Cape Town to speak on the Day of Affirmation. Though he had come to speak out against the country's official policy of apartheid, which segregated all blacks from all whites, his central message was more universal—that most of the world's great movements begin with one man. To an audience of 15,000, he said: "Few will have the greatness to bend history itself; but each of us can work to change a small portion of events, and in the total of all those acts will be written the history of this generation. . . . It is from numberless diverse acts of courage and belief that human history is shaped. Each time a man stands up for an ideal, or acts to improve the lot of others, or strikes out against injustice, he sends forth a tiny ripple of hope, and crossing each other from a million different centers of energy and daring, those ripples build a current which can sweep down the mightiest walls of oppression." The notion of ripples of hope became a kind of signature for Bob after that, inspiring tens of thousands of people to political involvement.

Whites were prohibited from touching blacks in segregated South Africa, so Bob, inspired by the civil rights marches back home, set forth on walking tours to shake as many black hands as he could. As word of his visit spread, blacks crowded around to touch him, and by the end of his trip, he was holding impromptu rallies with hundreds and hundreds of people. Margaret Marshall, a leader of students opposed to apartheid in South Africa, says Kennedy's visit gave the struggling movement hope. "He reminded us—me—that we were not alone. That we were part of a great and noble tradition, the re-affirmation of nobility in every human person. We all had felt alienated. . . . He put us back into the great sweep of history. Even if it's just a tiny thing, it will add up. He reset the moral compass, not so much by attacking apartheid, but by simply talking about justice and freedom and dignity—words that none of us had heard in, it seemed like, an eternity. He didn't go through the white liberals, he connected straight—by standing on a car. Nobody had done that. How simple it was! He was not afraid."[29]

After South Africa, Robert Kennedy took his disillusionment and insights about the bureaucracy of Washington and began to form a coalition of disaffected people around them. Harris Wofford believes that after his visit, he wanted to revolutionize the system, create a new kind of politics. The way the U.S. government was going about things became, in his mind, immoral.

As a member of the Subcommittee on Employment, Manpower and Poverty of the Senate Welfare and Labor Committee, Bob toured poor black towns in the Mississippi Delta. "He went into a foul windowless shack and found a starving child with a distended stomach," columnist Russell Baker wrote. "He held the child, talked to him, tried to arouse a response. Rats and roaches were on the floor. Kennedy just sat there, tears running down his cheeks."[30] The scene stayed with Bobby, and he told his children about it. He asked them to imagine what it would be like if they lived the way the children in the Delta lived, starving among rats. Bobby's moral imagination took the Kennedy legacy of concern for the dispossessed to its logical extreme, so that he began to feel what they felt. In his heart, he became one of them.

Bobby focused more and more on the inequities in America. He proposed a bill to promote industrial development in inner cities, increase welfare and social security benefits, and require cigarette manufacturers to put warnings in all their ads. Race riots continued to wrack the country in the summer of 1967, and Bobby testified about the need for gun control. Eunice Shriver once cut short critics who were questioning the genuineness of the anti-establishment "New Bobby." "What difference does it make, why waste time arguing about that? What counts is that all that energy, all that power, all that ability is being used for peace and for civil rights and for the poor."[31]

In the Senate, Bob and Ted both began to speak out against the immorality of the Vietnam War. Both senators had toured Vietnam, where they'd seen for themselves that things were not going as well as the government was reporting. Ted was the first to take a strong stand against further escalation, but it was Bob who had put him up to it, hoping to test out the waters for his own views. In a speech at Yale, Ted said, "I am an authority on violence—all it brings is pain and suffering, and there is no place for that in our society. . . . If you want to bring an end to war—then work to elect men who agree with you."[32] It didn't take long for Bob to mount the ramparts. In a major address on March 2, 1967, Bob said, "I can testify that if fault is to be found or responsibility assessed, there is enough to go around for all—including myself."[33] But he had changed his views, and now he saw the war as unwinnable. He asked the senators to picture the "horror" of the "ever-widening war" as "a mother and child watch death by fire fall from an improbable machine sent by a country they barely comprehend." He had become convinced that Johnson should stop the bombing of North Vietnam and start negotiating a political settlement. Vietnam, Wofford said, "was the crucible in which he found a new kind of courage—the courage to appear soft."[34] Bob Kennedy told people he had tamed his own "ruthlessness," and now he wanted to try to help tame the savageness at loose in the country.

After the Tet Offensive on January 31, 1968, when North Vietnamese and Viet Cong launched a coordinated attack all over the country, seizing many cities, the American public lost confidence in Johnson's prosecution of the war. Johnson continued to escalate the number of troops in Vietnam, so that by the beginning of 1967, more than 500,000 troops were committed, and Bob decided the only way to stop the war was to run for president against his brother's former vice president. He made his decision for spiritual reasons as much as political reasons. He said he wanted the save the soul of the country.

9

THE IMPOSSIBLE DREAM

Make gentle the life of this world.
　　　　　　　—*Bobby Kennedy, Indianapolis, March 31, 1968*

March 16, 1968: Bob announced his candidacy for the presidency in the same place Jack had, the Caucus Room of the Old Senate Office Building. He stood in the same spot and used the same opening words: "I am today announcing my candidacy for the presidency of the United States." He repeated his brother's trademark phrase during his remarks: "I think this country can do better." And he finished with four sentences written for him by his brother's speechwriter: "I do not lightly dismiss the dangers and the difficulties of challenging an incumbent President. But these are not ordinary times and this is not an ordinary election. At stake is not simply the leadership of our party and even our country. It is our right to [the] moral leadership of this planet."[1]

But from that moment on, nothing Bob did in his 1968 run for the presidency resembled Jack's 1960 campaign—or any previous campaign in American history. For 11 weeks, Kennedy and his entourage caromed around the country with reckless, frantic passion, unleashing animal energies everywhere they went. A "mobile riot," President Johnson labeled it. An "impossible dream," Senator George McGovern called it. It was "Jazz Politics" in writer Thurston Clarke's words—improvisational, emotional, unpredictable. Bobby would spend a majority of his time not in delegate-rich states but in America's poorest cities and neighborhoods, campaigning more like a revolutionary priest than a politician. He was on a crusade, not a campaign. He would *demand* to know what people were going to do for their country, rather than ask, as John had. He would promise to "close the gaps between black and white, between rich and poor, between young and old." He would tell Americans the hard truth about the state of their nation in 1968, even if it wasn't what they wanted to hear. And still, crowds would swarm him in city after city, climbing onto his convertible, grabbing his hair, tearing his shirtsleeves. Hysterical students would scream at him like he was one of the Beatles.[2] Bobby campaigned for 82 days like there were no certain tomorrow, ignoring death threats and shunning police escorts so he could be closer to people during the campaign.

Ted thought it was all a mistake.

In late 1967 and early 1968, when Bob was trying to decide whether to run, Ted was the leading voice against a bid for the presidency. Ted's reasons were both political and personal. Ted thought Bob ought to wait until 1972, after Johnson's tenure was finished, when he'd have a clean shot at the White House. If Bob ran in 1968 and lost in the primaries to a sitting president, Ted thought it would destroy his brother's chances later. He also just thought it was wrong for Bobby to run against his brother's vice president. Such a thing violated the rules of the game that were so important to Ted. But mostly, Ted feared his brother would meet the same fate Jack had. He and other close aides, such as Ted Sorensen, felt the Kennedy family had already paid a high enough price serving the country. "We weren't that far away from '63, and that was still very much a factor," Ted said years later.[3]

The person whose raging ambition had driven Bob so far toward this moment was now dead-set against it, too. Two days earlier, when Bob told his father he was going to run, Joe's head dropped to his chest in regret. He no longer wished to see three sons as president; he only wished to see the last two stay alive. The blowtorch was nearly out, and if Bob had only looked closely into his father's eyes, he would have seen the regrets Joe had over the high price he'd paid for his dreams. Jack's friend Lem Billings said later, "Bobby didn't know that his father was trying to stop this thing that had gotten started—this Kennedy thing of daring the gods. The two of them never understood each other on this."[4] Ted said he wasn't sure what Jack would have advised Bob to do, "but I know what Dad would have advised . . . 'Don't do it.'"

Jackie shared Ted's concern as well. "Do you know what I think will happen to Bobby?" she asked Arthur Schlesinger a few days after the announcement. "The same thing that happened to Jack. . . . There is so much hatred in this country, and more people hate Bobby than hated Jack. . . . I've told Bobby this, but he isn't fatalistic like me."[5]

Bob wasn't deaf to their concerns. He told Milton Gwirtzman that "nobody in my family wants me to run. No one whose political judgment I respect wants me to run. And not a single leader in the country wants me to run." He was especially attentive to Ted's advice since he now trusted his younger brother's political instincts implicitly. But Bob wasn't making a political decision, he was making a moral decision. "My brother thinks I'm crazy," Bob said. "He doesn't like this. He doesn't go along. But then, we're two different people. We don't hear the same music. Everyone's got to march to his own music."[6] Bob finally let himself be persuaded by those around him and pulled out of the New Hampshire primary. He still hadn't given up entirely on the idea, but for the time being he bowed to the majority opinion of his inner circle.

But then something extraordinary happened during a trip to California.

Bob accepted an invitation from union leader César Chavez to be in Delano when Chavez finished a monthlong fast affirming his commitment to nonviolence. On the way to the park where Chavez was to speak, Bob encountered 4,000 exuberant Chicano workers lining the road. They waved baseball caps at him and shouted "Bobby! Bobby! Un gran' hombre! Un gran' hombre!" as he took the stage.[7] With faces bathed in tears, they kissed Bobby on the hands and mouth. "You could see the blood," Chavez later said of Kennedy's hands, which had been badly scratched by workers reaching out to him.[8] They were devoted to Bob because he had visited them before and fought for their rights in Washington as a senator. He'd spoken out on their plight in California and supported their union, the United Farm Workers. And he was Catholic, just as they were. The reception went a long way toward erasing Bob's fears that he was an unpopular figure around the country because of his reputation for ruthlessness and ambition. "Do you know why we loved Robert Kennedy so?" Dolores Huerta, a United Farm Workers organizer, told a legislator. "Do you know why the poor love those millionaires John Kennedy and Robert Kennedy? It was their attitude. I think Ted has it, too. Robert didn't come to us and tell us what was good for us. . . . All he said was, 'What do you want? And how can I help?' That's why we loved him."[9]

Chavez was too weak from hunger to speak at the event, but his speech was read for him to the crowd. The words probably served as the final turning point for Bob in his decision-making process. "When we are really honest with ourselves," Chavez wrote, "we must admit that our lives are all that really belong to us. So it is how we use our lives that determines what kind of men we are. It is my deepest belief that only by giving our lives do we find life. I am convinced that the truest act of courage, the strongest act of manliness, is to sacrifice ourselves for others in a totally nonviolent struggle for justice. To be a man is to suffer for others. God help us be men."

Here was the new definition of courage Bob had been groping toward since his brother's death. It was new but familiar. Chavez was expressing the ancient creed at the very heart of Catholicism: The ultimate sacrifice one could make was to serve others—to die if necessary, as Christ had died, so that others may live.

Bob asked a campaign worker, Polly Fitzgerald, "If you had a choice of dying and going straight to heaven, or of living and taking your chances, which would you choose?" Polly said she'd live and take her chances. "Not me," Bob replied. "I'd still take the other." Translated into politics, his reawakened faith meant Bob *preferred* risking his life doing the right thing to any other existence. Such a life was worth living, more heroic and noble and even holy. The lettuce fields of California were Bob's Gethsemane. He knew he might die running for president, but he had decided it was worth that risk.

In the airplane on the way back to Washington, Bob was on fire, said Stewart Udall. "Yes, I'm going to do it," Bob told him. His mind was made up.

★ ★ ★

Just a few days later, Johnson barely outpolled the upstart antiwar candidate, Eugene McCarthy, in New Hampshire, 49 percent to 42 percent. Counting write-in votes in the Republican primary, the Minnesota Democrat had come within a few hundred votes of Johnson. The president was vulnerable, and Bob saw an open door that hadn't been there before. In Bob's mind, the results in New Hampshire only bolstered the case for entering the race because he considered McCarthy too pompous and incompetent to be president. Though McCarthy's campaign had sparked enormous enthusiasm among young voters, Bob thought he could carry the antiwar banner more successfully in the general election.

By now, Ted believed Bob had to run—for Bobby's own emotional well-being, as much as anything. But the youngest, most politically savvy brother was never convinced it was the right thing to do. "Bobby's therapy is going to cost the family $8 million," he quipped. Among all the Kennedy family what-ifs, it's hard not to include the question of how history might have been different if Ted's argument had won the day. Bob could very well still be alive if he'd listened to Ted. Johnson may very well have won a second term; and Richard Nixon may have never become president, saving the country the moral black hole of Watergate. If Bob had waited, Ted probably wouldn't have driven a car off a bridge after a party commemorating his brother's staff, and both he and Bobby very well may have been elected president, fulfilling

their father's prophecy. But for Bob, the moral imperative of stopping the
Vietnam War was all that mattered, and he had ego enough to believe he was
the only person who could stop it. For him, it was an ethical decision, not a
political one.

★ ★ ★

Ted and his brother-in-law Steve Smith, served as informal chairmen of the
campaign. Fred Dutton, an attorney who had worked in Jack's campaign,
became Bob's right-hand man and de facto campaign manager. No one person was really in charge, and the campaign structure was an organic, fluid
thing from the start. Joe, Bobby, Jack, Sargent Shriver and a host of veteran
advisers had intricately choreographed Jack's campaign for nearly four years
before he was "officially" running. Bob's campaign was planned in less than
a week.

Bob had already been scheduled to give a lecture at Kansas State University on March 18, so that's where he decided he'd deliver his first campaign
speech. Manhattan, Kansas, is a long way from Manhattan, New York, and as
the Kennedy team was flying in, many of them felt as if they were starting
their campaign behind enemy lines. Aides Jim Tolan and Jerry Bruno had
arrived earlier to get things ready, and they were "becoming more nervous
by the hour" as they took the temperature of the city.[10] Kansas was Republican country—Nixon had beaten Jack soundly in 1960—and Bruno was
worried that a hostile reception from the conservative students at KSU
could doom Kennedy's candidacy before it got off the ground. Kennedy
planned to come out strongly against the war in his speech, so he, too, expected to have to fend off heckles and boos from the midwestern crowd.

Fourteen thousand five hundred people crammed into Ahearn Field
House to hear what Bob had to say. Many of them were there to measure Bob
against his brother, but many were also there because they had decided the
country had gone off in the wrong direction after Jack's death. Bob was pleas-
antly surprised when he and Ethel walked in and the students cheered and
stamped their feet.

He opened with an apology. "Let me begin this discussion with a note
both personal and public," he said. "I was involved in many of the early decisions on Vietnam, decisions which helped set us on our present path. . . . I
am willing to bear my share of the responsibility, before history and before
my fellow-citizens. But past error is no excuse for its own perpetuation."
Loud cheers met his mea culpa, and seemed to give Bob confidence in his
message. "I am concerned—as I believe most Americans are concerned—that
we are acting as if no other nations existed, against the judgment and desires

of neutrals and our historic allies alike." His language would be echoed by Ted Kennedy almost 35 years later in protest of the invasion of Iraq. "War is not to be lightly undertaken, nor prolonged one moment past its absolute necessity," Bob declared.

His condemnations of the war were met by round after round of applause, and his voice grew with each one. He began pounding his fist on the lectern, shouting a line of John's repeatedly at the students. "I don't think we have to accept that here in the United States of America! I think we can do better in this country!" He finished by warning in a raised voice that "our country is in danger: not just from foreign enemies, but above all, for from our own misguided policies. There is a contest on, not for the rule of America but for the heart of America."

He raised his fist into the air, Che style, and promised "a new America!"

The reaction was tumultuous. Thunderous cheers went up and waves of students surged toward the platform, knocking over chairs on their way. They ripped Kennedy's shirtsleeves and grabbed at his hair. Instead of quickly slipping out a side exit, Kennedy waded straight into the crowd like a rock star entering a mosh pit. A *Look* magazine photographer standing on a platform was shouting over the heads of the mob, unable to believe his eyes. "This is *Kansas*, fucking Kansas! He's going all the way!"[11]

The crowd at the University of Kansas a few days later was even larger, a record 20,000 people, and more emotional than the one at KSU. On the plane ride back to Washington, Bobby huddled in Jack's overcoat and talked a hundred miles an hour. He asked columnist Jimmy Breslin, "Did you ever see anything like it? You can hear the fabric ripping," he said. "If we don't get out of this war, I don't know what these young people are going to do. There's going to be no way to talk to them. It's very dangerous."[12]

★ ★ ★

Bob took his campaign to the streets after that, bulldozing through 13 states in the next two weeks. "We're going to the people," said one of his aides.[13] Bob decided a televised campaign would send the wrong message to the people he wanted to reach. "Just as Tocqueville said that the people in a democracy reign supreme as the deities in the universe," he told an aide, "and just as you go to church to worship your deity—your God—so, too, when you seek the highest laurels in the country, you have to go before the people, where the power is. And you can't just do it by sitting in front of a TV camera . . . that's not what it's all about."[14]

Bob traveled without pollsters or marketing consultants or media advisers. He campaigned without much of a plan, making most of his decisions on impulse. He charged through Alabama and Tennessee, then on to New York, over to California, up through Oregon and Washington, and back to the heartland of Idaho, Utah, Colorado, New Mexico and Indiana. There was no bunting or elaborate backdrops or fancy stages. Adam Walinsky and Jeff Greenfield mostly wrote his speeches on the fly, and Bob often improvised his talks based on just a few notes. He spoke like Kerouac wrote—from the hip, stream of conscious, uncensored and uninhibited. Like so many people at that time, his primary interest was *authenticity*. Rather than flattering and cajoling his audiences, he lectured and harangued, calling out the better angels of their natures. He conducted spot polls among the crowds and did impromptu interviews of his own. His motorcades turned into parades, with children running alongside and crowds lining the highways for miles. Whenever he stopped, outstretched arms engulfed him as he stood on the backseat of his convertible, aides struggling to hold onto his legs so he wasn't yanked out of the car.[15] One motorcade across Indiana lasted nine hours. He often traced the contrails of his brother's campaign, but where John had drawn hundreds of people, Bob now drew thousands.

He told aides along the way he hadn't felt so alive in a long, long time. He saw a kind of redemption possible in running for president, both for himself and for the nation. He exhorted crowds to join him in experiencing the nobility of sacrifice. He thought the entire country might absolve itself of the sin of Vietnam through good works, just as his faith taught. By eliminating hunger and poverty, Bob told students at Ball State in Indiana, they could heal the wounds of Vietnam. "It is for us to turn this country to a path of honor, not through arms or wealth or force [but] by finding our own satisfaction in the conduct of our country."[16] Echoing César Chavez, he asked, "What other reason do we have really for [our] existence as human beings unless we've made some other contribution to somebody else to improve their own lives?" Bob pleaded with the students in Indiana to share his outrage over the inequities he was seeing wherever he traveled. "What really is our purpose in life?" he asked. "For all the advantages we have, don't we have a major responsibility and an obligation to those who do not have those advantages? Don't we have a major responsibility? Not the government of the United States, but the individuals have a major responsibility?"[17]

That spring, Arthur Schlesinger gave him a new title: the Tribune of the Underclass.

★ ★ ★

Thirteen days after Bob entered the race, Ted was sitting in an Indianapolis hotel room with a recruit, Gerard Doherty, eating a chicken sandwich and watching President Johnson on TV. Ted and Doherty had been meeting all day with coordinators around the state, trying to piece together an organization in just a few weeks for what would be Bobby's first test in a primary. On TV, Johnson was announcing a dramatic reduction in the bombing in North Vietnam and making an urgent appeal for negotiations. Then he said something that flabbergasted the two men. "With America's sons in the field far away, with America's future under challenge right here at home, with our hopes and the world's hopes for peace in the balance every day, I do not believe that I should devote an hour or a day of my time to any personal partisan causes. . . . Accordingly, I shall not seek, and I will not accept, the nomination of my party for another term as your president."

Johnson's polls had shown that McCarthy would thrash him in the upcoming Wisconsin primary, and the president had decided it was time to save himself the embarrassment of losing. The weekend before he withdrew, a Gallup poll indicated that Kennedy would beat him in a nationwide race. Johnson was not a man who liked to get into a fight he couldn't win. He took himself out of the contest before he was forced out. He also had come to realize that, even though he'd done more legislatively than Jack ever had, or than Bob and Ted had as senators at that point, he would never be as admired and loved as the Kennedys were admired and loved, and it stung him to the core. The architect of the Great Society ended his towering political career a bitter man.

"The mood was one of astonishment" in the Kennedy camp, Schlesinger wrote in his journal that day. There was "a certain perplexity and a general, non-exuberant, incredulous feeling that RFK would be our next president." In less than two weeks, Bob had accomplished his primary goal in running— to stop Lyndon Johnson from being reelected.

★ ★ ★

Nineteen sixty-eight came unhinged that spring. It was a year marked by days and weeks and months of rage. Kennedy was right about what was coming— the fabric of the country began to rip in a thousand places. Unprecedented race riots wracked the country, angry antiwar protests erupted on campuses, civilians were slaughtered en masse in the My Lai massacre in Vietnam, and beloved leaders met senseless deaths.

Just five days after Johnson's surprise announcement that he would not run again, a white racist named James Earl Ray fatally shot the Reverend Dr. Martin Luther King on the balcony of the Lorraine Motel in Memphis.

Bob had been scheduled to speak at a small park at Seventeenth and Broadway in Indianapolis that night, the heart of one of the most impoverished black ghettos in the country. By the time his plane landed, riots were already brewing in Memphis, and two aides, Burke Marshall and Joe Dolan, recommended that Kennedy issue a statement and cancel his speech. The reasons were simple: He might be shot.[18] Kennedy would have none of it. He told his staff he was going to Seventeenth and Broadway and he didn't want police going with him. Another aide, Frank Mankiewicz, urged him to give a very short speech. "It should be almost a prayer," he advised.[19]

Many of the 3,000 people gathered in the park that night had not heard the news because they had left for the rally before the shooting. But some of the people on the periphery had arrived later, and were already were itching for a fight. Walinsky and Mankiewicz had drafted a speech for the occasion, but Kennedy had other plans. He would speak spontaneously, he decided. From the heart.

His stage was the bed of a flatbed truck with a microphone in it. The night was so dark most of his audience was in shadow. He was all alone on his makeshift platform.

"Ladies and gentlemen," he began respectfully. "I'm only going to talk to you just for a minute or so this evening because I have some very sad news . . ." His voice caught for a moment, but he made it sound like a throat clearing. "And that is that Martin Luther King was shot and was killed tonight in Memphis, Tennessee."

Political journalist Joe Klein described the reaction as "screams, wailing—just the rawest, most visceral sounds of pain that human voices can summon."[20] As Bob began again, slowly, almost quietly, the screams died down: "Martin Luther King . . . dedicated his life . . . to love . . . and to justice between fellow human beings, and he died in the cause of that effort. For those of you who are black—considering the evidence evidently is that there were white people who were responsible—you can be filled with bitterness, and with hatred, and a desire for revenge. We can move in that direction as a country, in greater polarization—black people amongst blacks, and white people amongst whites, filled with hatred toward one another. Or we can make an effort, as Martin Luther King did, to understand, and to comprehend, and replace that violence, that stain of bloodshed that has spread across our land, with an effort to understand, compassion and love."

And then, with an unrehearsed honesty unheard of in politics now, he did something he'd never done publicly. He spoke of his dead brother. "For those of you who are black and are tempted to be filled with hatred and mistrust of the injustice of such an act, against all white people, I would only say that I can also feel in my own heart the same kind of feeling. I had a member of my family killed, but he was killed by a white man. But we have to make an effort in the United States, we have to make an effort to understand, to get beyond, or go beyond these difficult times."

Kennedy quoted an ancient Greek poet to his inner-city audience. "My favorite poem, my favorite poet was Aeschylus. He once wrote, 'Even in our sleep, pain which cannot forget falls drop by drop upon the heart. Until . . . in our own despair, against our will, comes wisdom through the awful grace of God.'" The silence deepened at that stage of the speech. Many of the people there remember the moment as one of the most stunning they've ever experienced.

Kennedy finished seven unscripted minutes by appealing to the crowd's deepest humanity. "Let us dedicate ourselves to what the Greeks wrote so many years ago: to tame the savageness of man and make gentle the life of this world. Let us dedicate ourselves to that, and say a prayer for our country and for our people."

Riots broke out in every major city in the country that night, but not in Indianapolis. Most of the crowd in front of the flatbed truck stood in silence after Bob's speech, some weeping. Others rushed the truck, reaching their hands up to him. They drifted away from the park quietly afterward, going back to their homes with bowed heads. Not a gun was fired in the city that night.

Associated Press reporter Saul Pett remembered Bob on the plane shortly after. "There would come a look in his eyes of the deepest kind of hurt a human can project. He was still feeling the loss of his brother. When he was away from the crowds and the noise and so forth, this look of what must have been eternal sadness came over him."[21]

Out of that sadness, however, Bob had forged an impromptu sermon on the hustings that has endured as a measure of what politics can be at its very best. "Nearly 40 years later," Klein wrote, "Kennedy's words [in Indiana] stand as an example of the substance and music of politics in its grandest form and highest purpose—to heal, to educate, to lead. Sadly, his speech also marked the end of an era: the last moments before American public life was overwhelmed by marketing professionals, consultants and pollsters who, with the flaccid acquiescence of the politicians, have robbed public life of much of its romance and vigor." Kennedy went on to win the Indiana primary, but it is not that victory he is remembered for. What Robert Kennedy left was not a legacy of political prowess or legislative triumph. The Indiana speech, and the very campaign itself, would be his legacy, and he seemed to have known it would be. He left something more individual than his other brothers have left, something each person who reads his words and learns about the 1968 campaign can find inspiration in. What Robert contributed to the Kennedy legacy was a forever-relevant example of unbridled humanity at work. In his campaign, Bob tried to become a living example of an awakened conscience, which was exactly what his brother had rhetorically summoned the country to in his inaugural. Bob answered John's call to service with his campaign, an 82-day act of love.

After Indiana, the Free-at-Last Tour zigzagged between success and failure, inspiration and amateurism. A week after winning Indiana, Bob won in Nebraska. McCarthy won the next two primaries in Wisconsin and Massachusetts and a heartbreaker in Oregon. Hubert Humphrey entered the race, complicating Bob's chances even further. Still, Bob motorcaded and whistle-stopped 12 to 16 hours a day, crisscrossing the country in a headlong sprint. But there was a shadow hanging over the campaign after Indiana. Bob had begun to believe that the contagion that had claimed King's life and John's might soon claim his as well. "I'm afraid there are guns between me and the White House," he told a friend of King's, the Reverend Walter Fauntroy.[22] But his fears didn't slow him down. He continued to campaign in an open convertible without Secret Service protection or police escort, still allowing anyone along the way to come up and touch him. Hays Gorey thought the campaign began to resemble a "slow-motion suicide" after the death of King. Bob simply viewed the dangers as a test of moral courage.[23]

It was in California that the campaign finally congealed politically. Bob's appeal to Hispanics, blacks and working-class whites translated into a majority of the votes in a major state. His pleas for a better, gentler country and his tirades against the immorality of the Vietnam War were starting to break through. Bob had made a believer out of many of his doubters with the sheer passion with which he campaigned.

At around midnight on June 4, Bob's impossible dream began to seem, for the first time, reachable. The late results pouring in from the California primary were starting to break in his favor. If Bob won California, he really thought he had a clear shot at winning the presidency. Kenny O'Donnell, a former classmate at Harvard, asked him if he thought he could go all the way. "I think I may," he said, adding, "I feel now for the first time that I've shaken off the shadow of my brother. I feel I made it on my own."[24]

When victory appeared to be in hand, the celebrations began to veer toward the combustible. These were celebrations of something bigger than a primary win. They were emotional coming-out parties for the undersung of America. In Los Angeles, when it became clear that Bobby had the votes, the crowd in his suite at the Ambassador Hotel went delirious. Bobby waltzed triumphant around the room. "People were celebrating, cheering each report that came over the television," says Ted Sorensen, a longtime aide to John F. Kennedy who was there that night. Bob and his closest friends and aides all rode a cloud down to the Embassy Ballroom for the victory celebration.

The mood in San Francisco was just as exuberant. Ted had flown out from Washington to stand in for his brother and thank the campaign foot soldiers who had secured Northern California. At midnight, he waded into the crowd at the municipal center and the workers went wild. "A great night," Ted proclaimed. "California is coming through for us!" As the liquored-up well-wishers in San Francisco watched on television, Bob nearly lifted the roof off the hotel in Los Angeles with a rousing victory speech. "I think we can end the divisions in the United States," he declared. "What has been going on over the period of the last three years—the divisions, the violence, the disenchantment with our society, the divisions, whether it is between the poor and the more affluent, or between age groups—that we can start to work together again. We are a great country, an unselfish country, and a compassionate country. . . . Now on to Chicago!"

As the speech ended in Los Angeles, Ted and his administrative assistant Dave Burke tried to wedge their way back through the revelers in San Francisco, having to push people out of their way out. Protestors up in the balcony screamed "Free Huey!" "Free Huey!"—referring to jailed Black Panther leader Huey P. Newton. Ted became alarmed at the smothering mob. Burke worried that the rally would turn ugly.

When Ted and Burke returned to their suite at the Fairmount Hotel and turned on the television, the announcer was talking about a shooting at the Kennedy rally. "We were lucky to get out of there," remarked Burke, adding that Ted needed better security in the future. But the shooting was in Los Angeles, not San Francisco. When Ted finally understood that it was Bob who had been shot, he just stared at the set, dumbfounded.

The crowd at the Ambassador was in an uproar. Ted's brother-in-law Steve Smith appeared on the screen imploring people to stay calm, leave the ballroom and go home. "I could not believe that what I had gone through five years earlier was happening again," says Sorensen, who had stayed behind in the hotel room. "I saw him speak, thank his supporters, conclude with the stirring words, 'Now on to Chicago!' which was to be the site of the convention that year, continued watching as the camera followed him off the platform only to hear the shots ring out, the commentators saying that Sen. Kennedy has been shot. . . . And there he was lying on the floor in a pool of his own blood."[25] Bob held a rosary given to him by a busboy.

Back in San Francisco, Ted Kennedy was utterly silent as he watched the madhouse on television. For long minutes, his expression remained unchanged. Finally, after what seemed like forever to Burke, Ted said simply, "We have to get down there."

Burke rushed down ten flights of stairs to the hotel desk to get help. He used a telephone in the assistant manager's office to call a perplexed American Airlines clerk, insisting that he needed an airplane immediately. Burke raced up and down the stairs three or four times in between calls trying to arrange a plane. San Francisco congressman Phil Burton eventually stepped in and called an Air Force major, who also balked at the request for a plane. "I am standing here with Senator Edward Kennedy, whose brother has just been shot and who may be the next president of the United States. You are at a point I call a career decision, Major. Either you get the plane or your career is over." Ted got the plane.

When Ted finally made it to the fifth floor of Los Angeles's Good Samaritan Hospital just after 3 A.M., Bobby was about to be taken in for three hours of surgery to remove bullet fragments from his head. A long bedside vigil began, the third such deathwatch in five years for the family. Friends and family members filtered in throughout the night. Outside, a somber crowd kept another vigil. Everyone knew he was going to die, they just didn't know when. Nonetheless, the crowd kept its composure and dignity. Witnesses don't remember any tears being shed prematurely.

"He was so happy last night," a man in the crowd who'd been with Bobby was heard to say. "He heard early that he was going to do all right and he kept walking up to people and saying, 'Later, we'll go up to the Factory for a drink. And tell so-and-so. I want him there. Tell him to be sure he comes with us. I'll chase Humphrey all over the country,' he kept saying. 'He won't be able to get away.'"[26]

Ted learned at about 5 A.M. that Bobby's brain waves had gone flat. A friend who came to pay his respects remembers Ted in the bathroom doubled over, "sort of leaning over the sink with the most awful expression on his face. Just more than agony, more than anguish. I don't know if there is a word for it." Nearly a day later, at 1:44 A.M., Thursday, June 6, Bobby was allowed to die. Edward Kennedy's worst fear had come true.

"I can't let go," Ted told one of his aides on the night of Bobby's death. "We have a job to do. If I let go, Ethel will let go, and my mother will let go, and all my sisters."

Ted returned to Washington in the plane with his brother's coffin a few days later. He kept a hand on the coffin all the way. Repeatedly on the flight back, he was heard to pledge "I'm going to show them. I'm going to show them what they've done, what Bobby meant to the country, what they lost." It was a promise that was to define the rest of his life.

Six of the Kennedy children gather for a family photo with Joe Sr. and Rose at Hyannis Port. From left are John, Jean, Rose, Joe Sr., Patricia, Bobby and Eunice. Ted is in front with a football. Photo courtesy of the John F. Kennedy Library and Museum

Ted (left) and Jack prepare for a sailing expedition on Nantucket Sound in 1946. Photo courtesy of the John F. Kennedy Library and Museum

Attorney General Bobby Kennedy, Senator Ted Kennedy and President Jack Kennedy confer in 1963. Photo by the Washington Post

(above) *Freshman Senator Ted Kennedy makes a speech in 1963 as his brother the president looks on. Photo courtesy of the John F. Kennedy Library and Museum*

(right) *President John Kennedy walks with his son John-John in the White House in 1963. Photo by the* Washington Post

The Senators Kennedy listen to a hearing together in March of 1967. Photo by the Washington Post

Ted Kennedy Jr., wearing a temporary artificial leg, leaves Georgetown University Hospital with his parents in 1973, thirteen days after his cancerous right leg was amputated. Photo by Harry Naltchaayn of the Washington Post

Senator Ted Kennedy pauses at the casket of Lance Corporal Geofrey Robert Cayer during a funeral ceremony at Arlington National Cemetery. Kennedy attended many of the funerals of Massachusetts soldiers who died in Iraq. Photo by Rich Lipski of the Washington Post

Senator Barack Obama listens as Senator Ted Kennedy endorses Obama for the democratic presidential nomination at American University on January 28, 2008. Behind Kennedy are Caroline Kennedy and Kennedy's son, Representative Patrick Kennedy. Photo by Gerald Martineau of the Washington Post

Senator Barack Obama, Caroline Kennedy and Senator Ted Kennedy respond to the crowd after Kennedy's endorsement of Obama at American University in Washington, D.C., on January 28, 2008. Photo by Gerald Martineau of the Washington Post

Senator Barack Obama and Senator Edward Kennedy leave the plane after landing in Boston for their final rally on February 4, 2008, before the Super Tuesday primaries. Photo by Preston Keres of the Washington Post

Caroline Kennedy arrives at the convention hall in Boston for the Democratic National Convention in 2004. Photo by Bill O'Leary of the Washington Post

Senator Edward Kennedy, flanked by his wife, Vicki, and son Patrick, makes a surprise return to the Senate in July 2008, just a few weeks after being treated for brain cancer. Photo by Linda Davidson of the Washington Post

ACT IV
TED

10

THE RELUCTANT PATRIARCH

Be not afraid of greatness. Some are born great,
some achieve greatness. Some have greatness thrust upon 'em.

—*William Shakespeare,* Twelfth Night

The memorable words Ted spoke during his brother's funeral in St. Patrick's Cathedral were by and large Robert Kennedy's own. "Few will have the greatness to bend history itself," Ted told the mourners, quoting Bob's speech to students in South Africa. "But each of us can work to change a small portion of events, and in the total of all those acts will be written the history of this generation. . . . Moral courage is a rarer commodity than bravery in battle or great intelligence. Yet it is the one essential, vital quality for those who seek to change a world that yields most painfully to change. And I believe that in this generation those with the courage to enter the moral conflict will find themselves with companions in every corner of the globe."

Toward the end of the eulogy, Ted plaintively summed up Bob's lasting impact. "My brother need not be idealized, or enlarged in death beyond what he was in life, to be remembered simply as a good and decent man, who saw wrong and tried to right it, saw suffering and tried to heal it, saw war and tried to stop it. Those of us who loved him . . ." His voice broke at the word "loved," and it seemed for a moment as if he wouldn't be able to finish. After the briefest of pauses, he kept on. "And who take him to his rest today, pray that what he was to us and what he wished for others will some day come to pass for all the world. As he said many times, in many parts of this nation, to those he touched and who sought to touch him:

> *Some men see things as they are and say why.*
> *I dream things that never were and say why not.*

A 21-car funeral train took Robert Kennedy's body from New York to Arlington, Virginia, after the service. Ted stayed in the last car, which carried the casket, for the duration of the trip. The train was scheduled to travel non-stop, arriving in Washington in about four hours. But Penn Central did not anticipate the 2 million people along the tracks, a 226-mile human line of grief. Many stood silently watching as the train slipped by, but many others were weeping, singing, holding up signs, waving flags and praying. A high school band in New Brunswick played "Holy God, We Praise Thy Name" when the train passed. After it had rolled by, they switched to "Taps."[1] Boats clustered at the railroad bridges along the way. Nuns standing in a yellow pickup truck sang Catholic hymns. Bridesmaids in a wedding party gathered at the side of the tracks and threw their bouquets at the last car of the train. The movable wake had to slow to half speed because of all the mourners, and after a northbound train killed two people on the tracks in Elizabeth, New Jersey, all other train traffic was halted.

Bob's casket was elevated on chairs inside the last car so people could see it pass.[2] Inside the train, Ethel and her oldest son, Joe, wearing one of his dad's suits, walked down the aisles shaking the hands of mourners on board. Ted would come out onto the back platform to acknowledge the crowd when the knot of people grew especially thick. His presence there startled some, as if they were seeing Bob's ghost. "After the train went through, people stood there transfixed for maybe five or six minutes," said one person watching. "It was difficult to leave."[3] "I hope this train ride never ends," someone else said. It was raining in Washington when the train finally arrived. Buses took the funeral party from the train station to Arlington. As Bob's last motorcade turned to cross Memorial Bridge to deliver his body to its resting place near John, hundreds of people who had collected at the Lincoln Memorial held candles aloft and flicked lighters at the rain as they sang "The Battle Hymn of the Republic." The moon was nearly full that night, and Arthur Schlesinger wrote in his journal that "one felt enveloped by the sadness."

Bob's oldest son, Robert Kennedy Jr., remembers going up to lie on his father's bed during the reception after the funeral. "He had pictures on his wall of my aunt Kick in her nurse's uniform during the war, and pictures of my Uncle Joe and Jack," Bobby Jr. recalls. "And I remember sitting there thinking, 'They all looked so young and they were all dead. . . . ' And I lay there and wept for probably an hour or more, and then my father's best friend, Dave Hackett, came in and sat with me. He just sat there silently for I don't know how long, maybe forty minutes or something. Then he said to me: 'He was the best man I ever knew.'

"That's the only thing that I remember. I don't remember after that."[4]

For the rest of the summer, Ted did what he often did after a Kennedy family tragedy. He went to sea. He would often just lie on his sloop and stare at the sky, a man dislocated and disconnected. He was oblivious to his wife and children for a time, unable to communicate his grief. "I couldn't talk to him," said Joan.[5] No one could. One of the first times that he attempted to return to his suite in the Senate office building, he found himself unable to enter, and drove back home. He thought it might be time to leave public service forever. "Maybe the country lost a lot from the death of Bobby and Jack," said Charles Spalding. "But Teddy suffered more than anybody."

"The burden fell like a thud on his shoulders when Bobby was murdered," says longtime Kennedy observer Tom Oliphant, a former *Boston Globe* columnist. "It fell so hard that his knees buckled at first."[6]

The only solace he seemed to find was out on the ocean, sailing by himself. "Sailing is one of his only real havens," said a Kennedy insider. "There are no cameras on the ocean. The phone doesn't ring. His life is not ruled by shoulds and oughts. And if you're a water person, like he is, you need that infinity of water." Senator John Kerry said, "I think he's never more at peace, and perhaps in some ways never more in touch with his family and his roots and his brothers than when he's out there sailing."

"The sea, the wind, the outdoors. It is the most renewing, healing place for him," said Kennedy's second wife, Vicki. "And always has been."[7]

But healing would not come that summer. There was no longer any grand design to the Kennedy dynasty, there was just Ted. He had now watched the early, violent deaths of three brothers and a sister. And the loss of his two brothers was also the loss of the two primary champions of the political ideals held tightly by his family value system, so Ted was put in a position of mourning both person and project, of grieving both the idea of Camelot and his own flesh and blood. As Arthur Schlesinger wrote in his journal on June 9, 1968, "We have now murdered the three men who more than any other incarnated the idealism of America in our time. Something about our social ethos has conferred a kind of legitimacy on hate and violence. One shudders at future possibilities."

Those future possibilities, the family feared, could very well ensnare Ted. Someone mentioned Ted's return to politics during the July 4 weekend at Hyannis Port, and Jackie rejected it out of hand. "Clearly she thinks he will be killed, too, if he takes a prominent role," Schlesinger noted.[8] After Bob's death, the *New York Times* set into type the advance obituary of Edward Moore Kennedy. He was not only the last brother, but in the family's eyes—and his own—he was a marked man.

Ted's own fears bubbled powerfully to the surface just a few months later on an infamous plane trip back from Alaska. Ted had replaced Bob on the Special Subcommittee on Indian Education, and a group of senators from the committee hopscotched all over the state in April 1969, visiting impoverished Indians and Eskimos. The cause of indigenous peoples had been Bob's cause, and now it was Ted's.

"We were going through that huge state, and we were looking at poverty in the Native populations," remembers Walter Mondale. "They had life spans half that of other Alaskans. Poor healthcare. Terrible alcoholism problems. So we're up there trying to see it and hear about [it], trying to develop some additional ways of dealing with these things. And we did make some progress," Mondale adds. "The problem was, on the trip home, apparently [Ted] had an extra pop that he didn't need."

Ted sat next to writer Brock Brower on the flight back, drinking whiskey steadily from a silver hip flask that had belonged to Bobby. Operating on little sleep and not much food, Ted suddenly burst out loud enough for the whole plane to hear, "They killed Jack and they killed Bobby and now they're trying to kill me. . . . they're trying to kill *me . . . !*"

It's hard to know exactly who Kennedy meant by "they," but he probably meant a vague amalgam of forces bearing down on him—his family, his party, brokenhearted Massachusetts citizens and devastated Americans across the country anxious to restore Camelot and their very image of their country. Bobby hadn't been dead an hour when Ted was urged to run for president. On the elevator down to the autopsy room, Allard Lowenstein said to him, "Now that Bobby's gone, you're all we've got."[9]

"I think part of him felt this huge responsibility to his family, to that national culture of people who wanted a restored Camelot," said Mondale. "And they were putting pressure on him all the time. I think part of him would just have soon avoided it." The pressure was particularly intense from party bosses in advance of the 1968 convention that summer. Political operatives had canvassed the party's voting delegates carefully enough to believe they had the votes to put Teddy somewhere on the ticket, at the bottom or maybe even the top, if he wanted it. "Teddy for President" signs were even made. But Ted was not ready.

"Do you know what it's like to have your wife frightened all the time?" he asked a reporter after drinks. "I'm not afraid to die, I'm too young to die."[10]

Rose Kennedy wrote a note about Teddy becoming president, according to biographer Robert Coughlan. "Never!" it said.

"He promised me . . . he promised me faithfully that he would not run," she told a writer for Hearst newspapers. "I told him I did not want to see him die, too, that I could not stand another tragedy like the deaths of his brothers John and Bobby."[11]

The family had already given the last full measure of devotion in their house, many times over. Ted was the last man standing in the family, and the women survivors said *enough*. "Something breaks," Rose told Coughlan, "and it just couldn't continue."

Ted faced an emotionally impossible choice: fail his party, fail to carry on his brothers' mantle and live; or carry that Kennedy standard forward honorably as a candidate for president and face probable death. Ted was asking himself: Do I shun my inherited role and survive, or do I honor my obligations and hope and pray that what has happened to all of my brothers and to Martin Luther King won't happen to me? The battle within his soul would rage for the next 16 years, pitting his own lust for achievement and his deeply held desire to please his father and honor his brothers against an instinctive will for self-preservation.

Emotionally, Ted was ill-equipped to approach a limelight political position with the same variety of tough political armor his brothers had. Ted had never been groomed for the role of leader. Ted was the Kennedy family's Peter Pan—his job within the hierarchy was never to grow up. The Kennedy family was already filled with kings when he came along; the playful prince had been the only spot left available. He wasn't just the younger brother in the family; he was the younger, younger, younger brother. He was the child who provided comic relief, who bucked the system and veered toward the black sheep model. There was very little chance that his family saw him as a fully grown adult before Bob's death.

Now, overnight, his roles in his family and in the political life of the country were being hastily and desperately reformulated for him. Suddenly, there was an expectation within his family that he would grow from the mental age of a 20-year-old to a fully focused adult at 36. But Ted had never had the rehearsal or training his brothers had. Nobody had ever groomed him for this. The country pined for a certain clonelike re-creation of the Kennedy brothers they had just lost. The need for that banner carrier led to an intense, grasping sort of adulation for Ted in the months to come.

After a dinner honoring Bob, *Washington Post* columnist Meg Greenfield wrote," It was obvious that the participants had come as much to cheer Edward as to mourn Robert. There is little quibbling about Teddy's qualities. If he is not as brainy as John, or as committed as Robert, he enjoys the political process." She quoted a top Democrat as saying "The kids like him because he's young and the blacks like him because of Bobby. The bosses will go for reform if it's the only way to get Teddy."

President Johnson once told Joseph Califano, "Teddy has the potential to be the greatest of the three."[12]

Washinton Post columnist Mary McGrory saw an emotional intelligence in Teddy that she had not seen in the other brothers, and she believed it served him well in politics. "He loves politics and is good at it. And I am referring here to politics in its very best sense: as a skill requiring generosity, compassion, sensitivity, a sense of fun and an ability to enjoy combat without getting uptight or nasty about it."[13] His emotional acuity would be the key to his political career over the coming years, and would begin to set him apart from the overpowering legacy of his brothers. But it would take years before he faced some of his own tightly held emotions.

Ted gained his sensitivity as a result of being treated with so much affection growing up. As the "light of the party," he was trained to be sensitive to the emotional climate of any room. Over the years, Rose trained her "baby" to be particularly attentive to emotional needs rather than material needs. Ted's interpretation of his role had always been to respond to his family with optimism and joy. He didn't really know how to do grief. He eventually would figure out a way to respond to the emotional needs of the entire country, but at the end of the summer of 1968 he had not arrived there yet. Instead, once he emerged from the initial shock of Bobby's death, Ted returned to and expanded the role he felt most comfortable with: taking care of the family.

In times of tragedy, Ted's father, Joe, had also fallen back on the solidity of his family, finding in them a loyalty and satisfaction that the political world had refused him. His most lasting achievement was his sons and daughters, and Ted relied on that same family dynamic. "He talked with great reverence about his father," said Ken Feinberg, a former chief of staff to Ted Kennedy. "He told me his father was a real family man and promoted family unity and harmony." Bob lost himself in his brother's causes after Jack's death. Ted lost himself in the cause of family. Following his father's example, he set himself the task of becoming a father and uncle of extraordinary commitment.

As early as the plane ride back from Los Angeles, "he stressed his increased family responsibility, both personal and political," said Jules Witcover of Newhouse Newspapers. Soon after, Ted asked his secretaries to call all the schools of his nieces and nephews to get a list of scheduled activities.[14] And then he began going to as many basketball games, track meets, school debates and soccer games as he could. Family governess Theresa Fitzpatrick said, "There were a lot of times when he'd be the only parent, certainly the only father, at some of these events. It would have hurt him to have missed something important—Senate business or no."

"If he was on the phone with an enormously important person, he would put that guy on hold to take a call from his children, or Bobby's kids, or whatever it was," recalls Tom Southwick, a former press secretary to Ted Kennedy.

In the summers, Kennedy began taking his children, nieces and nephews out to the Berkshires in western Massachusetts for an annual camping trip. He often took Ethel and all her children on cruises to Martha's Vineyard.[15] He took his nephew Joe to Spain for a summer vacation away from painful memories of his father. In the winters, "he'd dress up as Santa Claus for Christmas and give out the gifts," said Southwick. "He was a great father, not only to his own kids, but to Jack and Bobby's kids. They loved him and still do. He was their dad in a lot of ways."

Ted took his role as surrogate father to his brother's children so seriously that he would bow out of several presidential races in the years ahead when family members asked him not to run. Historian Doris Kearns Goodwin told a reporter that his role as head of the family was every bit as important to him as his role as family torchbearer. "He became not only the carrier of the political legacy, he became the carrier of the family."

All the Kennedy children say he is a good father and uncle.[16] "His kids and his brothers' kids are the only thing that make him happy," a friend said in the early 1980s. "He was like the Pied Piper," says Barbara Gibson, Rose Kennedy's personal secretary in the late 1960s. She remembers Ted organizing boating trips during family vacations.[17] "Wherever he was, there was a bunch of kids following him around." As the Peter Pan of the family, Ted had no trouble thinking the way a kid thought, imagining what their lives were like and connecting with them on their level. Bob had always been a teacher to his children; Ted became their playful camp counselor.

He did, however, put on the hat of disciplinarian when required. "When we got into trouble at school," recalls Christopher Kennedy, Bobby and

Ethel's son, "our mothers would call him to give us a tongue lashing. Believe me, he could scare you straight."[18]

Jackie had moved to New York to get away from all the memories and ghosts, so Ted was less involved in the lives of Caroline and John Jr. in the late 1960s and early 1970s. Worried about financial security, Jackie rushed into a marriage with Aristotle Onassis in 1968, much to the Kennedy family's displeasure. That meant Jackie's children now had a stepfather and financial support and no longer needed their Uncle Ted as much. But Ethel kept her children in Virginia, where Ted had just moved with Joan and his three children. He spent "just an enormous amount of time and energy taking care of them," said Southwick.

Ted was with Ethel when she went to the delivery room six months after Bob's assassination. He held her hand through her cesarean section, even giving suggestions to doctors during the procedure. Ethel named her eleventh baby Rory, a mix of Robert and Bobby, and took her to visit her father's grave on the way home from the hospital.[19]

All those nieces and nephews, sons and daughters would become part of Ted's legacy in the years to come as they each sought to extend the family heritage in unique ways. There would be tough years ahead for some, however, and Ted's dedication to the larger family sometimes came at the expense of his immediate one. His influence as a surrogate parent stretched only so far with 15 children in need of parenting, and the example he set as a role model would be a mixed one at best. His daughter Kara got in the bad habit of running away from home, and Patrick found himself abusing drugs early in his teenage years, prodded there by a complicated brain chemistry and his parents' fragile marriage. Some of Ted's nephews would also get into serious trouble down the road, succumbing to drug habits themselves. Some would lose their lives to freak accidents and unnecessary risks. Some would end up in treatment for alcoholism or addiction. And no one in the third generation would rise to the heights their fathers had. But none of them has ever said that Ted didn't try his hardest to be there for them.

Just before the Democratic convention, Kennedy mustered the courage to return briefly to the public sphere, driven by a desire to carry on Robert's fight against the Vietnam War. In a nationally televised speech at Holy Cross College in Worcester, Massachusetts, he told the crowd "there was no safety in hiding," and he would remain in public service. "Like my brothers before me, I pick up a fallen standard. Sustained by the memory of our priceless years together, I shall try to carry forward that special commitment to justice, excellence and to courage that distinguished their lives."

His speech, inspired by Bobby's antiwar passion, was his strongest statement yet on the Vietnam War, and his timing was aimed at Hubert Humphrey, the likely nominee. Kennedy wanted a rock-solid antiwar plank in the Democratic platform in memory of Bobby, and he got it. When antiwar demonstrators laid siege to the Chicago convention a few days later, the images on television made it look like a revolution had broken out on the streets. Many inside the convention hall wondered "what might have been" if Bob had lived, or Ted had run. Would their broad appeal have becalmed the storm before it broke, keeping the election out of Nixon's grasp? Many Democrats thought so, and several party warlords blamed Ted for the loss that November.

Friends say Ted seriously considered running, but emotionally he could not bring himself to the task.

But the tragedy of his brother's death had increased his resolve to work for progressive causes. After more than six months of hibernation, he found a way to leverage his heir apparent status within the party into a leadership post in the Senate, which would set him up well for the next presidential contest in 1972. By then he figured he might be ready. As he would many times over the next 40 years, he had found a way to take advantage of the emotional support for his fallen brothers to advance his own agenda. He didn't miss a political opportunity so much as he fashioned the opportunity into a bid for an office he was more comfortable with—the majority whip job in the Senate, the number two leadership post. Ted was a savvy enough politician not to try to become Robert or Jack right away. Instead, he tapped into the power of their legacies to increase his own ability to better complete those legacies.

In January 1968, as Richard Nixon was ascending to the presidency, Ted's colleagues voted him in as the youngest majority whip in the history of the U.S. Senate. His campaign for the position was scarcely five days long. A reporter at the time who had covered all three brothers was certain that neither Jack nor Bobby could have won the same post because of their impatience with Senate protocol.[20]

At 36, Ted Kennedy was now in the cockpit of congressional power. Pundits of the day saw a politician with a blazingly bright future. Ted was showing plenty of ambition and nerve already, but no sharp edges or baggage so far.

"Let's face it," wrote Mary McGrory. "Teddy is a Kennedy without problems."

His honeymoon would be over forever in just six months.

11

THE TORCHBEARER

The perfect is the enemy of the good.

—*Ted Kennedy*

At 10:56 P.M. on July 20, 1969, Neil Armstrong stepped off the last rung of the ladder bolted onto the side of the *Eagle* and dipped his boot into the dusty Sea of Tranquility. "That's one small step for man, one giant leap for mankind," said the first man on the moon. Buzz Aldrin joined Armstrong a short time later, describing the lunar surface memorably as "magnificent desolation."

On the same day John F. Kennedy's moon walk challenge was fulfilled, his brother was busy trying to explain to police how his Oldsmobile had plunged off a humpbacked bridge on Chappaquiddick Island, drowning the woman in the passenger seat. The *Boston Globe* actually gave the Chappaquiddick story more dramatic play than the moon landing that Sunday. In the days that followed the accident, Ted Kennedy would find his own not-so-magnificent desolation as hostile reaction to the accident settled around him permanently. For many Americans, that week in July marked the beginning of the fall of the house of Kennedy.

Some of the people close to Kennedy said they had seen the crash coming for some time. While Ted had begun to steadily and methodically build his public life in the Senate that spring, his private life had skittered around like a loose top. After the drunken outburst during the Alaskan plane ride in April of 1969, the network of "Honorary Kennedys" that had grown up like a tightly woven spider web around John, Bob and now Ted became alarmed. Many wondered whether he was suffering from a delayed reaction to his brothers' deaths and the burden of their legacy. John Lindsay of *Newsweek*, who had been a fan of Robert's, put together a memo for distribution inside the office concluding that, emotionally, Ted was slipping out of control. Lindsay had noticed mood shifts, sudden bouts of tears, drinking before public events and a tendency to leave sentences unfinished.[1] "Does he drink? Sure Teddy obviously drinks," said Richard Goodwin in 1969.[2]

It had always been his role to be the boisterous, happy buffoon. And expectations certainly had changed now that he was patriarch and torchbearer. But friends began to notice an intensity of desperation in Ted that spring. His drinking was more regular, his driving wilder than usual and his affairs more blatant. An Associated Press reporter wrote that he was submerging his grief in "frantic activity," driving at breakneck speeds to dozens of events a day as if an increase in velocity might somehow help him outrun his grief.[3] Ted had always been a fast and reckless driver, collecting a number of speeding tickets throughout his life. In law school he had earned the nickname "Cadillac Eddie" by speeding down Virginia's country roads in his battered Oldsmobile convertible. Ted drove as if no harm could come to him, or he simply didn't care if it did.

Where Bob had assuaged his survivor's guilt with a purposefully reckless campaign, Ted seemed to be doing so with a deliberately reckless nightlife. Ted had always chased women as if it were a competition with his brothers to tally the most conquests, but now he did so without any care about getting caught. "He's the least discreet guy on the Hill," an old congressional friend said. "I have told him ten times, 'Ted, you're acting like a fool. Everybody knows you wherever you go. . . . Jack could smuggle girls up the back way. . . . But you're not nearly as discreet as you should be. He looks down with a faint smile and says, 'Yeah, I guess you're right.' But he never listens."[4] At the time of the accident, Ted reportedly had a girlfriend named Helga Wagner, the wife of a San Francisco businessman.[5]

Ted was looking for relief from his responsibilities and burdens anywhere he could find it. *Life* reporter Sylvia Wright warned her editors: "He's living by his gut; something bad is going to happen."

The party on Chappaquiddick Island off Nantucket was one more round in the endless Irish wake Ted Kennedy committed himself to on the night of Bob's death. He was paying his respects to Bobby's "boiler room girls," six women who formed the nerve center of information for the presidential campaign. Ted attended such events out of a sense of duty as the last heir. He had missed the first office party for the women right after Bobby's death, so he felt an obligation to make an appearance for this one.

Looking back with 40 years of hindsight, it's easy to see a pattern repeated in Ted Kennedy's darkest moments. Both Chappaquiddick and, later, a Palm Beach incident that ended in a rape accusation against his nephew William Kennedy Smith, happened on the heels of events where Ted was forced to wallow too long in memories of his dead brothers. In the Palm Beach scandal in 1992, Kennedy was wrestling with the recent death of his brother-in-law Steve Smith, a loss that ripped the scabs off old psychic scars concerning his brothers. Seeking to drown his pain, Kennedy instigated a round of bar-hopping with his son and nephew. Though Ted was not directly involved in the later incident that led to rape charges, the mix of late-night boozing, bad Kennedy memories and a fresh scandal landed the senator on the front of every tabloid in the country.

"That's just something he doesn't like to deal with," a press secretary once said. "I've seen it happen so many times in the past: Things are going fine, he's very loose and relaxed, and then somebody brings up the Kennedy legend stuff, or asks him something about Camelot or carrying the torch, and he freezes. He absolutely freezes. His eyes glaze over and that muscle on the right side of his face starts to twitch and then it's all over, buddy. He pulls back into his shell and you've had it."[6]

Ken Feinberg, who worked for Kennedy for five years as chief of staff, says he never mentioned his brothers once.

The endless reminiscences about Bob during the Chappaquiddick party fed an emotional stew that was already on a low boil. Stir in alcohol, and the recipe for disaster is nearly complete. On several such occasions, Ted described a feeling of walls closing in on him, of "too many blue suits" around, and a desperate need for solitude. "I think I know him pretty well, well enough to realize that he was—he was not exuberant," said Charlie Tretter, a Boston lawyer who was there. "He was not having a helluva good time."[7]

At about 11:15, after at least two rum and Cokes and far too many Bobby stories, Kennedy decided he'd had enough. He told his driver Jack Crimmins he wanted the keys to his Oldsmobile. He planned to make a dash for the last ferry to Edgartown at midnight and drop off one of the guests, Mary Jo Kopechne, at her hotel. Kennedy told Crimmins that Kopechne wasn't feeling well and had asked for a ride.

What happened then only Ted Kennedy knows, and it may be that not even he knows for sure.

He said later, in a report to police, that he took a wrong turn on his way to catch the ferry and drove a half mile down Dike Road in the dark, plunging his Oldsmobile off the doglegged Dike Bridge into a tidal estuary below. Kennedy can't remember how, but he managed to get out of the car and swim or float to the surface of the water. But Mary Jo was trapped in the car. Kennedy said he made several attempts to dive down and pull her out before he collapsed from exhaustion. After a 15-minute rest, he returned to the cottage where the party was still going and climbed in the backseat of a car. He summoned Joey Gargan and Paul Markham, telling them there had been an accident. They drove back down to the bridge, and Joey and Paul stripped down and tried to dive to the car and free Mary Jo, but could not.

"Senator Kennedy," Gargan told Burton Hersh, "was very emotional, very upset, very disturbed, and he was using this expression which I have heard before, but he was using it particularly that night. 'Can you believe it, Joe, can you believe it, I don't believe it, I don't believe this could happen, I just don't believe it.'"[8]

A later report by Kennedy's doctor diagnosed "a temporary loss of consciousness and retrograde amnesia," and noted "impairment of judgment and confused behavior are symptoms consistent with an injury of the character sustained by the patient."

Kennedy's political reputation may have survived the accident intact at that point if someone had immediately contacted the police and there had been every possible effort made to get Mary Jo out of the water. But they didn't. No one reported the incident for ten hours. At 1:00 in the morning, Kennedy swam across the 500-foot cut to Edgartown and returned to his hotel, a strange decision that later seemed to confirm accusations raised questions of a cover-up. If no ferry operator was involved, Kennedy could claim to have been at the hotel in Edgartown at the time of the accident. His actions that next morning supported those suspicions. He made small talk with hotel guests and made no move to report the accident until Gargan and Markham arrived. His delay was not the action of a man worried more about Mary Jo than himself.

What Ted Kennedy could never admit was that he probably lost control of his sanity temporarily that night. Another person vital to the entire Kennedy project had died, and he was directly responsible. And it had been another death he felt powerless to stop, just like the deaths of his brothers and sister. His reaction had been paralysis and disassociation more than panic or guilt. He said later he expected Mary Jo to come walking up the road at any minute. It's as if he wasn't fully conscious of what had happened, that his concussion-jangled nervous system shut down after so much shock. "It was just a nightmare," Kennedy said to Markham when he arrived the next day, "I was not even sure it happened."[9]

What Ted's mother, Rose Kennedy, could never understand is why neither Joe Gargan nor Paul Markham got help.

"I do not understand why Joey Gargan or Markham did not report the matter to the police even if Ted did not have sense enough or control enough to do so—especially when the body of the girl was in the car," said Rose. "That is what seems so unforgivable and brutal to me."[10]

Mary Jo's mother held a similar view: "No matter how you look at it, it was an accident. What hurts me deep is to think that my daughter had to be left there all night. This is why we had so bitter a feeling toward Markham and Gargan. . . . I think Kennedy made his statement when he was still confused. In the state he was in, I do believe he couldn't think clearly. I think he was taking all this bad advice, and it just continued for days."[11]

What many people around the country couldn't understand in the coming months was the lack of a thorough investigation. No autopsy was performed on Mary Jo's body, and the next day, when Kennedy finally did go to police, he was not asked any questions.

An inquest in January came to two conclusions: Kennedy lied when he said he was taking Mary Jo to Edgartown, and Kennedy's "negligent driving appears to have contributed to the death of Mary Jo Kopechne." Kennedy could have been charged with manslaughter, but instead received a two-month suspended jail sentence for leaving the scene of an accident. "No man stands above the law," Kennedy would tell Richard Nixon in a few years during the Watergate hearings, but during Chappaquiddick, it appeared to many people that one man did.

When Ted Kennedy finally made a nationally televised speech about the events, more people watched than had seen Neil Armstrong walk on the moon. Ted referred to "the Kennedy curse" for the first time during his speech, as if he were the victim of a metaphysical evil beyond his control rather than directly responsible for what happened. And he forever altered the Kennedy legacy that day by invoking a passage on courage from his brother John's book. By doing so, Ted inadvertently highlighted his own inadequacy in comparison to his brothers. From then on, Ted would be regarded as the lesser Kennedy in most people's minds. A mountain of achievements in the next 40 years would still not erase that impression wholly. At that moment, the Kennedy legacy became more of a burden than a blessing for Ted.

Many of the honorary Kennedys and loyalists to Bobby and John turned on Ted after Chappaquiddick. Ted Sorensen deleted most of his references to

Ted Kennedy's bright promise from *The Kennedy Legacy: A Peaceful Revolution for the Seventies*, which was already in bound galleys.[12] Ted Kennedy never seemed to forgive himself, either. Al Simpson of Wyoming remembers an encounter with Kennedy when Simpson first arrived in the Senate in 1979. "I hadn't been there two months, when I'm in the subway with him. As he stepped off, this woman said. 'Huh! Senator Kennedy, how do feel about what you did to that poor woman in Chappaquiddick?' And he never changed his expression," Simpson remembers. "He said, 'It's with me every day of my life.'"

Rose never discussed the incident with Ted. "Teddy had everything," she said later. "He goes out one night in an accident and everything is smashed. As I say, it just seems as though, I realize that from Shakespeare, how much destiny decides, really."[13]

Ted's marriage to Joan may have been a casualty of Chappaquiddick as well. "No one told me anything," Joan said later. "Probably because I was pregnant, I was told to stay upstairs in my bedroom. Downstairs, the house was full of people, aides, friends and lawyers. And when I picked up the extension phone I could hear Ted talking to Helga. Ted called his girlfriend Helga before he or anyone told me what was going on. It was the worst experience of my life. I couldn't talk to anyone about it. Nothing ever seemed the same after that."[14] A month after the accident, Joan would have a miscarriage.

"For a few months everyone had to put on this show, and then I just didn't care anymore. I just saw no future. That's when I truly became an alcoholic," she told Laurence Leamer.

But Ted's home state wasn't ready to give up on him yet. Toward the end of his 17-minute speech, he asked Massachusetts voters if he should resign. Ten thousand telegrams arrived at the Kennedy compound the next morning asking Ted to stay. Massachusetts would remain forever loyal to their Emerald Kings.

Tom Southwick, who was Kennedy's press secretary at the time of the tenth anniversary of the accident, believes Kennedy never changed his story over the years, as many people alleged, and insists there was never any cover-up. "I have a feeling that if Paul Kirk had been there, or somebody more used to standing up and saying this is what we need to do, this is the right thing, that it might have come out differently," Southwick said. "People ask me about it sometimes, and I say, look you can make a judgment about what happened that night and say, he was wrong, and therefore he shouldn't be president, whatever, but there's no cover-up here, there's no deception, this was not a girlfriend."

Many years later, Ted told a reporter for *Time* magazine that he'd told people all he could about the accident. "People may not believe me or accept some of my answers. But the idea that the people who were there that night are holding back some secret is just all wrong. The essence of the event for me is that the girl is dead. There is nothing else for me to say."[15]

The accident of longevity seems to have slowly erased much of the blot Chappaquiddick left on the Kennedy legacy. Many young people around the country who know of Ted because of his endorsement of Barack Obama said they had never heard of Chappaquiddick. Its relevance to his career fades as the impact of his accomplishments grows and new Kennedys take their place in the Obama administration. If Ted's dream of universal health care passes within the next few years, the once-dreaded epithet of Chappaquiddick may forever become a footnote.

After Chappaquiddick, however, the private lives of politicians began receiving a new kind of scrutiny in the media. No longer would there be any gentlemen's agreement to look the other way on private indiscretions. Chappaquiddick rewrote the rules for the media, introducing the justification that what a politician does in private has direct bearing on his public life. Washington became a less swinging town as a result, more C-Span than *Mad Men*. If an incident like Chappaquiddick had occurred before John Kennedy was president, it's likely he would never have been elected because the press would have been much more likely to reveal his indiscretions.

Ted spent the days and weeks after Chappaquiddick in the protective cocoon of his family. He told his father what happened, but no one is sure Joe ever understood. "Dad, I'm in some trouble," Ted said, according to his father's private nurse. "There's been an accident and you're going to hear all sorts of things about me from now on. Terrible things." His father gripped his hand and pressed it to his chest, unable to respond. "Dad, I've done the best I can. I'm sorry."[16]

Within three months, Joe Kennedy began refusing food and his body started wasting away. Soon he wouldn't get out of bed. The family began to gather for a deathwatch, and on the last night of the patriarch's life, Ted slept in a sleeping bag on the floor in his father's room. Jackie stayed, too, sleeping fitfully in a chair, a blanket over her legs. Joe Kennedy died the next morning while Rose and the children were saying the "Our Father." It was just a few days before the sixth anniversary of Jack's death. Joe Kennedy had lingered eight years after his first stroke, and in that time the myth and legend he'd willed to life died multiple deaths before his uncomprehending eyes. Lamented Sargent Shriver, "Without you none of us would be anything."[17]

★ ★ ★

After enduring so much loss, Ted had all the makings of a forever tragic figure, doomed to collapse under the weight of his family's legacy and his own character flaws. But he simply refused to play the part.

He certainly lost some of the clout his last name had carried in the months after he returned to the Senate that fall, but Ted's promise to honor his brothers was a tough flame to douse. The depth of his commitment to their unfinished agenda was stronger than any thoughts of bowing out. He faced a merciless press in his 1970 reelection campaign, but that didn't keep him from stumping on street corners and in airport waiting areas, enduring the insults of hecklers day after day so that he might continue his work. Those who thought Ted could never survive Chappaquiddick, and they were probably in the majority, didn't fully understand the power of his commitment to his brothers. Massachusetts, however, must have had an inkling. They gave him another term.

A diminished profile in the Senate allowed, paradoxically, more of Ted's own profile to emerge. Chappaquiddick peeled away the necessity of expending so much energy upholding the Kennedy family's pomp and veneer as the dutiful son. He'd inadvertently destroyed the carapace of reputation and history that imprisoned him, and now he began surfacing a new identity wholly his own. No longer performing for his father or brothers, the only person he needed to be true to was himself.

He began locating that unique identity in the nooks and corners of the Capitol, not on its stages. By 1971, he'd lost his job as majority whip to Senator Robert Byrd, but the loss forced him more deeply into committee work and the one-on-one relationships where he was most effective. His aim was to spread himself among as many committees as he could, amassing power independent of the leadership of the Senate and independent of the party itself, really. In committees, he began to build extraordinary expertise as a get-'er-done legislative craftsman. Kennedy found himself in the coach seats of committees for the first time, rather than first class, and he found friends there who were willing and eager to work with him. He built his political presence after Chappaquiddick by slow accretion rather than the bold strikes his brothers had employed. And he began winning his fellow senators back over by humility and hard work.

"Work, that's the only real defense for him, he's working terribly hard again, too hard maybe," his legislative assistant, Dave Burke, said at the time.

"But it seems to help."[18] Colleagues and staffers were struck by how much work Kennedy could accomplish in a day despite all that had happened to him. "Why is he so driven?" another former Judiciary staffer asked. "Because when you've got a legacy like his, you're one step ahead of the shadows. He's competing with myths."[19]

"He's like a shark—not in the negative sense, but rather in the fact that he's got to keep moving all the time," said Thomas M. Susman, who spent 11 years on the Judiciary staff. "That's part of Ted Kennedy's metabolism."[20]

For the next 40 years, perpetual motion became his coping mechanism, as if he through sheer diligence might be able to outrun and overcome the legacy of tragedy.

At the heart of his operation and his drive for redemption for the next few decades was a simple, steadfast symbol of his work ethic: The Bag.

Every afternoon, the battered black briefcase was packed at the senator's office with memos, invitations, papers to sign, research to read, mail to open. Staffers treat The Bag as if it were alive, as in "The Bag is leaving now."

And every morning, no matter what demands his nightlife made, Kennedy returned The Bag with everything in it finished: notes on memos, mail answered, documents signed. The senator did his homework.

"I don't think people understand how hard he works," said Shrum. "I'm not a big memo writer, but lots of people are, and he would take home this giant bag of memos, and still does, every night. And they come back with annotations every morning. Every single one."

The Bag now holds a place of reverence in the annals of the Senate. When Kennedy's memorial institute is built next to the JFK Library, surely The Bag will be on display front and center, encased in glass.

In the 1970s, Kennedy also got in the habit of holding "issue dinners" at his house, during which he moderated Socratic debates among experts to determine how to proceed on legislation. Such dinners gave birth to most of Kennedy's greatest social reforms over the next decades.

And Kennedy found two immediate ways to get things done with a diminished reputation. He deputized his powerful staff to do more of the heavy lifting and he started giving credit to other senators for bills he initiated. Carey Parker, a 24-year-old Harvard Law School graduate, joined the staff in 1969, and not long after drafted a memo making the case for lowering the voting age to 18 from 21. At the heart of his argument was the observation that if 18-year-olds were old enough to be sent off to Vietnam, they ought to be old enough to vote.

Kennedy circulated Parker's memo to friendly senators and issued it as a press release. Warren Magnuson of Washington liked Parker's idea, and he and Majority leader Mike Mansfield of Montana agreed to sponsor the proposal. Kennedy believed Mansfield's prestige in the Senate would carry the day better than Kennedy's diminished reputation might. Kennedy signed on as a cosponsor, however, and spoke eloquently in defense of the proposal on the floor. The measure passed quickly, but ended up before the Supreme Court. The justices decided the lower voting age was constitutional, but also decided it only had jurisdiction over federal elections, not state.

No one wanted two separate rolls of voters, however, so advocates for the states urged Congress to amend the Constitution to make the voting age universal. The Twenty-Sixth Amendment, which originated in Kennedy's office, was ratified on July 1, 1971. Kennedy may not have sponsored the bill, but by empowering Carey and greasing the skids for Mansfield and Magnuson, he made it happen. The bruised, post-Chappaquiddick Kennedy ego had actually served as an asset in the cooperative work required to make sausage in the Senate.

Carey Parker still works for Kennedy 40 years later, perhaps the ultimate example of the extreme loyalty Kennedy's staff members show for their boss because of the generous amounts of responsibility he bestows on them. Kennedy often supplemented the pay of his staffers with his own funds, which made it possible to hang on to real talent. He also never hesitated to call on Bobby and John's ex-staffers or the best-in-the nation experts at Harvard and MIT. Kennedy's staff would become huge—nearly 100 professionals and several dozen interns—and legendary, a kind of auxiliary branch of government. They helped turn Kennedy into a unique kind of power center, beholden only to himself. "Other Senate offices aspire to run the same kind of political operation, but they don't have the same Prussian precision that Kennedy's staff does," a Hill aide told a *Washington Post* reporter.[21]

"Kennedy uses staff people the way Pony Express riders used horses: Ride 'em hard and then leap to another horse," said Thomas M. Rollins, former staff director of the Labor Committee. "He's a genius at managing people."[22]

Marshalling all his ample resources, Kennedy started getting things done in the 1970s despite himself. Many observers have argued that Kennedy didn't really come into his own as a legislator until after he lost to Jimmy Carter in the 1980 Democratic presidential primary. But his string of achievements before then belies that particular interpretation.

The causes he pursued most passionately, of course, were Bobby's causes, which lay before him like bread crumbs and vapor trails. He didn't pursue those issues just in memory of his brother, however, because by 1970 they were already his causes, too. What Bobby's death did was give those causes the obligation of holy writ, as if they were part of a deathbed request.

Ted took Bobby's daughter Kathleen with him when he went to speak about Robert's concern for Native Americans at graduation exercises for Rough Rock, an experimental Navajo school in Arizona.[23] Soon after, in February 1971, he introduced a bill to give Indians more of a voice in the education of their children.

"It was part of helping people who need a break," said a cosponsor of the bill, Walter Mondale, during a 2008 conversation with the author. "There's a sad and in many ways tragic history to American Indians. And this naturally would be something he would be very concerned about. So what we did, we passed a strong Indian education act to give control over education to the parents, not to outside experts. We ended the elementary boarding schools on some of these reservations. They're cruel institutions that take six-year-olds away from their parents to make 'good white people' out of them. And we did a lot of other things to try to make life better for Indians."

Ted also pushed forward his brother John's arms control agenda by speaking on the subject in Moscow and pressing Soviet leader Leonid Brezhnev for a complete ban on nuclear testing. He also succeeded, at Joan's request, in winning an exit visa for the great Soviet cellist Mstislav Rostropovich during one of his trips to Russia. "He would use the power of his name and his personality to do things that made people's lives better," said Southwick.

On January 4, 1973, Kennedy was finally able to push his party to go on the record favoring an end to the Vietnam War, an attempt to finish what Bobby started in his 1968 campaign. Ted's resolution, a version of which House Democrats adopted 154–75, declared that no more money should be appropriated "for U.S. military combat operations in or over Indochina, and that such operations be terminated immediately."[24]

Ted also carved out a few issues of his own in the 1970s.

On August 27, 1970, he officially launched his career-long crusade for a universal health care program. "We must begin to move now to establish a comprehensive national health insurance program, capable of bringing the same amount and high quality of health care to every man, woman and child in the United States," he announced on the floor of the Senate.[25] It was a phrase he would repeat and a bill he would introduce in every Congress for the next 46 years and 23 Congresses. "We used to call it S–3," said Walter

Mondale. "It was the third bill introduced every Congress for as long as I can remember. And it became kind of the symbol of national health care."

Ted hired a Harvard Law School professor, Stephen G. Breyer, to look into deregulating the airline industry so that cheaper carriers could enter the market and fares might be set by the market, rather than artificially by the Civil Aeronautics Board (CAB). With Breyer's help, Kennedy succeeded in eliminating the CAB, clearing the way for dramatically more airline routes, more competition among carriers and cheaper fares. Breyer, like so many of Kennedy's staffers, went on to even greater things. He now sits on the Supreme Court.

Ted also initiated the first congressional investigations of the Watergate scandal, an effort that ended when an independent counsel took over. After Nixon and Watergate, criminal justice became a big issue in the 1970s, and Kennedy got interested. He was also still thinking of a run for the presidency at some point, and he wanted a solid position on law and order he could point to as a candidate.

What intrigued him the most was criminal sentencing reform. "Disparity," clarified Ken Feinberg, the superlawyer Kennedy hired to push the reform through. "Poor black offenders getting longer sentences or harsher punishment than those who were white collar or white." Kennedy saw sentencing reform as an opportunity to be bold, to do something constructive that would reduce sentencing disparity.

With the sentencing reform effort, Ted also began a courtship of powerful senators on the other side of the aisle as a means of getting things done. Ultra-conservative senators like John McClellan of Arkansas, who had been Bobby's boss in the late 1950s, became key allies in the rewrite of the country's sentencing laws.

From Kennedy's point of view, there was a lot of inequality in sentences because of racial issues. From the point of view of McClellan, who headed the Senate Judiciary Committee on Criminal Laws, there were a lot of liberal judges who were letting people off. Before the sentencing laws were rewritten, judges could sentence people to whatever terms they wanted. If you were black in the South, and you got convicted of a federal crime, you might do 30 years, whereas if you were black in San Francisco, convicted of the same crime, you might do 6 months. "There was no rhyme or reason to it," said Southwick.

The bill that Kennedy and McClellan eventually pushed through ended parole in the federal prison system, created a United States sentencing commission to monitor sentencing guidelines and instituted a finite range of punishments that could be doled out for each specific crime. "So there are a lot of people who otherwise would have been sentenced to unfair sentences—too lenient or too harsh—who are now going to serve the time that they should serve no matter where they are convicted in the country," said Southwick. "You know, millions of lives have been affected by that. Yet nobody knows Kennedy rewrote the criminal code."

It took eight years for Kennedy to get it all passed. "If you can't get it all, increments," noted Feinberg, explaining Kennedy's legislative philosophy. "Incremental reform. He has confidence that once the incremental reforms are put in place, they will work. And [people] will come back for more. So he was always willing to bargain hard, make demands, work out the best good you could get short of the perfect."

It may be that Ted's own imperfections gave him a greater tolerance for the inevitability of imperfection, an appreciation for gray areas and the necessity of baby steps when walking toward the promised land. The lives he'd lost had increased, for him, the value of *something,* however bastardized, over *nothing*—a piece of the pie if you couldn't get the whole pie. His own imperfections also allowed him to better tolerate those in others, so that he always kept open the possibility of forgiveness for his opponents, perhaps because he so badly needed it himself.

"He has political DNA," said Feinberg, "where you can agree or disagree with him, but it is never personal." The imperfect prince was a role he could get his arms around.

Despite building successes in the Senate, the personal tragedies continued unabated for Ted. In November 1973, just days before the tenth anniversary of Jack's assassination, a cancerous tumor was discovered just below the knee in his 12-year-old son Teddy Jr. The only way to ensure that the cancer would not spread was to have the leg amputated.

Upon the recommendation of doctors, Ted waited until the day before the surgery to tell his son he had cancer. Teddy asked if he was going to die, and Ted and Joan assured him that he wouldn't, but told him he would have to lose his leg. Everyone in the room cried. Ted tried to explain all the things Teddy could do with an artificial leg, including skiing, sailing and camping. Teddy Jr. had inherited the Kennedy stoicism. He talked about the future matter-of-factly and told his mother to stop crying.[26]

Just after the surgery, Ted rushed to Holy Trinity Church a few blocks away to fill in for his brother at the marriage of Robert's daughter Kathleen to David Townsend. Kathleen had suggested postponing the wedding, but Ted would have none of it. As he escorted his niece down the aisle, he told her how happy his own wedding had been and made sure she knew how proud his brother would have been.[27] At the end of the Mass, after Ted had given his niece away, the congregation celebrated with a rousing round of "When Irish Eyes Are Smiling."

After the ceremony, Ted returned to the hospital. He tried to keep his son distracted during his recovery with presents, cards and surprises. One day he brought the whole Redskins offensive line into the hospital to visit. Ted usually slept in his son's hospital room during his stay. As the weeks went by, doctors found evidence of much deadlier bone cancer cells mixed in with the less-lethal ligament cancer cells. Teddy's prognosis worsened, and Kennedy went on the offensive.

He visited cancer research centers, consulted other doctors and called together experts for a four-hour meeting to discuss experimental treatments. Ted heard about a doctor named Edward Frei III at Children's Hospital in Boston who had successfully treated 21 children with bone cancer using a then-experimental treatment that would become known as chemotherapy. Frei had used massive doses of a drug called methotrexate, which killed all fast-dividing cells. Radiation, which had already been established as a cancer treatment, was the best alternative to the new treatment, but Kennedy decided to try the chemo.

Two years of treatments began. Every three weeks, Teddy Jr. flew to Boston with his mother or father and would lie still for six hours while methotrexate was dripped into his arm through an IV. The experimental chemotherapy was followed by injections of a vitamin called citrovorum, which Ted learned to inject himself at home so he and Teddy could get back to Washington Sunday night.

Thanks largely to Ted's aggressive hunt for experimental treatments, his son survived. By March, Teddy Jr. was skiing again. In the years to come, whenever he found out about a friend who had cancer, Ted would call up and recommend doctors he knew from all the research he'd done.

When speechwriter Bob Shrum's sister-in-law was diagnosed with breast cancer, Ted called Bob and told him that she needed a doctor he knew at the University of Pennsylvania. It was someone who had worked for him years before, and was now one of the leading oncologists in the world. "He really didn't know [my sister-in-law] at this point," said Shrum. "He'd met her once." Kennedy kept tabs on her treatment, and recommended other doctors along the way. She got better and Kennedy hired her to work in his office, where she worked from 1997 to 2006.

Former chief of staff Ken Feinberg has his own story, as does every person who has ever worked for Kennedy. Twenty years ago, Feinberg's father was failing with a heart condition, and Feinberg was concerned about the level of care his father was receiving at a small hospital in Florida. "I mentioned it to Senator Kennedy. A call was made and my father was transferred to a better hospital in Miami," Feinberg said. "The greatest thing he does, and it has nothing to do with his legislative skill, is just that. The things he does behind the scenes, quietly, for friends, constituents, family members, that never get publicized."

A number of years after Chappaquiddick, columnist Murray Kepton observed that if Ted Kennedy was to be forever known only for Chappaquiddick, "in the arrogance of our conviction that we would have done better than he did in a single case, we exempt ourselves from any duty to pay attention to the many cases where he shows himself better than us."

12

A CAMELOT TOO FAR

Sometimes a party must sail against the wind. We cannot afford to drift or lie at anchor. We cannot heed the call of those who say it is time to furl the sail.

—*Ted Kennedy, Memphis, December 9, 1978*

Ted Kennedy was frustrated.

He paced like a caged lion along the glass partition in the customs area of Washington's Dulles Airport. He and several American servicemen were on one side of the glass wall, and on the other side waited the Vietnamese wives and children the servicemen hadn't seen for five to seven years. The women's eager eyes pleaded silently with Kennedy, and he was fast losing his patience. The refugees had just flown from Hanoi to Bangkok to Manila to Los Angeles, filling in all the necessary paperwork along the way. They had finally arrived at Dulles, and the immigration people wouldn't let them through. *Wouldn't let them through.* Kennedy couldn't believe a years-long bureaucratic odyssey and a trip halfway around the world had stalled in its final steps.

"We could see them, they were right there," remembers press secretary Tom Southwick. "We could see them through the glass! And the immigration people were saying we won't let them through. They don't have the proper documentation."

Bureaucrats were thwarting Kennedy's grand plans for an airport reunion, and he was furious. For a man in perpetual motion, involuntary idleness—waiting for a late plane, getting stuck in traffic, being tied up in red tape—was the seventh level of hell.

As the chairman of the Judiciary Committee's Subcommittee on Refugees and Escapees, Kennedy had become very active in refugee issues toward the end of the 1970s. And he had personally negotiated with Vietnam to get this particular group of Vietnamese wives and children of American servicemen—Vietnamese women and children who had been left behind after the fall of Saigon—back together with their husbands and fathers.

The United States didn't recognize the new Communist government of Vietnam at the time. The immigration officials didn't see how they could honor documents from a country the United States didn't have relations with. An aide was on the phone to the State Department to try to get them to intervene, and Kennedy had started to pace. "He was at the airport, ready to greet these people. I have pictures of this!" exclaims Southwick. "You can just see him thinking, what am I gonna *do?*" said Southwick. "He's got this determined look on his face."

Finally, Kennedy couldn't stand it anymore He asked Southwick one last time what the status was. "And I say, you know, the State Department, we haven't gotten anything through."

And then Kennedy says, OK, that's it, and he walks right around the glass partition and takes the hand of the first little girl there and says, "Follow me." And the immigration people just stand there dumbfounded. "What are they going to do, arrest the chairman of the Subcommittee on Refugees and Escapees?" asks Southwick. "And so he just took that whole group and walked them right through."

The embraces, squeals and tears that followed were the stuff of a Frank Capra movie. With Kennedy as their escort, the families walked out of the airport reunited and untouched by bureaucrats, ready to begin their new lives in America. Here was a case when Kennedy's disregard for the law, his belief that the law perhaps did not always apply to him, worked to the everlasting advantage of a handful of interrupted families.

A short time later, Kennedy rode his rage to passage of a bill that tripled the number of refugees allowed into the United States annually. Kennedy felt strongly that the United States had created the mess in Southeast Asia and therefore had an obligation to do all it could to clean up the detritus, to mend the lives broken by the war and find homes for its refugees.

In a speech at Georgetown University, Kennedy demanded that Jimmy Carter do more for refugees in Cambodia, too. "Cambodia is on our conscience," Kennedy said. "We cannot escape the moral consequences of our actions during the Vietnam War which helped to launch the descent into hell of that once beautiful and peaceful land."

That same day, Carter announced that he would send more aid, and his wife, Rosalynn, planned to visit refugee camps there.[1] But it was Kennedy who had goaded him into action.

Behind Kennedy's challenge to Carter lay something deeper than just a difference on refugee policy. Kennedy had begun to believe that Carter was letting the flame of idealism his brothers had lit fizzle, that his leadership was no longer lifting America's sights. Kennedy felt Carter was sending a "can't-do" message about the power of public service rather than restoking the optimism his brothers had once inspired. "You had a whole sense that the notion of government or the capacity of government to do anything that was purposeful or meaningful was being destroyed," said Bob Shrum, Kennedy's speechwriter at the time.

Kennedy's fears congealed when President Carter went on national television in the summer of 1979, in the midst of runaway inflation, long gas lines and a shaky economy, to deliver a speech on "a fundamental threat to American democracy."

The threat "was nearly invisible in ordinary ways," he told the American people. "It is a crisis of confidence. It is a crisis that strikes at the very heart and soul and spirit of our national will. We can see this crisis in the growing doubt about the meaning of our own lives and in the loss of a unity of purpose for our nation."

The speech became known as Carter's "malaise" speech, and it drove Kennedy nuts. Press secretary Tom Southwick watched it with the senator on the night of July 15, and "afterwards he just shook his head, because this is not leadership as he understood it," said Southwick. "It really got him. So counter to the Kennedy approach." Kennedy spent two hours on the phone complaining to friends and party leaders about the speech.[2] He told them it sounded like Carter was blaming the American people for his own problems within his administration. Carter was projecting his own "crisis of confidence" onto the country as a whole. He was globalizing his own failure. It was leadership by knocking down rather than building up, which, to Kennedy, was no leadership at all.

"The essence of political leadership," Kennedy would say a short time later, "is basically challenge and response. Constantly, that's sort of the central element in terms of my makeup, and I think in terms of politics you are trying to challenge and move the process, and then you are getting response to the challenging again. In this country, I think it is an essential aspect of the soul of this society, and one of the things that's made it sort of great. And it seems to me that that is sort of what Democrats have been about."[3]

In Kennedy's mind, his family's principles *were* the party's principles, and Carter was forsaking them. In the years after John's death, Kennedy had never really found anyone he thought was true enough to his family's principles, to John and Bobby's principles, which he now saw as the core of liberalism. Lyndon Johnson for a while, yes, but certainly not Carter, and not Walter Mondale, though Kennedy had campaigned for Mondale and Geraldine Ferraro in their doomed bid in 1972. And he did not find it in Bill Clinton with his triangulated liberalism either, though the two were close friends and accomplished an enormous amount together. Kennedy really hadn't trusted anyone else to be the guardian of the liberal agenda his brothers set until Barack Obama's arrival on the scene in 2008. For 40 years, Kennedy never believed anyone else could bear his brothers' torch as truly as he himself could.

It was his sense that the party was slipping off its moorings that propelled Kennedy into the presidential race of 1980. Carter could probably have kept Kennedy out of the race if he'd tried to appease him on health care reform, but disagreements raged there, too. After Carter's malaise speech, senators begged Kennedy to run. "He had a lot of his colleagues in the Senate, many of whom did not come through with endorsements later, saying you gotta do this or we're going to lose a whole lot of Senate seats," said Shrum. They were worried about getting reelected if the top of the ticket got trounced. Senator John Culver from Iowa, who had been Kennedy's roommate in college, led the effort to pressure Kennedy into running. Polls showed Democrats preferring Kennedy over Carter by margins of more than two to one.

"I think he responded to that more as a sense of obligation to the constituency he represented and to his colleagues than out of any overwhelming ambition to be president," said Southwick. But Shrum takes issue with the notion that Ted was reluctant to run and did so only to try to save the party. "I think that's all a pile of hooey," Shrum said. "I think he wanted to run. This stuff about he really didn't want to be president is ridiculous. He *wanted* to be president. I don't think he'd ever anticipated it would be by repeating the RFK thing and running against the incumbent president of his own party. And in fact the safer thing for him to do would have been to just wait, as he had once counseled Bobby to do." But Kennedy did not wait. He was the guardian of the Kennedy legacy, and protecting that legacy was paramount.

He found more and more forums in which to criticize the president's leadership. After Carter refused to push forward universal health insurance, saying the costs were too great, Kennedy responded, saying "National health insurance is the great unfinished business on the agenda of the Democratic Party." Carter wanted to increase the military budget at the expense of social spending, putting the burden of fighting runaway inflation on those least able to pay for it. Kennedy told an audience, "The poor and the cities may be out of political fashion this year, but they still have a rightful claim on public policy," and "Someone has to speak for them. Someone has to stand against the temporary tides of reaction—against a politics and a Presidency that may see injustice, but then quietly looks away."[4]

Carter reacted to it all by telling several congressmen at a White House dinner that if Kennedy ran, he would "whip his ass."

In all his discussions with family and friends and advisers about whether to run or not, Ted never explored the impact Chappaquiddick might have on his campaign, and it was a breach in his strategy that he was never able to repair. His inability to face the powerful emotions Chappaquiddick unleashed in himself and others meant that his own campaign was ill-prepared for their implications. Even before his campaign got under way, the press—and Carter— seized on the issue, and never let go.

Reports about John F. Kennedy's womanizing were starting to surface at the time, as well, and reporters who had known about them, such as Ben Bradlee of the *Washington Post,* were being criticized for keeping them secret for so long. As a result, journalists who had been friendly to John and Bobby were tougher on Ted so they wouldn't be perceived as pro-Kennedy mouthpieces. Worse than that, Ted became the brunt of all the hatred and resentment that the other brothers had inspired, so that he was not just fighting his own fights in running for president, but the old fights of his brothers, too. "Now that he is down it is coming on strong and mean-minded from those who want to be sure that he is made to suffer because the Kennedys have always had so much," the *Washington Post* wrote. It was an era of deconstruction, and the deconstruction of Camelot had begun.

The rewritten rules of journalism and the politics of the press came most powerfully into play during a Roger Mudd interview of Kennedy for CBS News.

"Roger was seen as a friend of the Kennedys," said Southwick. "He played tennis with Ethel. He was invited to Hickory Hill a lot. And he was sort of seen as a friend of the family. So he needed to do two things. He needed to prove he was a hard-bitten news guy, and he needed to prove he was no friend of the Kennedys. And so this hour-long special he did on CBS accomplished both of those, using what I thought were some very unfair journalism tactics."

Southwick had set up an a photo op for Mudd with Kennedy *before* Kennedy had announced that he was getting into the presidential race, but the documentary didn't run until *after* everyone knew he was running.

"Roger comes to me and says, we need some photos of the senator walking on the beach down in Hyannis," said Southwick. "This is maybe in October. So we'll have the crew come down, take some photos, and we'll be gone."

The morning of the photo shoot, Kennedy came downstairs to find Mudd and his crew had set up in his living room, and the camera was rolling. And Rogers said: "Senator, tell us about Chappaquiddick."

"Kennedy didn't know it was coming, he didn't know it was going to be an interview," said Southwick. "I had been told it wasn't going to be an interview. That it was just a photo opportunity. And they used that footage."

Kennedy wasn't prepared. Ted's staff had always worried about his talent for non sequiturs in interviews. Listening to Ted Kennedy talk off the cuff has been compared to listening to AM radio while someone is channel surfing, all static and broken sentences, but occasional bursts of music as well. Type in a transcription of one of his informal conversations and the grammar check on your computer will convulse with "fragment" warnings, begging you to fill in the text with a few verbs. "God forbid if he should go off text," said one insider. But his inability to articulate an answer, or articulate anything at all in the Mudd interview, was of another order. It revealed a man who hadn't come to terms with Chappaquiddick himself, who had never faced down many of the demons he carried.

In the finished documentary, while Kennedy is trying to explain what happened at Chappaquiddick and his feelings about it ten years later, a shot from the driver's seat of a car, driving along the road to the infamous bridge, rolled across the screen. "A reenactment," said Southwick. "And I don't know whether the lighting that night was good enough for cameras. I suspect not. They put a lot more light on that road than there was that night. I just thought it was kind of a cheap trick."

During the "photo op" session, Mudd also asked, "Senator, why do you want to be president?" And once again, Kennedy wasn't prepared.

"Kennedy had not formally announced at that point," Southwick said. "And he knew that if he said I want to be president because of X, Y and Z, it would trigger all these federal election laws. If you are a formal candidate for president you are responsible for money that is raised and spent in your name. If you're not yet a formal candidate, you are not responsible. He was very concerned about that because even though the documentary wasn't going to run until November, he knew that if he told Roger 'I want to be president because of this,' he would effectively be announcing for president when the legal issues weren't resolved, the structure wasn't in place." Kennedy wanted to control his own announcement. He wanted to make the announcement himself, not hand that moment over to Roger Mudd.

"So he kind of hemmed and hawed around it," said Southwick. The interview made it look as if Kennedy couldn't explain why he wanted to be president, implying, in some people's minds, that he thought it was just his by divine right.

"When you got to that Mudd interview, it was very revealing," said Walter Mondale, Carter's vice president. Mudd "hit him with softball questions. I think deep down he couldn't think of anything. And I think Roger gave him a second chance to clean up, and he answered that worse. I think he had, deep down, some mixed feelings about whether he really wanted to go for it or not. I think part of him would just as soon have avoided it."

"It was like, I want to be president because the sea is so deep and the sky is so blue," Mudd said later.[5]

Kennedy was just as fumbling when it came to discussing his marriage, which was also filled with problems he hadn't ever really faced.

"Are you separated or are you just . . . what?" Mudd asked.

"Well, I don't know whether there's a single word that should . . . have a description for it. Joan's involved in a continuing program to deal with the problems of . . . of alcoholism, and . . . and she's going magnificently well, and I'm immensely proud of the fact that she's faced up to it and made the progress that she's made. And I'm—but that progress continues, and that . . . it's the type of disease that one has to . . . to work."

The interview aired on November 4, just three days before Kennedy planned to officially launch his campaign. The reaction was so universally bad that it may be Kennedy never recovered. It was a clear warning that Kennedy's candidacy would be judged as much by the personal as the political, if not more so.

And, as if that weren't enough, that same night Iranian students overran the U.S. Embassy in Tehran, seizing 60 American hostages in a crisis that would last until the very last day of the Carter presidency, altering the dynamics of the race dramatically. The playing field had tilted dramatically before Kennedy had even gotten out of the tunnel.

 ★ ★ ★

When Kennedy did formally announce his candidacy on November 7, 1979, he did not do so in the Senate Caucus Room, where his brothers had announced theirs. In a small gesture of either independence or deference, Ted chose instead Boston's Faneuil Hall, evoking the hopes and history of his hometown and his family. His mother, his nieces and his nephews filled the hall, making it clear to all that, for the third time in 20 years, this was not just a man but a family running for the highest office in the land.

"Before the last election, we were told that Americans were honest, loving, good, decent and compassionate," Kennedy reminded the crowd gathered in the hall. "Now, the people are blamed for every national ill and scolded as greedy, wasteful and mired in malaise. Which is it? Did we change so much in these three years? Or is it because the present leadership does not understand that we are willing, even anxious, to be on the march again?

"The most important task of Presidential leadership is to release the native energy of the people," Kennedy said. "The only thing that paralyzes us today is the myth that we cannot move."[6]

There was no media honeymoon for Kennedy's candidacy, no trial period for him to work out the kinks in his organization. The spotlight was full on from day one, and as a result the "campaign was just a miserable, horrible thing," complained one aide, mainly because of the specter of Ted getting shot and the media's resulting bloodlust.

"By choosing to campaign for the presidency next year, Sen. Edward Kennedy permits his fellow citizens to enjoy the guilty pleasure of guessing at his chance of being murdered," wrote essayist Lewis Lapham in *Harper's Magazine* in December, 1979, just to cite one example. "Prolonged over a period of months, the intoxicating horror of this calculation will impart to the election the excitement of a gladiatorial show in the Roman arena."

More than 150 members of the press put in requests to cover Kennedy, and all of the networks wanted their own cameraman on him all the time, rather than agreeing to a pool, as was traditionally the case. "The networks were there in case he got shot," said one media source.

Southwick remembers a troubling episode early on. "Bob Kerr from NBC came out to Kennedy's home uninvited, went into the house, sat down with Patrick Kennedy who was 7 years old, and started interviewing him with a camera, saying 'Are you concerned about your father's safety?'"

Kennedy himself was never fully aware of the jockeying. He knew there was a real possibility he might get shot, but once Rose and his children had given their blessing, he had decided the risk was worth it. He was realistic about the threat, but didn't let it dominate, said Southwick.

"You took precautions," said Shrum. "We had a doctor with us everywhere we went. We had ambulances in most places. The memory was there. But you just lived with that." Early polling showed that a number of voters who were inclined to vote for Kennedy were concerned about the threat to his life, and indicated they were going to vote the other way because they didn't want the trauma.

After Bobby's death, Secret Service protection was de rigueur for presidential candidates, not just presidents. Jimmy Carter made sure Kennedy had a full Secret Service detail two months before he was in the race.

★ ★ ★

Carter had put Iowa forever on the political map with a surprise victory in the caucuses there in 1976. With polls showing that Kennedy was favored, lightning struck again for Carter in 1980, and he beat Kennedy two to one. Voters were rallying around the commander in chief in a time of crisis, just as they would with President Bush after 9/11. Kennedy's inner circle of advisers voted on whether Kennedy should quit right then and there. The vote was 4–4. "The vote is one to nothing." Kennedy then said. "I'm going to run."[7]

"We lost a whole bunch early on. We lost Iowa, we lost New Hampshire, which was effectively the end of the campaign, but he wanted to keep going because he felt he had a constituency," said Southwick. "You know there are a lot of parallels with Hillary. Millions of people vote for you, give you money. Do you fight until the bitter end on their behalf? Or do you say, 'gee, for the good of the party, I'm going to bow out.'"

John had called Ted the family's best campaigner, but through the hazy lens of nostalgia, Democrats remembered Jack and Bob as extraordinary, superhuman campaigners, and somehow Ted was not measuring up. Author Garry Wills, in his book *The Kennedy Imprisonment*, memorably makes the point that expectations for Kennedy were impossibly high. "Kennedy was being forced, every day, to demonstrate that he was not as good as his brothers. His effort at recommending himself worked to condemn him. He could not make the counterclaim, that his *brothers* were not as good as his brothers, that Camelot had been a fabric of political unreality. In this campaign, Kennedy was like the last climber in a human chain going up a mountainside, tied to the prowess of the four men above him. But then, in rapid succession, all four men fell, and the very strength that had been drawing him upward now hung a dead weight below him. Each time he stirred to go higher, he just slipped back. The 'Kennedy legacy' had become a very literal burden, [and] made his life a constant labor with death."[8]

And both the president and the press kept reminding voters of the ghost of Chappaquiddick in the much-haunted campaign, criticizing Kennedy for his efforts to soft-peddle the accident. Carter ran ominous television ads raising "trust" and "character" issues about Kennedy.

Jimmy Breslin, in the *New York Daily News*, wrote, "What was required here was an old-fashioned Catholic confession: 'Bless me, Father, for I have sinned . . . ' And when that confession is made, you talk about yourself, first person, as the sinner. You don't say the sins were committed by some guy standing on the side someplace; you were there and you did it, so tell what you did and how you feel. Do not try these little shifts and evasions to give the impression that perhaps it wasn't you who did it in the first place."

Ted's twenty-year-old daughter, Kara, was leafleting in New York City when someone said to her, "You know, your father killed a young woman your age."[9]

Joan's fragile state and her strained marriage with Ted were also factors in the campaign, as was Ted's reputation for womanizing. Ted was carrying a lot of baggage with him around the country. But beyond all that, it appeared that Kennedy had simply waited too long. The bloom was off the Kennedy dynasty in the hearts of Americans. For many of the younger-generation Kennedys who had grown up believing the family had a unique place in America, it was hugely disillusioning to find that they were met frequently with hate, anger and indifference while campaigning. Ted Kennedy received ten letters a day that were considered possible death threats.[10] "I think there is a deep resentment of the Kennedys in the land," Arthur Schlesinger wrote in his journal on March 20. "I guess we like dynasties up to a point, but then begin to hate what are taken as dynastic pretensions and expectations. Ted Kennedy is the victim of the same backlash that destroyed TR Jr. in the 1920s and FDR Jr. in the 1950s." America has always fed itself on stories of Horatio Alger underdogs making it to the top, reaffirming the preeminent belief that anyone with enough piss and vinegar can make it. The Kennedys had tapped into that anything-is-possible ethos when John first ran for office, but by the time Ted took his turn, the Kennedys represented not a rise in aspirations but rather a kind of decaying aristocracy. In its heart of hearts, America really did prefer democracy to monarchy.

★ ★ ★

After Ted's losses began to mount, however, the candidate felt freer to say what he thought. Kennedy with his back against the wall has always been a spectacle worth watching, and in defeat, once again, Kennedy found his voice. "I know Sen. Kennedy wanted to go out there and say what he really thought and really go out and fight on the issues he really cared about," Shrum said. "So that's what he did."[11]

Kennedy became an outspoken advocate for women. He promised to put a woman on the Supreme Court, legislate equal pay for women and push through government-sponsored child care for working women. Kennedy attacked Carter more strenuously on his handling of the hostage crisis and the

Soviet invasion of Afghanistan. He held a fund-raising event with Los Angeles's gay and lesbian community, the first time a presidential candidate had ever embraced gays. He took it as his mission to articulate the liberal principles he believed the Democratic party ought to represent, and from which he had never strayed.

"I have a personal hypothesis that he lacked confidence in his ability to be president," one aide told Burton Hersh, "and one of the reasons why his performance improved so drastically was in inverse relationship to how much he thought he had a chance to be president. The less he thought he could win the better a candidate he was."[12]

And then a funny thing happened. He started to win a few. In late March, as Bob Shrum was preparing a withdrawal speech, New York gave Ted a landslide victory, 59 percent to 41. Connecticut voted for Kennedy that same night, 47 percent to 41 percent. Shrum tore up his concession speech and wrote a victory speech instead. "Can you believe this?" Kennedy said to him. "Can you believe it?"

The last big showdown was a Super Tuesday precursor on June 3, when California, New Jersey, and Ohio voted, along with five smaller states. Ted won big, claiming both California and New Jersey and three of the five smaller states. His overall delegate haul was 372 to Carter's 321, but he lost Ohio by 7 percentage points. It was too little too late: Carter had enough delegates at that point to clinch the nomination. And yet Kennedy vowed to fight on to the convention, where he hoped to repeal "the robot rule" that required delegates to vote as they had previously pledged in the primary. Kennedy wanted to throw the convention wide open now that he had a bit of momentum. He thought the contest might finally be breaking his way.

Kennedy's closest advisers, including his campaign manager and brother-in-law Steve Smith, would tell him the numbers didn't add up. "And he'd say, 'Let me tell you the numbers that concern me: the numbers of unemployed in this country, the numbers of people without health insurance . . . the number of people who can't afford to buy a home or can't afford to send their kids to college. That's what concerns me, and I'm going to carry their cause to this convention,'" according to Shrum.[13]

At the convention in New York, however, delegates voted to uphold the "robot rule," and Kennedy's candidacy was stilled.

But once again, in defeat, Kennedy showed himself at his best. When he took to the stage at Madison Square Garden, Ted spoke more about Kennedy-like principles than about Carter. The president's Chappaquiddick ads had put Kennedy in no mood for conciliation. "I am asking you to renew our commitment to a fair and lasting prosperity that can put America back to work," Kennedy said to the delegates. "This is the cause that brought me into the campaign and that sustained me for nine months across 100,000 miles in 40 different states. We had our losses, but the pain of our defeats is far, far less than the pain of the people that I have met." He made a brief statement acknowledging Carter's win, but the speech is best remembered for its emotional closing, which had nothing to do with Carter. For the first time during the entire campaign, Kennedy spoke of his slain brothers.

> Someday, long after this convention, long after the signs come down and the bands stop playing, may it be said of our campaign that we kept the faith. May it be said of our party in 1980 that we found our faith again.
>
> May it be said of us, both in dark passage and in bright days, in the words of Tennyson that my brothers quoted and loved and that have special meaning to me now:
>
> *I am part of all that I have met*
> *Tho' much is taken, much abides*
> *That which we are, we are—*
> *One equal temper of heroic heart . . . strong in will*
> *To strive, to seek, to find, and not to yield.*

And then he concluded with the passage that became his signature: "For me, a few hours ago, this campaign came to an end. For all those whose cares have been our concern, the work goes on, the cause endures, the hope still lives, and the dream shall never die." To Shrum, who penned the words, "it was an embodiment, an expression of hope, an affirmation that the Democratic Party actually did have a mission and a vision for where the country should go."[14] The crowd at the Garden ignited in a demonstration that lasted half an hour. "It was one of the most powerful moments I've been a part of," said author Rick Atkinson, who was there covering the convention for the *Washington Post*. "It was the most electrifying speech that I'd ever heard personally. His delivery was just perfect. Absolutely spot on. Brilliant. It just resonated. People were crying because, I think, it was so evocative of the dead prince."

It was the highlight of the convention.

The lowlight came on the final day. Mondale still has bad memories of it. Rather than take Carter's hand and raise arms together in unity on the podium, as he'd practiced doing with Bob Shrum earlier, Kennedy arrived late for the celebration, shook hands with Carter and retreated to the back. Carter was livid.

"While Kennedy's speech at the national convention was fantastic, his appearance that last night on the platform was not fantastic, it was weird, I thought," said Mondale. "And it really hurt us." Rather than a party reconciled and unified to defeat Ronald Reagan, the Democrats finished the convention looking divided and angry.

"All the press criticized him for not being up there and not raising the hand," said press secretary Southwick. At a party for staffers in McLean afterward, however, Kennedy took Southwick aside and said, "Look, the press is all over me for appearing unenthusiastic, but I didn't want to stand up there and overshadow Carter. This was his moment. He should be at the front of the stage. That's why I was in the back. I didn't want to be upstaging him. I thought the best thing to do was to stand behind him, and stand in the back. I don't know why they are all pissed off at me."

The feelings were so raw after two months in the trenches that no matter what Kennedy did, it probably would have been interpreted in the wrong way. Or it may have been that Ted Kennedy did not know how to lose. He was the first of his generation of Kennedys to lose an election, and after that night it had to be apparent that likely no Kennedy would ever command the nation again. His quest to restore Camelot had failed.

Twenty-nine years later, however, Kennedy's defeat looks more like a blessing than a loss to many of those who support his goals. If Kennedy had somehow won the nomination and the general election, which is probably unlikely, given the strength of Reagan's appeal and the Republican ascendancy that year, he would have had eight more years in politics at the most. His influence would have ended then. Instead, Kennedy's influence continues even now as a legislator. "Imagine if Teddy Roosevelt had been able to stay in office 43 more years than he did," said Southwick. Kennedy's "influence is much much greater than it would have been had he become president."

Merrill Peterson, professor emeritus at the University of Virginia, is the author of *The Great Triumvirate,* a study of the senatorial careers of Daniel Webster, Henry Clay and John C. Calhoun in the years before the Civil War. "I said to a colleague recently that he [Kennedy] might be the greatest senator of them all," Peterson told the *Boston Globe.* "Not just because of the time served but because of his excellence. . . . I can't help with him but recall what a Philadelphia man once told Daniel Webster, when Webster was thinking of a presidential bid. This man advised him against it. He told Webster that he could be a senator until he died and still have a great career. And that's what happened."[15]

Mondale, who is still friends with Kennedy despite everything, agrees. "After 1980, when he gave up the presidential race for all practical purposes, I

think he was probably an even better legislator, because he had all that seniority now." Mondale said in a telephone interview with the author in 2008.
"He had the presidential itch under control and he could concentrate on his
Senate goals, and I believe he became an even better senator. Having dropped
the presidential subthemes, he was able to broaden the caucus of people who
would work with him. He let it go."

Kennedy still wanted to be president after 1980, but he was and always
would be hogtied by a deep sense of his own unworthiness in comparison to
his brothers. So many of the campaign's problems were self-inflicted that
Kennedy may have believed in his gut that if he actually became president, he
would somehow be dishonoring his brothers, inappropriately treading on
their sacred ground. Kennedy had to find a way to burnish and carry on their
legacy while creating a unique one of his own.

Camelot may have been gone forever, but there is another, forgotten
character in that story that Jack and Jackie treasured so. At the very end of
the play, a young lad named Tom of Warwick appears on the battlefield
eager to fight alongside King Arthur. He knows all about the legend of
Camelot, the Round Table, Lancelot and the Holy Grail. The king listens to
the lad recount his very own deeds, and a broad smile of epiphany spreads
over his face. Arthur realizes that his brief shining moment has a second
chance after all.

He orders the lad *not* to fight, but rather run behind the lines as the battle rages, *remembering*. Arthur exhorts the boy to go forth afterward and tell
the world about Camelot, spread its news far and wide, so that Camelot
might live forever. The king knights Tom of Warwick then and there, then
send him on his way. Grow old, he pleads with the boy as he departs. And
run.

13

THE MINOTAUR

Beastliness reflects the bloodlines, that inspiration which years ago tempted Lewis Lapham to term Edward Kennedy a "Minotaur," a cross-breed of man and mythology, "a creature who carries with him all the 'opposed principles' that are the family legacy."

—*Burton Hersh*, The Shadow President

*Do I contradict myself? Very well then I contradict myself,
I am large, I contain multitudes.*

—*Walt Whitman*, Song of Myself

In January 1981, Ted Kennedy's life changed in three decisive ways. A Republican president, Ronald Reagan, took up residence in the White House; Republicans took control of the Senate, meaning that for the first time in his career, Ted Kennedy was in the minority and Ted's slowly disintegrating marriage to Joan finally came to an end.

"With regrets, yet with respect and consideration for each other, we have agreed to terminate our marriage," Ted and Joan said in a statement released on January 21. "We have reached this decision together, with the understanding of our children and after pastoral counseling."

Although they'd tried to present a unified front during the campaign, Ted and Joan hadn't had a marriage to speak of in many years. Joan had moved back to Boston in the fall of 1977 in order to, in her own words, "lead a life of her own." They were essentially separated, but for political and religious reasons, they never considered announcing the fact. Ted flew up occasionally for dinner, but that was about the extent of their relationship. Though

Joan had made attempts at reconciliation several times, Ted's philandering and Joan's drinking had sundered their bond irrevocably.

When Ted asked Joan to come down to Washington to talk about what role she would play in the campaign, she had been met by a political panel, not a husband. Ted had arranged a meeting involving a psychiatrist, three doctors, Eunice and Ethel in addition to himself. Generously, Joan agreed to campaign, in part to try to reconnect to her husband and rise to the exalted role she had always hoped to have within the Kennedy family. But once the campaign ended, Ted didn't need her anymore. After the convention, they'd flown back to Washington together for a party for campaign workers and Secret Service agents. On the flight back to Hyannis Port from Washington, the plane stopped at Montauk Point on Long Island, and Ted got off, leaving Joan by herself again to finish the trip. She said she knew then and there that the marriage was over.[1]

Ironically, the campaign had given Joan confidence that she could survive on her own. She'd stayed sober while on the trail with Ted, and felt better about herself than she had felt in years, probably because Ted really had needed her. She was at her best during the times Ted needed her the most and when her role was clear within the oppressive Kennedy hierarchy. She had risen to the challenge, attending many important events during the campaign and generally serving her husband well. She was proud of how she'd done. "I guess I felt like I could go it alone," she said some years later.[2]

Ted was not necessarily stronger afterward. Newly divorced, newly in the minority and fresh off a losing campaign that had seemed to repudiate not just him but his entire family, Ted started the new decade with several more pieces of baggage on top of his already ridiculously large load. Richard Burke, Ted's administrative assistant from 1978 to 1981, remembers longtime aide Larry Horowitz telling him "Rick, there's so much scar tissue on that man, don't even attempt to try to ever think that he's ever going to change or that anybody is going to be able to help him."[3]

One small response Ted made to it all was to start smoking. He favored giant Davidoff cigars, imported from Geneva, and smoked them straight through committee hearings in the Capitol that winter, driving other participants mad. Orrin Hatch, the upright Mormon Republican senator from Utah who ascended to the chairmanship of the Labor and Human Resources Committee in the new majority, remembers Ted using his cigars as a kind of stick to poke the ruling party in the eye. Ted, after all, was an opposition leader now.

"You could normally tell whether we were fighting by the amount of smoke he would send my way," said Hatch, whose religion forbids smoking and drinking. "If our differences were great, I would have to sit there, my head enveloped in cigar smoke, as we worked through amendment after amendment. Ted would lean back in his chair, puffing away, knowing he was giving me a headache that was more than just political. I would try to plow my way through without giving him the satisfaction of seeing my irritation."[4]

Another member of the majority party, Alan Simpson of Wyoming, put up with the dry, acrid smoke for weeks while he and Hatch were drafting new immigration laws in the 1980s. Finally, Simpson couldn't stand it anymore. Ted showed up at his door with a cigar in hand, and Simpson said, "Ted, you can bring anyone or anything, or any idea into this office. But you cannot bring that cigar."[5]

Hatch and Simpson had every reason in the world to thwart and undermine Kennedy, yet they would all become the closest of friends in the ensuing years. For Hatch especially, Kennedy stood for everything he opposed.

"I came to Washington to fight Ted Kennedy," said Hatch. To most conservatives, Kennedy represented all that was wrong with liberalism. He wanted the federal government to forever act as a parent to the poor and the dispossessed, no matter what the cost. Reagan and his revolution thought government was the main problem, not the solution, and he had been elected on a vow to cut the size of government dramatically, weed out the pork and shut down the influence peddling in Washington. Kennedy was also an adulterous drunk in the minds of most conservatives, morally corrupt and undisciplined. To many Republicans, his legislation on abortion, gays and "women's liberation" perfectly reflected the situational ethics of his personal life. Kennedy was the liberal libertine they loved to hate.

"Ted is a passionate liberal, an East Coast Democrat. I'm a Rocky Mountain compassionate conservative," said Hatch. "Kennedy's personal life has been rife with controversy and well-publicized problems. Other than making the *National Enquirer's* list of possible space aliens in Congress, my personal life has never been of public interest."[6]

Yet Hatch and Kennedy found themselves forced to work intimately together on the Labor Committee. Kennedy purposefully chose to become the ranking minority leader on Labor because he thought there he would be in a better position to oppose cuts in social programs he believed the Reagan administration wanted to eviscerate. Many Democrats in Congress responded to the writing on the wall by moving to the right to accommodate the new mood, but Kennedy absolutely would not.

"Goddamn it," Bob Shrum said in an interview with Burton Hersh, "whatever criticism people have of this guy, remember that in the early eighties, when everybody else was running for cover, he absolutely refused to. He stood up on stuff that was tough to stand up on."[7]

Kennedy knew, however, that he would need to form new alliances to keep the Republicans from completely wrecking all his work. The pragmatic Hatch knew he needed alliances to succeed in his new position, as well.

"When I became chairman of the Labor and Human Resources Committee, back in 1981, with the advent of Reagan, well, up to that time, hardly any self-respecting Republican would go on the Labor Committee, because it was totally liberal," said Hatch. "With the advent of Reagan, seven of the nine Republicans on the committee were conservative." But the other two Republicans voted with liberals on social issues. And Kennedy had seven Democrats on the committee, which meant in reality Kennedy still had the edge.

"I knew I couldn't run the committee without Ted Kennedy," said Hatch. "I went to Ted, and I said, look I can't run this committee without you. You know it and I know it. You've got the ideological edge nine to seven even though we're in the majority. I need your help."

Kennedy said, "Well, Orrin. I'll be happy to help you. There are some things I can't do; there are some things I just have to stand up for. But otherwise I'll help you."

Thus was born one of the strangest and most productive alliances on Capitol Hill. What began as a relationship of political expediency developed into a deep friendship as the two titans counseled each other through personal setbacks. Together, they also pushed back a bit against the rising tide of partisanship that was engulfing Washington. It was also an alliance that would, in a decade, save Kennedy's career.

"It was kind of a wary friendship at first," said Hatch. "Kennedy actually saw that we could work together. He's the type of person who, if you reach out to him in friendship, he'll grasp it. Gradually, we became very good friends. He recognized if he worked with me he would get some of his ideas through when they were in the majority."

They found common ground in compassion. Orrin Hatch held the very first Senate hearings on the AIDS epidemic in 1986, during which he hugged an AIDS victim from Utah in an effort to end widespread fears that the disease could be transmitted by touch. Kennedy responded with several hearings of his own, pushing the Reagan administration to allocate more money for AIDS care and research. Hatch and Kennedy teamed up on the Ryan White AIDS Act, which established the largest federally funded program for people living with HIV and AIDS.

"We found that we had a mutual interest in health care," recalls Hatch.

Hatch's support of Kennedy on the Americans with Disabilities Act was the key to its passage in 1990. He also helped Kennedy renew the health center program that had been his first major legislative victory in 1965.

Kennedy and Hatch also cosponsored the State Children's Health Insurance Program (SCHIP) that ensured coverage for 9 million uninsured children. The Hatch-Kennedy partnership on SCHIP was the glue for the first balanced budget amendment in 40 years. SCHIP was attached to the balanced budget bill, and Democrats couldn't vote against the balanced budget because SCHIP was in there. And fiscally conservative Republicans couldn't vote against SCHIP because they wanted a balanced budget.

"I was up on the dais when we were voting, and one of the leading Republicans said to me: 'Orrin, I hate this bill.' And then he voted 'Aye.'"

Hatch's Mormon faith, which directed him to love and help those who couldn't help themselves, intersected providentially with the strong Catholic ethos of the Kennedy family. The team of Hatch and Kennedy co-sponsored bills on mental health, Alzheimer's research and religious freedom. They established standards for mammography, regulated prescription drug advertising and food safety and codified the requirements for access to life-saving medicines. They also collaborated on the creation of the Eunice Kennedy Shriver Institute on Child Development. And in 2008, while Kennedy was undergoing radiation and chemotherapy treatments for brain cancer, they put the finishing touches on a new national service plan that would provide college tuition help to more than 200,000 people who volunteer a year or two of service to their country.

"We're finding today that lot of young people do not serve," Hatch said recently, sounding a lot like John F. Kennedy. "They don't serve in the military, they don't give service to the government, to communities, to charitable organizations. A lot of them will never see the Peace Corps and some of the other service agencies. So we're trying to come up with a bill that will encourage young people to give two years of service."

Kennedy forged alliances with many other conservatives in the early 1980s in a strategy that would soon make him the Senate's most productive member. When he couldn't preserve a social program, rather than lose the program altogether, he would propose a replacement that was more palatable to Republicans.

With Dan Quayle, he pushed through the Job Training Partnership Act as a replacement to the Comprehensive Employment and Training Act. The act was a hybrid kind of program, enlisting private industry groups in providing jobs.

With Robert Dole's help, he renewed the Voting Rights Act of 1965. He worked with Strom Thurmond on a crime control bill that toughened sentencing, reformed bail requirements and embraced preventive detention.

With Simpson, he would rewrite the nation's immigration laws.

Simpson remembers a call at about one in the morning the night of the 1980 election, when it was clear the Republicans were going to be in the majority. "Ted Kennedy calls, says congratulations for the majority. He said, 'I gotta come over as soon as I can.' I said, 'OK, come on in.' And Kennedy said, 'Look, I've been handling immigration and refugee matters for 17 years, all by myself. Strom's chairman now, so if you'll talk to Strom and ask him to set up a subcommittee on immigration and refugee policy, I'll loan you my staff, I'll help you train yours. There are no politics here. If we can't do an American bill instead of a Republican or Democrat bill, then we don't have anything anyway.'"

Kennedy and Simpson worked closely together after that for years. "If you're a legislator, you gotta form such alliances," Simpson said, even if they aren't very palatable to folks back home. "If you're satisfied to clip ribbons and make speeches, you're not worth anything in the U.S. Senate. It's a deliberative body. The purpose of being there is not to be an administrator; it's to be a legislator. And [Kennedy] knew that. He would work with anyone. He had special relationships with everybody in some way on the other side of the aisle. And the longer you're there, the only way you ever succeed is to align yourself with somebody who's 'unpopular' in your district or your state. People in Wyoming used to say, 'Oh God, you worked with Ted Kennedy.' Up in Massachusetts, they'd say what the hell are you working with Simpson for? It was a two-way street.

"He knew the game," Simpson adds. "He taught me a lot about hearings. He said, Be sure when you have a hearing that you get the toughest people on the other side. Don't just set up hearings where you can play cozy and get your side said and tear the ass off everybody else and look good. So that you'd get a full hearing without a bunch of bias and tripe, that's just your side. A hearing just for the hell of it so you can pound on the opposition, and beat it to death, show off and gain nothing because the other side hasn't been presented."

Later, Kennedy would team up with John McCain to rewrite immigration laws again, and together they would push the Patients' Bill of Rights through the Senate.

He enlisted Nancy Kassebaum in passing a bill that allowed for the portability of health insurance.

With the help of Republicans Robert Stafford (VT) and Lowell Weicker (CT) on the Labor Committee, Kennedy kept Reagan from consolidating dozens of federal programs into seven block grants to states and cities, though spending on the programs was cut. Kennedy preserved school-lunch subsidies, thwarted cuts to Social Security, saved legal assistance to the poor and ensured the continuation of low-income fuel assistance.[8] What Reagan did change, Kennedy made sure he got his fingerprints all over. He became the country's keeper of traditional liberalism.

He also created his own war chest in the 1980s, the Fund for a Democratic Majority. The personal political action committee allowed him to invest in selected senatorial candidates, influencing the makeup of the Senate as well as its output.

Since he no longer could hold hearings without the authorization of a committee majority, Kennedy invented a new vehicle, the "forum." He often booked the Senate Caucus Room for such quasi-hearings and still had enough clout to attract a crowd.

Instead of lamenting the limits on the depth of his power, he simply widened its breadth. Ignoring the traditional limit of two major committees per senator, Kennedy used his clout in 1982 to get a seat on the Armed Services Committee, where he still sits today. From there he could throw a monkey wrench into Reagan's massive defense buildup. He called the proposed B–1 bomber a "supersonic Edsel"; the MX, "a missile without a mission"; the Strategic Defense Initiative, "the lone ranger in the sky."[9]

He wrangled a spot on the Manpower Subcommittee and began visiting U.S. military installations around the world. He got into the weeds of defense appropriations, focusing on the social issues that had always been important to him: day care, health care, education and wage levels.

"Instead of cutting off food stamps to our own people, let us cut back the feast of military aid to fatten dictatorships around the world," he urged Democrats at their midterm convention.[10] He preached the liberal mantra that U.S. support for strongmen like Panama's Manuel Noriega in the name of stability actually spurred revolutionary challenges around the world, creating more instability instead of less.

Kennedy took to the world stage with a vengeance in the 1980s, often acting as an unelected second president.

In 1984, at the invitation of Episcopal archbishop Desmond Tutu, he retraced Bobby's footsteps to South Africa, attempting to visit antiapartheid leader Nelson Mandela in his jail cell. "We visited the jail, but we couldn't get in," said Bob Shrum. "We left the bust for the Robert F. Kennedy Human Rights Award against the prison fence." Many years later, Mandela told Kennedy that he knew he had been there because word had been spread inside the prison. Knowing the world was paying attention was hugely important to him at the time, Mandela said.

Kennedy did stay with Tutu in his humble bungalow in Soweto, becoming the first white man ever to sleep in the embattled township.[11] Kennedy remembers Tutu's Nobel Prize sitting right next to his bed.

Bob Shrum wrote a speech to echo the "ripple of hope" address Bobby had given 19 years earlier, describing the fight against apartheid as the continuation of the great fight for civil rights around the world. "To any who turn their heads, who pretend that they do not see, I reply: Let them read, as a I have read, the repressive words of South Africa's statutes. Like an earlier generation that saw the construction of the Berlin Wall, let them look at the clear barrier of discrimination against black people here. The barrier is not always built of bricks or mortar or barbed wire, but it is starkly visible everywhere. And if anyone doubts that it is wrong, let them come to Soweto. Let them go to Onverwacht; let them go to Crossroads; let them got to Branfort—let them ask Winnie Mandela."[12]

But the speech was never given. A hundred demonstrators from a militant antiwhite group loyal to slain activist Steven Biko vowed to disrupt Kennedy at the Regina Mundi Cathedral in Soweto if he gave the speech. South African officials were worried about riots. "I remember how heartbroken Bishop Tutu was, even though he understood that we couldn't do it," said Shrum. "There were real security concerns that a lot of people might get hurt. Kennedy decided that giving a speech was not worth somebody getting killed or seriously hurt." Bobby had faced similar concerns and went ahead and spoke anyway, but Ted had been touched by too much violence.

Ted traveled the country just as Bobby had, but this time ABC News and NBC News teams trailed him, showing the world what apartheid really looked like. Bishop Tutu believed that the increased attention generated by the trip stoked an international movement toward sanctions against the South African government.

It was Ted Kennedy who introduced a sanctions bill in the U.S. Senate when he got back. And he fought hard for it, criticizing President Reagan personally for his inaction, recruiting Republicans to the bill, staging forums on the subject, fine-tuning legislation over and over and introducing new legislation when the first try got bogged down. Reagan vetoed the bill when it finally passed and, for the first time since the War Powers Act was enacted over Nixon's veto in 1973, Kennedy mustered an override. As the roll call was taken in the Senate, black representatives stood vigil in the back of the chamber and civil rights leaders watched from the galleries. Kennedy won his two-year-long fight by 11 votes.

Britain followed suit with sanctions, and pressure built around the world. Within three years, Nelson Mandela was freed and apartheid was ended.

"I had always been somewhat reluctant to go down there," Kennedy said in an interview later, "because I thought my brother Bob's trip had been such a powerful visit, with so much substance and symbolism, sort of like a bell that was continuing to ring. I didn't want to interfere with the chimes."[13] Yes, Bobby had spoken memorable words, but it was Ted who had acted on them.

Kennedy also opened up his own diplomatic relations with Russia, empowered by the potency of his name and the possibility that at any time he might become the next president. He felt he had a mandate inherited directly from his brothers, who both had visited the Soviet Union frequently. Each time he went he won exit visas for refuseniks, gave speeches on the usefulness of democracy, and pressed for improvements in arms control during meetings with the general secretary. His role has never been that of go-between for the president and the general secretary, however; it has always been much more freelance than that.

A Soviet defector, Vasily Mitrokhin, in 2002 revealed a series of secret meetings between Kennedy's proxies and the KGB in the early 1980s.[14] According to a letter from KGB chief Viktor Chebrikov to General Secretary Yuri Andropov on May 14, 1983, Kennedy wanted Andropov to know that he was worried about the state of relations between the United States and the Soviet Union. He proposed a series of steps "to counter the militaristic politics of Reagan." The proposals were relayed to the Soviets in 1983 by former senator John Tunney, speaking on Kennedy's behalf.

Among the ideas was a suggestion that Andropov invite Kennedy to Moscow for a personal meeting. "The main purpose of the meeting, according to the senator, would be to arm Soviet officials with explanations regarding problems of nuclear disarmament so they may be better prepared and more convincing during appearances in the USA," Chebrikov wrote in the letter.

Essentially, Kennedy wanted to give the Soviets some PR tips. He also suggested that Andropov organize televised interviews in the United States in August–September 1984, right before the general election. "A direct appeal by the General Secretary of the Central Committee of the Communist Party of the Soviet Union to the American people will, without a doubt, attract a great deal of attention and interest in the country." Kennedy was prepared to ask

Walter Cronkite and Barbara Walters to visit Moscow for such interviews. He made it clear that it was important the initiative be seen as coming from America, not vice versa.

Some conservatives who have seen the Mitrokhin papers, which now reside at the Woodrow Wilson International Center for Scholars, have cried "treason" over the contacts. Kennedy's overtures may indeed have violated the Logan Act, which prohibits American citizens from engaging in private diplomacy with a foreign government with the intention of influencing public policy. But the law, which has been on the books since 1799, is rarely enforced.

At the very least, Kennedy was trying to work around Reagan, creating a direct channel between the Soviets and the American people, and may have been hoping to influence the election that year via the Soviets. But Soviet leader Andropov died before he ever responded to the invitation.

When Mikhail Gorbachev became the Soviet leader, Kennedy actually became an important back channel between the White House and the Soviets. The Soviets went to Kennedy first when they were thinking about destroying their intermediate-range ballistic missiles, and Kennedy and his friends and representatives helped broker the Intermediate-Range Nuclear Force missile treaty.[15] Secretary of State George Schultz acknowledged Kennedy's contribution when the treaty was signed in 1988.

Kennedy essentially went about creating his own shadow government in those long years he spent in the minority. With the Senate's sails in the hands of the enemy, Kennedy found his way to the back of the boat and grabbed onto the tiller. It's almost as if Kennedy refused to accept at some level that he hadn't been elected president.

In October of 1984, he gave one of the best speeches in his life at Liberty Baptist College, the epicenter of the Reverend Jerry Falwell's conservative Christian empire, the Moral Majority. Building on his brother John's famous campaign speech on the separation of church and state, Kennedy laid out one of the clearest, most thoughtful descriptions of the proper relationship between morality and government ever expressed by an American politician. It's an address that is often included on lists of America's best 100 speeches of the twentieth century.

Ted couldn't stop the Reagan revolution in the 1980s, but he certainly slowed it down, redirected it and in many cases stalled it completely. By conducting his own foreign policy, by erecting parliamentary roadblocks, by relentlessly marking up bills, by staging mock hearings and press conferences, by blocking conservative appointments like that of Robert Bork to the Supreme Court, Kennedy ran a successful rearguard action against Reagan's efforts to dismantle his life's work. In doing so, he succeeded in keeping intact much of the social agenda his brothers had articulated and he had help put in place.

But it was grueling work. Throwing sand in the machinery was not the same as moving mountains. And there was a price to be paid. As the public man valiantly held his ground, the private man felt it shifting like quicksand beneath him.

Work was the easy part for Ted Kennedy. Work was a place where there was some sanity and structure. "This was not an easy family," said one insider. Since Joan was in Boston, and Ted was in McLean, he was both mom and dad for Teddy and Kara. Patrick had chronic asthma, and more than anyone, feared for his father's life. Ted would bow out of another presidential run in 1984 largely because of Patrick's concerns. And then Joan descended back into alcoholism. In 1988, she crashed her car into a fence on Cape Cod and was ordered to attend an alcohol education program. Joan would relapse frequently over the next decade despite the presence of a full-time caretaker. At one point, desperate to avoid detection, she took to secretly drinking mouthwash and vanilla extract, which had enough alcohol in them to satisfy her relentless craving. Just a few years earlier, she had been found after a relapse passed out on a Boston sidewalk with a concussion and a broken shoulder.

"I remember very clearly growing up in my family whispering in my household as my mother suffered tremendously from this disease of alcoholism," said Patrick Kennedy. Both of Kennedy's sons, Teddy Jr. and Patrick, have now undergone treatment for alcoholism.[16]

"When you've grown up around it, you get a distorted view of alcoholism," Patrick Kennedy said. "Denial creeps in and you think, 'Well, so long as I'm not doing that, I must be alright,'" he said.[17]

Joan's alcoholism and the demands of all the family's other nieces and nephews on their last remaining father figure made growing up in the Kennedy house a sometimes difficult, hollow experience.

"No one can convince me, from what this disease has done to my mother or what this disease has done to millions of Americans like her that I have witnessed, let alone that I have witnessed in my own personal life, that people have chosen this life," said Patrick. "Voluntarily. No one voluntarily chooses to live the kind of painful, sordid, destructive life that people who are alcoholics and addicts or people who are depressed or people who suffer from schizophrenia or bipolar disorder, any number of mental illnesses, obsessive compulsive disorder, any one of those illnesses, no one can convince me that that is a voluntary choice on their part."

What is left unsaid is how much Ted Kennedy's own drinking affected his children. In February 1990, writer Michael Kelly came out with a devastating piece in *GQ* that presented Kennedy as an unrepentant Lothario, drunkenly prowling Georgetown at night for one-night stands with his partner in horseplay, Senator Chris Dodd.

What was remarkable about the stories recounted by Kelly was how public Kennedy was with his recklessness. John had been deviously discreet with his affairs; Bobby's are still a matter of question; Ted didn't seem to care. He and Dodd once played a game of "waitress toss" with an unsuspecting server, throwing the lightweight woman back and forth between the two of them, and in 1985 they threw down each other's autographed pictures in La Colline restaurant on Capitol Hill and performed a Mexican hat dance on top of them.[18] Kennedy was caught in flagrante delicto with a lunch companion on the floor of La Brasserie restaurant in 1987; and he was photographed on top of a brunette in the well of a speedboat in St. Tropez.

Burton Hersh, who had good access to Ted and his staff at the time, wrote in his 1997 book *The Shadow President* that some of the senator's aides "found themselves bird-doggin' a live prospect across a crowded reception, under orders to recommend a drink in the back of the senator's limousine, or even—there were verified claims—a line of coke."[19]

Suzannah Lessard wrote an article for *Washington Monthly* entitled "Kennedy's Woman Problem, Women's Kennedy Problem."[20] She pointed out the contradiction between Kennedy's advocacy of women's equality and his behavior at night. "Kennedy's womanizing is widely known to many women who have been approached themselves and to reporters and others who have been around Kennedy and have seen the pattern in action. The type of womanizing that Kennedy is associated with is a series of short involvements—if they can be called that—after which he drops the lady. It suggests an old-fashioned, male chauvinist, exploitative view of women. . . . It gives me the creeps."

Of course womanizing was a deep-seated family pattern, born of a pre-feminist era when none of the women the Kennedy brothers married stood up to their husbands and demanded a stop to it. Ted was straddling two eras, but finding out that society would no longer put up with the behavior in which his father and brothers indulged themselves. The country had changed, and it was time Ted changed, too.

Another reporter who spent time with Kennedy during the period says he is convinced that Kennedy was an untreated alcoholic. He never drank during the day, but he drank every night. During a two-hour stretch the reporter watched him down two drinks of Scotch, two of vodka and, with dinner, three glasses of red wine, a fairly normal night for Kennedy.

One adviser wondered to Burton Hersh if there weren't an element of self-sabotage to Ted's drinking. "If you get drunk regularly in public with various important personalities, there has be an element of self-humiliation present, doesn't it?" Survivors are careful about their dead one's legacies. They don't wish to diminish them in any way by actions of their own. It may be that, as Ted's successes mounted in the Senate, he made certain outside the chamber that his star would never rise above his brothers'.

A staffer for Senator Byrd who knew Kennedy during the 1980s put it more simply: "He was not a happy person before Vicki."

"I like him so much," said Hatch at the time. "I'm just going to send the Mormon missionaries to him to straighten out the rest of his life."[21]

Yet Ted Kennedy got up and went to work every day. In the 101st Congress while Reagan was president, he pushed 54 bills into law, the most enacted by the Labor Committee since Johnson's Great Society. While Reagan's successor, George H. W. Bush, was president, Kennedy helped pass a new Civil Rights Act, which overturned seven Supreme Court decisions that Kennedy saw as rolling back the gains of the civil rights movement.

In 1990, Bush signed the landmark Americans with Disabilities Act that Kennedy had cosponsored. Kennedy also won an increase in the minimum wage under Bush and passed the National Military Child Care Act, which established the child care system for the entire Department of Defense. He also made it possible for women to serve as combat pilots.

And he attended hundreds of piano recitals and soccer games during the same period, always available to help a family member into rehab or out of a tight spot.

In 1986, Democrats recaptured the Senate. Nine out of the 11 incoming freshmen Democrats received money and advice from Kennedy's political action committee.

Though his Tabloid Ted private life provided ample ammunition to his political antagonists in the 1980s, no one has ever been able to recall an instance when drinking appeared to impair his work or his role as patriarch. Somehow he always managed to keep the often opposite-moving rivers of his life—his work, his nightlife, his family—all separate during his bachelor years.

Until Palm Beach.

14

FOUR FUNERALS
AND A WEDDING

*For unto whomsoever much is given, of him much shall be required;
and to whom men have committed much, of him they will ask more.*

—*Luke 12:48*

Ted Kennedy's most memorable speeches are all eulogies. In the 1990s, the demand was such that Kennedy employed a eulogy writer to help him craft the appropriate words. Ted often struggled to hold back tears when delivering these final tributes and his voice almost always broke during delivery, but in the end he usually willed himself through. There is probably no one better qualified at trying to make sense out of death.

During Steve Smith's eulogy in 1991, however, Ted Kennedy broke down time after time, stopping in midsentence, starting again and finally summoning his son Patrick to come to the pulpit to take over.

Steve, the husband of Ted's sister Jean, was yet another lost brother. "He was an extra brother, really," Kennedy would tell a judge, of all people, in a few months time. "We lost a brother in a war. When Jean married Steve, we had another brother. And when Steve was gone, something left all of us."

In addition to managing Ted's campaign and helping organize both Jack's and Bobby's runs for president, Steve had managed the entire Kennedy financial estate for a number of years. He'd come from a wealthy, political family himself—his grandfather had built a shipping fortune and served three terms in Congress—and had put his own political ambitions aside in service of his brothers-in-law. Steve and Jean had built their own home in Hyannis Port to be near the center of gravity in the Kennedy family. For 30 years, the chain-smoking ladies' man had been, for Ted, a crisis manager and best friend.

On the Easter weekend after this death, members of the family collected at La Guerida, the faded Kennedy hacienda at Palm Springs that Joe Kennedy had bought in 1933. The newly widowed Jean had also invited Bill Barry, a friend and former bodyguard who had knocked the gun out of Sirhan Sirhan's hand after Bobby's murder. As on the night of Chappaquiddick, the weekend started as a belated memorial, surfacing too many difficult memories for Kennedy.

"We were visiting on the patio after dinner," Kennedy testified in the trial that was to result from that night's events, "and the conversation was a very emotional conversation, a very difficult one. Brought back a lot of very special memories to me, particularly with the loss of Steve, who really was a brother to me and to other members of the family. And I found at the end of the conversation that I was not able to think about sleeping. It was a very draining conversation. . . . So we left that place, and we went out. We went to Au Bar's.

"I wish I'd gone for a long walk on the beach instead."

At the bar, his son Patrick and his nephew Willy Smith both picked up young women who eventually found their way back to the Kennedy compound that night.

Just before four in the morning, while Patrick and Michele Cassone were cuddling in one of the downstairs rooms, Ted appeared at the doorway in his knee-length, striped nightshirt to say goodnight. He was "just there with a weird look on his face," Michelle told the *Boston Globe*. "I was weirded out." She told the *Globe* that she informed Patrick, "I'm out of here," and asked him as he walked her to her car, "Does your father embarrass you?" But she later testified that instead of leaving at that moment, she went out on the beach with Patrick and fooled around.

Out on another part of the beach, Willy Smith was having sex with 29-year-old Patricia Bowman. He said it was consensual, but the next day she filed charges against Smith, alleging rape. Police came by the next day to ask questions and were told by Barry that Smith and Ted had left, though Ted was out on the beach at the time and did not leave until Monday. Willy and Patrick had left the compound early Sunday.

Many of the newspaper stories that came out in the days that followed made it sound like Ted was responsible for the whole gothic affair. "Ted's Sexy Romp" read the *New York Post*'s main headline. *Time* magazine called Kennedy "a Palm Beach boozer, lout and tabloid grotesque." Jay Leno had a field day, asking on NBC's *Tonight Show* "How many other 59-year-old men still go to Florida for spring break?" The normally friendly *Boston Globe* scolded Kennedy for leading his son and nephew astray. Another publication put it simply: "His Career is Over."

It has always been standard journalistic procedure not to print the names of alleged rape victims, but in this case a tabloid, the *Globe,* paid $1,000 to a friend of Bowman's who had been at the bar, and Bowman's name was published soon after by NBC News and the *New York Times.*

"The whole thing turned into a media free-for-all," said the *Boston Globe*'s John Aloysisus Farrell. "This is the first instance that I can remember where the reporting in the supermarket tabloids made it to the newspaper tabloids and spilled through the wire services into the mainstream press so quickly."

The Kennedys themselves had dissolved the wall between traditional political power and media celebrity. It was movie mogul Joe Kennedy who invented the celebrity politics that was now coming back to bite Ted. The Kennedys were no longer a public political treasure—it was clear in the coverage of Palm Beach—but a kind of "public cultural bauble," in the words of an insightful *Boston Globe* profile.[1] A certain reverence for political figures had been permanently replaced, thanks to the Kennedys, by a competition to air every gossipy detail of the private lives of politicians, with many media outlets no longer distinguishing much between fact and opinion. Rumors and half-truths were reported side by side with facts in the Palm Beach story; indiscretions that weekend were magnified and distorted into crimes.

What is known for sure about Ted Kennedy's role was that he took his son and nephew out drinking. Eighteen years hence, it's hard to find much other fault with Kennedy's behavior that night. The press wasn't reacting to one incident, however, but to years of reported indiscretions that swirled around Kennedy. This one happened in real time, and participants were talking.

Friends said Ted was shaken by Palm Beach. "You can't go through an experience like this and not make up your mind that you are going to be a little more attentive to your behavior," he told John Farrell of the *Boston Globe.*[2] But he insisted still that he did not have a drinking problem.

In the span of ten years, Ted personally squandered much of the mythology of the Kennedy family in American culture. It was that loss he cared about more than any of his own. This was not just a political career at stake. Kennedy was playing for history, more than his brothers ever got a chance to, and their legacy was his. It was time to try to preserve himself so that, once and forever, he might preserve that legacy itself.

In desperation, Kennedy turned to his old Mormon Republican friend Orrin Hatch.

"Ted came to me when the media was all over him because of what they considered to be his less-than-desirable image," said Hatch. "And I helped him. And he knows it."

Ted asked Hatch if he would field requests from reporters for comment. Hatch agreed, but warned him that he had to stop drinking. "It's no secret that we've had some heart-to-heart talks. He changed his life. There's no question he listened to me and started to change."

An inquiry was lodged with the Senate ethics committee into whether Kennedy's conduct reflected poorly on the Senate, but was dismissed a week later. A trial for Smith was scheduled for late 1991, and Kennedy was subpoenaed to testify. Polls in Massachusetts plunged from 70 percent approval rating for Kennedy to 40 percent overnight. For the first time in nearly 30 years, Ted seemed in danger of losing his Senate seat.

It was a moment when Kennedy needed to step out of his brothers' enormous shoes and admit to himself, and his constituents, that he was all too human.

As the late political essayist Walter Karp once wrote: "Kennedy is—a Kennedy. Great clouds of windbaggery befog and blind him, are bellowed forth to befog and blind him—the 'Camelot legend,' the 'Kennedy legacy,' the 'presidential destiny.' That was what he needed most to overcome—that sense that not only do Kennedys not cry, they do nothing that is not grand and royal and operatic and of great ritual import to the nation."[3]

Kennedy decided, in that moment, that he needed to publicly confront his behavior, something he'd never been able to bring himself to do before. He sensed something dangerous and permanent in the air.

"I recognize my own shortcomings," Kennedy said in an extraordinary speech at Harvard's Institute of Politics at the Kennedy School of Government on October 25. "I realize that I alone am responsible for them, and I am the one who must confront them.

"Unlike my brothers," Ted added, "I have been given length of years and time. And as I have approached my sixtieth birthday I am determined to give all that I have to advance the causes for which I have stood for almost a third of a century."

Sitting anonymously in the packed audience that day was a 38-year-old lawyer who had pushed Ted hard to make the public atonement. Her name was Vicki Reggie, and she and Kennedy had been quietly dating for four months.

It was a match that probably saved Kennedy's reputation for history, not to mention his poll numbers.

Vicki Reggie had crossed paths with Ted Kennedy for 22 years. Her father, a retired judge and lawyer, helped deliver Louisiana for vice presidential candidate John F. Kennedy at the 1956 Democratic convention, and the two families had been friendly ever since. Still, Ted had never paid much attention to Vicki, who was 20 years his junior. They were from different generations. Then Vicki invited Kennedy to a fortieth-anniversary dinner she was having for her parents. They soon began an old-fashioned kind of courtship, full of flowers and laughs. Kennedy lavished attention on her two young children. He would sometimes arrive at her house before she got home from the office, and he was usually on the floor making animal sounds with the girls.

Ted had finally met someone with a no-nonsense will to match his own, but the bond between the two may be based on a shared appreciation for laughter more than anything else. Friends say Vicki has a grand sense of humor, which often reveals itself in her willingness to match Kennedy's pratfalls and pranks step for step. At Ted's annual "off-the-record" Christmas party for his staff, Vicki skipped in dressed as a little girl, with a braided blond wig, as Ted entered costumed as Barney the purple dinosaur. They danced to the *Barney* theme song together, and reportedly brought the house down.[4]

"They love to have fun," said Linda Douglass, a television journalist. "If they know it's someone's birthday, they'll get up and instantly create a hilarious song and sing it. You rarely see that level of fun and devotion in a couple."[5]

Kennedy proposed at the opera.

"When he decided to marry Vicki, I was out in California," remembers Hatch. "I was at a big fund-raiser, and got a call. They said, 'Ted Kennedy's on the phone and he sounds very agitated.' This was a 500-person fund-raiser I was speaking at. So I went down to the plaza, and I thought his mother had died.

"I said, 'What's the matter, Ted?'

"'Oh nothing, I just wanted you to be the first person to know. I'm going to get married.'" Hatch told him it was just what he needed.

Ted and Vicki wed in a small, private ceremony a year after the Harvard speech, in 1992. Hatch wrote a love song for them, called "Souls Along the Way."

"I get a call over the July 4 weekend from his boat," said Hatch. "Kennedy says, 'I just played that song for Vicki and she's sitting on the edge of the boat crying. She loves it so much.'"

Vicki was the person who was finally able to anchor Kennedy's life for him. And like a good fairy summoned in at the last possible second, she gave the Kennedy legacy a second chance.

The success of Ted's public life and his private life, however, still affected each other inversely in early 1992. The moment he found some stability in his personal life, he suffered through one of his lowest moments in the Senate. With Palm Beach still hanging over him, Kennedy was muzzled during the Judiciary committee hearings on Anita Hill's charges of sexual harassment against Republican Supreme Court nominee Clarence Thomas. Liberal groups were furious at Kennedy's silence, but when he finally did try to speak up, Republican members attacked him personally. Arlen Specter called Kennedy a hypocrite. "We do not need characterizations like 'shame' in this chamber from the Senator from Massachusetts." Oddly, Orrin Hatch took a cheap shot in defense of his party's nominee: "Anybody who believes that," he said about a statement of Kennedy's, "I know a bridge up in Massachusetts that I'll be happy to sell them." (Hatch told reporter Adam Clymer a few minutes later that he meant to say "bridge in Brooklyn," and had the Congressional Record corrected.)

The Senate confirmed Thomas 52–48, and liberals immediately laid blame at Kennedy's door. Columnist Anna Quindlen wrote, "He let us down because he had to; he was muzzled by the facts of his life." Other columnists wondered if Kennedy had lost too much clout to be an effective advocate for liberal causes.

Massachusetts voters were beginning to wonder the same thing.

When Kennedy testified at William Smith's rape trial that December, he came across as sympathetic and statesmanlike. He had already gained a new centeredness thanks to Vicki. He spoke nobly of his legacy, like a wounded survivor, reminding millions of viewers of all his family had suffered through and meant to the country. His testimony was clearly tangential to the charges, and the prosecutor treated Kennedy with kid gloves.

The case devolved quickly down to a "he said, she said" face-off between Bowman and Smith. The jury acquitted Smith of the rape charge, but half of the public didn't believe him innocent. Three other women had given sworn

depositions describing assaults by Smith, but the statements were not allowed at the trial. The whole Palm Beach incident still hung like a dark, slow-
to-dissipate cloud over Kennedy. A *Boston Globe* poll the following spring
found that only 38 percent of the electorate believed that Kennedy deserved
another term.

In response to Kennedy's new vulnerability, a formidable challenger sur-
faced in Massachusetts for the first time in Kennedy's career. Mitt Romney
was a wealthy venture capitalist with a Harvard MBA and a father who had
been governor of Michigan and secretary of Housing and Urban Development (HUD). Romney, who was also a leader in the area's Mormon Church,
quickly positioned himself as the face of the future.

Back in Washington, Kennedy got more bad news early that summer.
The health reform package he had worked so many years to bring forward
and had planned to campaign on was collapsing. With a sympathetic president in Bill Clinton, Kennedy thought he had his best chance in years to
make universal care happen. The president had even campaigned on health
care, using the slogan: "Every criminal gets a lawyer, how come every person
doesn't have a doctor?"

The problem was, for the Clintons, it hadn't been much more than that,
a campaign slogan. No serious attempt was made to estimate what universal
care would cost before Clinton took office, and there had been no real attempt to pull specifics together before inauguration. President Clinton put
Hillary in charge of the plan but made it clear that a tax increase was unac-
ceptable. Political realities set in fast.

Many people involved at the time said Hillary Clinton went about her
healthcare campaign in an arrogant way, failing to consult with Congress
adequately. There was an assumption by the Clintons that all Democrats
would line up behind them. That was not the case at all. In the Senate, there
were competing bills rather than one coordinated effort, and one of those
alternative bills was Kennedy's plan, Health America. Clinton's campaign
was never coordinated with Kennedy's or with other legislators' plans. "It
was essentially in competition with other folks rather than trying to do
something collaboratively," remembers Dr. Jay Himmelstein, a health policy
specialist at University of Massachusetts Medical School who worked on
Kennedy's plan. And Hillary didn't bother thinking about reaching across
the aisle, either, said Himmelstein. She thought she had the votes without
reaching out. In other words, she didn't know the folkways of Washington
as well as Ted did.

It was also a relatively public process, which had the unwanted side effect of exposing Hillary, as the first lady, to criticism of overreaching. It was

Senator Hatch who dismissed Clinton's plan as "a blueprint for socialized medicine."

Hillary's ambitious campaign alienated members of the coalition Kennedy had cobbled together over so many years in his slow march toward universal care. The failure of her plan was also a setback for his. Kennedy tried to salvage pieces of it in the next few months with his own bill, but Republicans saw only a "pasteurized version" of the Clinton bill. Nancy Kassebaum, head of the Health Committee, doomed the effort when she said, "The Kennedy bill is rather like a casserole made from the leftovers of the previous evening's meal."[6] Just as he was fighting for his political life, his best chance in years to fulfill the cause of his life slipped away.

Kennedy abandoned his effort to finish a new health bill when Jacqueline Kennedy's Onassis's non-Hodgkin's lymphoma took a turn for the worse. Hospitalized for a month, Jackie asked in early May to return to her Fifth Avenue apartment to die. Ted and Vicki visited her there May 17 and 18 as reporters stood vigil outside in the rain. The night of May 18, as Ted and Vicki were flying back to Washington, Jackie died with John Jr. and Caroline at her bedside.

Once again, Ted was called on to give a eulogy.

At St. Ignatius Loyola Church on Park Avenue the following Monday, Kennedy reminded the mourners of Jackie's strength after Jack's death.

"During those four endless days in 1963, she held us together as a family and as a country. In large part because of her, we could grieve and then go on. She lifted us up, and, in doubt and darkness, she gave her fellow citizens back their pride as Americans."[7]

"She made a rare and noble contribution to the American spirit," Kennedy added. "She graced our history. And for those of us who knew and loved her, she graced our lives."

She was buried next to President Kennedy in Arlington.

Kennedy's campaign in Massachusetts got off to a slow start that summer.

While Kennedy campaigned on the streets, person by person, in the same way he always had campaigned, Romney used his wealth to stump electronically through massive television buys. And it was working. A fusillade of television advertisements presented Romney as a telegenic, clean-cut scoutmaster and Kennedy as an aging relic who could barely lift himself off a park bench.

"The answers of the past aren't working anymore," Romney announced in his best speech of the campaign, after he had sealed up the Republican nomination. "Thirty-two-year-old social problems like our welfare system that Ted Kennedy helped create just isn't working for us."[8]

When Kennedy's long roster of friends and staffers heard he was in trouble in Massachusetts, they rushed in to help. Carol Mosely-Braun of Illinois, Barbara Boxer and Dianne Feinstein from California and Barbara Mikulski from Baltimore all flew in for a fund-raiser; Bob Shrum, then a high-powered political consultant, jumped into the fray to ramp up Kennedy's TV advertising; David Burke, who had headed ABC News and CBS News after leaving Kennedy's staff, came in to keep Kennedy on message; Ranny Cooper took time off from her New York public relations job to help manage the campaign with Michael Kennedy, Ted's nephew. Dozens of former aides turned up to knock on doors, do advance work for an event or just ride around with Kennedy, keeping him on schedule.

Senator Tom Harkin of Iowa started raising money for him; Hillary Clinton raised $250,000 on September 23; less than a week later, President Clinton raised $750,000. Kennedy also took out a $2 million mortgage on his house to try to match the $8 million war chest Romney had assembled.

A collection of refuseniks whom Ted had gotten out of Russia threw a thank-you rally for him at Brandeis University.

The surprise of the campaign was Vicki, who insisted on aggressive opposition research to fight back against Romney's attacks. Her political instincts proved invaluable as the campaign ramped up.

Bolstered by the support of so many friends, Kennedy began to rise to the occasion, campaigning with verve. He was also starting to enjoy himself as he made the rounds once more. He invoked his long legacy in a speech at Faneuil Hall that was interrupted 57 times by applause. "I stand for the idea that public service can make a difference," Kennedy reminded Massachusetts.

"We ran on who Kennedy is," said Shrum. "We never ran away from that. Healthcare, education, freedom of choice."[9]

New campaign ads emphasized his devotion to constituent services over the years. One ad reminded voters that when a factory closed in Southbridge, Kennedy won the community a Defense Department accounting school. Another round of ads orchestrated by Shrum took advantage of the opposition research Vicki had ordered up, accusing Romney's companies of providing no health insurance for workers, and quoting other workers who had lost their jobs after Romney's firm took over their companies.

On camera, laid-off workers from the Indiana firm AMPAD redefined Romney for Massachusetts voters: "I don't like Romney talking about creating jobs. He took all ours away." "He cut our wages to put money in his pocket." "I would like to say to Mitt Romney—if you think you'd make such a good senator, come out here to Marion, Indiana, and see what your company has done to these people."[10]

A busload of AMPAD workers traveled to Massachusetts to follow Romney around.

By early October, polls were back up. Kennedy was regaining the upper hand.

But then Kennedy got some help he didn't need. Ted's nephew Joe called Romney a member of a "white boys' club" and charged that the Mormon Church "has a belief that blacks are second-class citizens . . . women are second-class citizens." Romney called a press conference to say that Kennedy had betrayed his brother John's legacy. He reminded voters of John's stirring speech to Methodist ministers calling for religious tolerance in 1960. Shrum hastily arranged a conference call and told Ted bluntly that he had to disown Joe's statements.

"Are you saying I should just walk off the field with my tail between my legs?" Kennedy asked Shrum.

"No," Shrum came back immediately, "I'm saying you should put your tail between your legs and *run* off the field as fast as possible."

There was a long silence, Shrum remembers. Then Kennedy told Shrum to get a statement ready reiterating his position that religion had no place in the campaign.

Kennedy called Shrum back a few minutes later to tell him he sometimes felt like firing him. But Kennedy said his brother John had always advised him to have "two or three sons of bitches" around who weren't afraid to disagree.[11]

Kennedy's poll numbers continued to rise, and it began to look fairly certain that he would hold onto his job. That's when Boston's two newspapers, the *Globe* and the *Herald,* joined together in a unique arrangement to demand that the two candidates debate. The campaign had steadfastly avoided debates thus far, seeing no clear advantage if Kennedy was out front. Washington aides argued against debates, too, worried that Kennedy would face embarrassing questions about his personal life and might stumble badly. Shrum agreed. He felt that Kennedy was back in control and didn't need to risk an unformatted appearance.[12] Burke, however, thought Kennedy would trounce Romney in a debate, and Cooper believed Kennedy would lose the *Globe* endorsement if they didn't agree.

Kennedy made the choice to debate. He no longer had anything to hide.

The Kennedy team prepped for five days.[13] Shrum posed questions and David Smith posed as Romney, even imitating some of his mannerisms during mock debates. Shrum had found out about a likely line of attack involving an alleged sweetheart government deal that the Kennedy family had on a commercial property in Washington. The land had been purchased through a blind trust, and Kennedy didn't even know about it. But Shrum was sure Romney would bring it up to counter all the AMPAD criticism. He practiced a response with Kennedy that Shrum thought might just win the debate in a single sentence: "Mr. Romney, my family did not go into public service to make money—and quite frankly we've paid a price."

The night before the debate, a friend who'd been with Kennedy since the beginning of his career snuck extra-wide podiums into historic Faneuil Hall to cloak Kennedy's girth next to the trim and tall Romney.[14]

The next afternoon, Kennedy spent a long time by himself at the JFK library, "communing with ghosts," in the opinion of Dave Burke.[15]

Ironically, Kennedy came into the contest the underdog, just as he had been 32 years earlier in his only other competitive race for Congress. Romney's effort to portray Kennedy as a "tongue-tied, blowzy aging incompetent" with "enough baggage to keep a bellhop busy for life," as *Boston Globe* columnist Bella English put it, had lowered expectations for the incumbent.[16] The national press corps showed up in force, thinking they just might witness the end of Teddy's career. It was a deathwatch again.

Three million people tuned in to watch, more than had watched the Super Bowl in Massachusetts that January.[17] Right from the opening, it was clear that the debate would be a referendum on Kennedy's entire career, on his character, on his trusteeship of the Kennedy legacy. The format allowed reporters to directly question Kennedy about anything. The central query hanging in the balance was one most people never have had to ask themselves: Had his life been *worthwhile*?

The questions about Kennedy's personal failings came early, eliciting boos from the audience. But Kennedy was prepared this time.

"Every day of my life I try to be a better human being, better father, a better son, a better husband, and since my life has changed with Vicki, I believe the people of this state understand that the kind of purpose and direction and new affection and confidence on personal matters has been enormously reinvigorating. And hopefully I'm a better senator."

Romney was asked to respond to the same question, "What is your greatest personal failing?"

He spoke of his missionary work as a young Mormon. "I've spent hundreds of hours in hospitals across the state, working with sick people, consoling them—"

The moderator Ken Bode cut him off: "This was a question about your greatest personal *failing*." The audience broke out laughing.[18]

Something shifted after that. Romney's blow-dried saintliness didn't connect with the crowd in the way that Kennedy's humanity did, and Kennedy dropped his defensiveness afterward. The crowd was on his side again.

Romney attacked Kennedy for the television ads that impugned his business record. "When will it end?" he asked. Kennedy saw an opening to use the line he and Shrum had practiced, and even improve on it. He responded to Romney's complaint by pointing out that Romney had done exactly the same thing with his TV ad accusing the Kennedy family of profiting on the land deal.

"Mr. Romney, the Kennedys are not in public service to make money. We have paid too high a price." At that point, Shrum said, "the ignition of applause almost blew the roof off Faneuil Hall."[19]

Kennedy went on to recount his achievements on health care, woman's rights and civil rights. In the second debate, the breadth of Kennedy's legislative experience shone through even more. Nearly every time Romney offered up a new, innovative proposal, Kennedy talked about how he had been hammering away on similar legislation for years, reciting all the hurdles he'd already cleared out of the way. Kennedy pointed out that a Romney proposal to give tax credits to employers who hire welfare recipients was already on the books. "It's not working very well," he added.[20] The debates turned into a Kennedy tutorial for Romney on the intricacies of effecting change in the complicated skunk works of the Senate.

Romney never recovered.

On the eve of the election, Kennedy spoke at a final, outdoor rally in West Roxbury. "I am looking forward to the outcome of that election tomorrow," Kennedy said. "I want to tell every one of you that the day after tomorrow, I am going to begin again a fight for health care reform, to fight for jobs and programs. I am not going to sleep, I am going to continue that fight until there is the kind of economy, the kind of jobs, the kind of education, the kind of health care, the kind of respect for the individual that is so much a part of our Democratic tradition."

The next day, Massachusetts voted 1,265,997 to 894,000 to give Kennedy six more years to finish what his brothers had started.

★ ★ ★

By January 1995, the time had come for another eulogy, this one for the matriarch of the family. Steely spined, sweet-tempered Rose Kennedy finally succumbed to pneumonia on January 22, at the age of 104.

Thousands of people lined the roads and overpasses as her coffin was conveyed from Hyannis Port to St. Stephen's Church in Boston, where she had been baptized in 1890. Hundreds of mourners stood outside the church listening to the service over loudspeakers.[21]

"I had to walk down the middle of the street there were so many people standing there," remembers Orrin Hatch, who sat in the front rows with the family.

Cardinal Bernard Law made the point in his homily that Rose Kennedy's history had been America's history. "Few lives have been so intertwined with the joys and sorrows of our nation's life as has hers."

In his own eulogy, Ted called his mother "the glue that held the family together. . . . whatever any of us has done—whatever contribution we have made—begins and ends with Rose and Joseph Kennedy. For all of us, Dad was the spark. Mother was the light of our lives. He was our greatest fan. She was our greatest teacher." His voice broke once more when he said he expected that, in heaven, she would "welcome the rest of us home someday."

Kennedy developed a new legislative weapon after 1994: patience. He'd been through so much and survived for so long that he was no longer easily upended by the loss of the majority, a setback on health care, or a new death in the family. For the rest of his years he would focus on solutions more than politics—and more than himself, for that matter.

At the time, he liked to tell a story to emphasize his new attitude:

Three geography teachers were interviewing for a job. The school board had a two-thirds vote requirement to choose someone, and was bitterly split over whether the earth was round or flat. The first teacher goes in to the room to be interviewed and comes out a few minutes later, saying "I didn't get the job." The other two ask why not, and she says, "Well, they asked me if I thought the world was round or the world was flat, and I told them, obviously, the world was round, that's how I'm going to teach it, and they didn't like that."

The next one comes out and says, "Well, they didn't like me either."

"What did you tell them?" the last candidate asks.

"I told them I thought the world was flat."

And the third person walks into the room and says, "I'll teach it anyway you want it, round or flat." She got the job.

"I'm interested . . . in practical solutions, in getting this done," Senator Kennedy told Adam Clymer at the time. "I'm ready to teach it round or teach it flat."

He was unbound from his brothers' legacy after 1994, more a witness to it than a slave of it. Kennedy rose to the height of his powers in the next decade, still driven by his brothers' agenda but no longer imprisoned by it. He was his own man.

When Newt Gingrich took over as Speaker of the House with his ten-point Contract for America the following January, the House passed the whole thing within 100 days. Kennedy organized the resistance in the Senate, and not a single bill made it through.

Kennedy figured out that it was important to be the last person to see Clinton before the president made a decision, and became one of his closest advisers. During Clinton's pivotal budget talks with Congress in the fall of 1998, Kennedy chased him down to make sure he didn't buckle. The standoff with Gingrich marked the beginning of Clinton's own resuscitation.

"You couldn't have a better friend," Clinton said in an interview after Kennedy helped him weather his impeachment trial. "I mean he is loyal. People have been loyal to him, and understanding, and he's had to ask for forgiveness a time or two. His advice is always simple. It's just sort of get up and go to work, just keep going, and remember why you wanted the job in the first place."[22]

Over the next two years, Kennedy won an increase in the minimum wage in a hostile Senate, and he found a way to pass the Kennedy-Kassebaum bill, which guaranteed access to insurance to all who lost or left jobs, or had pre-existing medical conditions.

In 1997, Kennedy and Hatch crafted their bill to insure half of the country's 10 million uninsured children. Kennedy had taken another incremental step toward his elusive goal of health care coverage for all.

While politics became more and more of a science, involving media consultants, attack ads and microtargeted surveys, Kennedy was still working in the medium of *people,* forging coalitions around shared interests and a deep desire to get things done.

"The point is to have some positive impact on people's lives," he told the *Boston Globe.* "The danger as a legislator is that you get involved with just passing the bill. You can lose the context of what passing the bill means, and then you're just shuffling papers, and you lose that emotional contact. Maybe some people could do it. I think I'd run dry pretty quick."

It was Kennedy's emotional acuity that finally redeemed him, paradoxically, since it had been his emotional fragility that had nearly doomed him. His brand of emotionally responsive politics was ultimately his own creation. He could not be the tough war hero like Joe. He could not be the hard-driving, movie-star figurehead for the family like Jack was. He would turn out to be particularly laughable as a moralist—that was Bobby's role. Instead, he found his greatest success in his family and in politics through close, productive relationships.

With Vicki as ballast, his humanity became an epic thing on the Hill in the next decade. When Caroline Kennedy was interviewing candidates for vice president as head of Barack Obama's search committee for a nominee she said she was overwhelmed by stories from people she interviewed about personal acts of kindness done by Ted.

"When my mother died," Orrin Hatch recalls, "Ted and Vicki flew out to the service. I didn't ask them to come. It was in a Mormon Chapel. There were 500 or 600 people there. I was the one who did the sermon that day. And I directed a little bit of it at Ted. I couldn't help but give him a little bit of a hard time, even at my mother's funeral."

"Seventy-eight people died on that 9/11 Boston plane that was going to California that hit the World Trade Center," remembers Ken Feinberg, Kennedy's former chief of staff. "Seventy-eight Massachusetts residents got on that plane at Logan Airport on 9/11, when the plane took off they all died. Senator Kennedy telephoned every single one of the families who lost a loved one on 9/11. And commiserated with them on the phone. Every one."

After a particularly bruising floor fight with Republican Al Simpson, Kennedy went to an antique shop to get Simpson a gift.

"He's a classical old collector of ship etchings and portraiture, loves antiques, knows 'em." Simpson recalled in a telephone interview with the author in 2008. "He found a 44-star flag. There were very few of them because five states came into the Union within eight months after that. He framed it and sent it to me, and wrote: "'To the Kid from Cody, a great friend and a great senator even if he still seems to be playing with 44 stars in his flag.'"

Always generous, newly stabilized, Kennedy began in the 1990s to add a fresh piece of inspiration to the Kennedy legacy: the virtue of perseverance. Big brother John had challenged people to do something for their country. Bobby had called on them to care for the dispossessed. By the example of his durability, Ted exhorted them to never, ever quit.

"He was forced from the rhetoric of moral outrage and into the incremental nitty-gritty of social justice," wrote Charles Pierce of the *Boston Globe*. "He learned to plod, because soaring made him look ridiculous."

"It's really 3 yards and a cloud of dust with him," said his son Patrick.

Before the transformative decade came to a close, Ted was called upon to give yet another eulogy for a family member. One hundred and five Kennedys were gathering at the Cape for the wedding of his brother Bobby's last child, Rory, when John Jr.'s Piper Saratoga airplane went missing on a moonless night. As the family waited for news, the wedding tent was converted into an outdoor chapel, hosting Sunday Mass and prayers for the missing. There was no celebration that weekend. Instead, television anchors lamented the probable loss of "America's prince" and the brightest hope of his generation of Kennedys.

The wreckage of the plane wasn't found until the following Wednesday, off Martha's Vineyard, where John and his wife, Carolyn, had been flying her sister, Lauren Bissette. There were no survivors.

"Ted was John's dad in every way," said Al Simpson. "And Ted would say to him, 'Now don't fly your damn plane to meetings in Boston by following the coast.'" But John had not always heeded his uncle's advice.

John had served with Ted on the board of the Institute of Politics at Harvard's John F. Kennedy School of Government. Many in the family believed he was the rising political star in the family, blessed with the good looks and charisma of his father. There had even been talk that John might inherit Ted's seat one day.

Once again, obituaries were written for the Kennedy legacy and the family's impact on American history. Once again, a vague dream of Camelot's restoration was dashed.

A private Mass was held at St. Thomas More Church in New York on Friday, July 23. President Clinton, Hillary and their daughter Chelsea were among the 500 mourners.

"We dared to think," Ted said at the conclusion of his eulogy, quoting Yeats, "that *this* John Kennedy would live to comb gray hair, with his beloved Carolyn by his side.

"But, like his father, he had every gift but length of years."

Of all the sons of Camelot, only Ted Kennedy seems to have been granted that particular bequest.

15

HIS FINEST HOUR

I look forward to a great future for America—a future in which our country will match its military strength with our moral restraint, its wealth with our wisdom, its power with our purpose. . . . And I look forward to an America which commands respect throughout the world not only for its strength but for its civilization as well.

—*John F. Kennedy, a month before he was killed*

In November 2003, Ted Kennedy drove out to Arlington Cemetery, where his two brothers are buried, to attend the funeral of a Bedford, Massachusetts, boy killed in the Iraq War. It was a crisp fall day, and the leaves were mostly gone from the 100-year-old oak trees. The necklaces of white markers looked as if they continued on over the gray hills into infinity. In the span of 45 minutes, Kennedy heard "Taps" in the distance at least eight times.[1] Twenty-eight funerals would be held that day. "You're there, you get caught up in the emotion, and you know what's going on," Kennedy said.

Private First Class John D. Hart always knew he wanted to be a soldier. He had belonged to Bedford High's rifle team and junior ROTC program. Longtime friend Ben Chambers recalls sneaking out with Hart at 2 A.M. to plaster Army stickers around town. Hart enlisted in September 2002, less than a year after 9/11, because he wanted to make a difference. He joined the 173rd Airborne Brigade in northern Iraq in the summer of 2003. Trained as a paratrooper, he was immediately thrown into ground patrols instead. Several firefights later, he'd earned a Combat Infantryman Badge. He would go on to earn the Bronze Star. His courage wasn't a thing anyone questioned, but John still had a problem with the Army. He didn't think the brass was keeping the grunts safe enough. He called home later that fall and told his father, Brian, that the Humvees he was driving in didn't have bulletproof shielding or metal doors. In some cases they didn't have any doors at all. He asked his father for help getting more body armor for soldiers, and armor for the Humvees. "As soon as Brian hung up he told me what John had said," recalls Brian's wife, Alma Hart, "and he's pacing back and forth across the living room, [asking] who should we contact what can we do that won't have feedback on John without getting John into trouble."[2]

A week later, just after John's twentieth birthday, a 6 A.M. knock awakened Brian and Alma Hart. A policeman, a local priest, and an Army officer were at the door to deliver the news. "When he died, all his ammunition had been spent," the unit commander had written in a letter to Hart's parents. Hart's convoy was ambushed near Kirkuk, and John died when a hail of bullets hit him inside his Humvee. "Your son gave everything he had for the safety of others. . . . As a commander, I struggle to find words that adequately capture the depth to which we honor Private First Class Hart."

"John was dead," said Alma, "and it was, OK, we can do anything we need to do now. They can't hurt us any more than this." Brian Hart translated his grief and anger into action. He learned all he could about soldiers killed in unarmored Humvees. He found out which defense contractors made add-on armor. He pulled together a network of soldiers, families and defense contractors to lobby for armored Humvees. And that day in Arlington, he talked to Kennedy.

"The Kennedys had been a gold star family before I was born," said Brian. Ted "remembers where his mother was, where his father was, when they came and told him his brother Joseph was killed. We share a wound that doesn't heal. And a deep abiding love for this country."

Kennedy agreed to call hearings, and within six months, all troops in Iraq had body armor. "To that I owe the senator," said Hart. The Marine Corps ordered $9 million worth of bulletproof Humvee door panels after the hearings, and the Army doubled its order of heavily armored Humvees from its contractor. Hart went to work after that getting armor for trucks driven by National Guard soldiers. Then he learned the Army had a shortage of in-field tourniquets, which the Army's own studies showed could prevent 15 percent of deaths in the field. With a push from Hart, the army started issuing them to every solider in 2006. Kennedy successfully attached an amendment to the $81.26 billion emergency supplemental passed in October 2006 that gave the Pentagon $213 million to continue producing the highest number of armored Humvees possible.

"These people have suffered as much as people can suffer, the loss of a child," Kennedy told a *Washington Post* reporter, his voice trembling. "And they've turned this grief into the ultimate love of country. Nothing could mean more to me than this."

Kennedy has dozens of similar stories he could tell, but Hart's stands out for him. The video tribute at the convention in Denver included a brief interview with Hart as a testimonial to Ted. The father's story in a way mirrors Kennedy's own lifelong struggle to alchemize tragedy into salvation for others. A day before the invasion began in March 2003, Kennedy introduced a bill to guarantee that families of reservists and National Guard members would continue to receive health coverage despite being called for active duty. On May 22, 2003, he and Senator John Kerry co-sponsored an amendment that ended the Army's ban on paying for relatives to visit their wounded loved ones. Kennedy was inspired by the story of Sergeant Vanessa Turner, whose family couldn't visit her after she developed a life-threatening illness while serving in the Gulf. Kennedy was determined to ensure, in whatever way he could, that servicemen and women got what they needed.[3]

But none of his humanitarian efforts were what Kennedy was proudest of when it came to the Iraq War. Rather, it was his unrelenting, vocal opposition to the war from the beginning that he was proudest of. In 2007, Kennedy said: "My vote against this misbegotten war is the best vote I have cast in the United States Senate since I was elected in 1962."

On the August day in 2002 when Vice President Dick Cheney began the country's march to war, he did so without showing President Bush the speech he would use as his starting gun. When Cheney told the president he would be explaining the administration's new post-9/11 military strategy at the national convention of the Veterans of Foreign Wars in Nashville, Bush merely responded, "Don't get me into trouble." Standing beneath giant hanging stars in front of a curtain drenched in red, white and blue light, Cheney told the gathered vets that the best way to prevent another 9/11 was to attack the world's problem areas *before* they attacked the United States. "The risks of inaction are far greater than the risk of action," he said. And his suggested first target for action was Iraq.

Cheney quoted Richard Nixon's secretary of state, Henry Kissinger, saying that "the imminence of proliferation of weapons of mass destruction, the huge dangers it involves, the rejection of a viable inspection system, and the demonstrated hostility of Saddam Hussein combine to produce an imperative for preemptive action." If the United States could have preempted 9/11, we would have, no question, Cheney told the vets. "Should we be able to prevent another, much more devastating attack, we will, no question. This nation will not live at the mercy of terrorists or terror regimes." Cheney was articulating Bush's new national security strategy, which declared that the threats from weapons of mass destruction and global terrorist networks were so novel and dangerous that the country should "not hesitate to act alone, if necessary, to exercise our right of self-defense by acting preemptively." The Bush Doctrine was born, and the veterans applauded enthusiastically.

Bush's own secretary of state, General Colin Powell, and others in the State Department said later they were "blindsided" by Cheney's speech "and were just as surprised as everyone else," according to one administration source.[4] Ted Kennedy was also taken aback, warning the president that no preventive action should be taken against Iraq without the consent of Congress, which Bush agreed to seek a few days later. As he often would in the unfolding Iraq debate, Kennedy made reference to his brothers as a precedent for caution on Iraq. "Forty years ago, we had the Cuban Missile Crisis," Kennedy said.[5] "The urgency in Iraq is not more urgent than that which faced us forty years ago." President Kennedy "presented that evidence and gained overwhelming political support. It seems to me that that's the clear precedent for this now."

Kennedy believed his brothers—still his historic touchstone 34 years after their deaths—had found a better response to a new kind of threat in October 1962 than Bush had found. John and Bobby had to create a new, "more enlightened foreign policy" to deal with the changed world after World War II. That foreign policy combined military, diplomatic and economic components. Deterrence and containment were adopted to keep the Soviet Union in check. A preventive "invasion" of Cuba had been urged by some military leaders at the time of the Cuban Missile Crisis, but John Kennedy had rejected their advice. Kennedy came to believe, after the Bay of Pigs fiasco, that the standard military options did not work in the Cold War.

Ted Kennedy believed the country needed to make a similar shift after 9/11. "September 11 taught us that we are vulnerable, not invincible," he said. "We learned in that instant that we were no longer immune from the festering hatred of peoples ten thousand miles away. With such new and deadly enemies able to reach our shores, we needed a new definition of national security. Instead, the military aspects of the War on Terror became the single-minded focus of our foreign policy," he added. "Rather than looking forward and developing a new concept of national security, we reverted defensively and fearfully to policies of earlier times."[6]

Kennedy didn't think Bush and Cheney had made a persuasive case for war yet, but after Cheney's speech he thought he had to act fast. He urgently began hosting a series of dinners for generals, defense department officials and other military thinkers. He wanted to hear from all sides as the debate heated up. Kennedy also pushed for Senate Armed Services Committee hearings on the subject of Iraq. In four public hearings held in September, several retired four-star Army and Marine Corps generals cautioned about attacking Iraq at that time. "I was inclined to support the administration when we started the hearings in the Armed Services Committee," Kennedy said. But "it was enormously interesting to me that those that had been—that were in the armed forces that had served in combat—were universally opposed to going," he added. "I mean we had Wes Clark testify in opposition to going to war at that time. You had General [Anthony] Zinni. You had [Major] General [William] Nash. You had this series of different military officials, a number of whom had been involved in the Gulf I War, others involved in Kosovo and had distinguished records in Vietnam, battle-hardened combat military figures. And, virtually all of them said no, this is not going to work."[7] General Joseph Hoar, the former commander of Central Command, told members a case had not been made to connect Al Qaeda and Iraq. General Clark, former Supreme Allied Commander Europe, testified that Iran had closer ties to terrorism than Iraq. He pointed out that Iran has a nuclear weapons development program, and it already has a missile that could reach Israel.

The public hearings went largely unnoticed by the media. Some of the testimony was classified at the time for national security reasons, including Secretary of Defense Donald Rumsfeld's statement, "there are weapons of mass destruction north, south, east and west of Baghdad."

In response to that statement, the chairman of the committee, Senator Carl Levin (D-MI), asked Rumsfeld, "Well, we're now providing this information to the inspectors aren't we?"

"Oh, yes, we're providing that," Rumsfeld answered.

"But are they finding anything?" Levin replied.

"No."

Kennedy kept asking Rumsfeld, "Well, if they're not finding any of the weapons of mass destruction, where is the imminent threat to the United States security?"

Rumsfeld insisted that the weapons were there, they were just being moved around. He said intelligence had been passed along to teams of inspectors, but by the time inspectors got to the sites, word had leaked out and the weapons were hidden.

"It didn't make sense," Kennedy said later.

If the testimony at the hearings was better publicized, Kennedy thought, more people might be persuaded to proceed cautiously, the way he had been. He told his staff to gear up for a series of speeches on the Iraq issue. He planned to tell the world about the generals' testimony.

On September 19, the president sent to Congress a two-page proposal for an Iraq War resolution. His approval rating hovered right around 80 percent at the time. Anything he proposed was likely to be popular with a still-frightened America.

During an Armed Services Committee hearing that same day, Kennedy began to publicly express a host of doubts. "As of today, many questions remain unanswered. Is war the only option? How much support will we have in the international community? How will war affect our global war against terrorism? How long will the United States need to stay in Iraq? How many casualties will there be? War must always be a last resort, not the first resort."[8] Amid worries on both sides that the debate over Iraq was being politicized to win votes in the congressional elections that fall, Kennedy announced that he would make a major address on the issue on September 27, the Friday before debate was scheduled in Congress on Bush's resolution. Kennedy had urged caution only in sound bytes and floor statements thus far; he hadn't addressed the issue in a substantive way yet. His speech at Johns Hopkins University's School of Advanced International Studies was the first of dozens on Iraq policy he would make over the course of the next five years. His goal was to change the public debate about the war.

Kennedy was introduced at Johns Hopkins by Francis Fukuyama, who had been the first prominent conservative intellectual to question the Bush Doctrine of preventive war. When Kennedy took the podium, he wasted no time getting to his point. "America should not go to war against Iraq unless and until other reasonable alternatives are exhausted," he began. "I am convinced that President Bush believes genuinely in the course he urges upon us." However, the president and his supporters must "resist any temptation to convert patriotism into politics. It is possible to love America while concluding that it is not now wise to go to war. . . . We must ask what is right for country and not party."[9]

Kennedy argued that the Bush administration should first win a new resolution from the United Nations demanding that Iraq give UN inspectors unconditional access to suspected weapons development sites. He referenced the comments of the generals he'd listened to during his dinners: "It's an open secret in Washington that the national uniformed military leadership is skeptical about the wisdom of war with Iraq. They share the concern that it may adversely affect the ongoing war against Al Qaeda and the continuing effort in Afghanistan by draining resources and armed forces already stretched so thin that many reservists have been called for a second year of duty and record numbers of service members have been kept on active duty beyond their obligated service." Quoting Armed Services Committee testimony by Generals Hoar and Clark, he warned that a war in Iraq would, in Clark's words, "supercharge recruiting for Al Qaeda." Kennedy then made the case that, even if Saddam Hussein had weapons of mass destruction, that fact alone did not warrant going to war. "We have known for many years that Saddam Hussein is seeking and developing weapons of mass destruction," he said. "But information from the intelligence community over the past six months does not point to Iraq as an imminent threat . . . or a major proliferator." The speech was a clarion call for caution from a man who had lost a brother in a war, watched intently as another brother averted a nuclear war and helped another brother make the case for the immorality of the Vietnam War. It was a passionate argument that the idea of preventive war defied America's historical traditions. Every possible problem Kennedy raised in his speech—from America's loss of esteem in the world, to the possibility that Iraq could become a hotbed of terrorism after an invasion—emerged in the aftermath of the invasion.

But nobody listened.

Two days before Kennedy gave his speech, the *Washington Post* had observed in a front-page article how dozens of congressional Democrats "are frustrated with their leadership for rushing to embrace President Bush's Iraqi war resolution and fostering an impression the party overwhelmingly backs a unilateral strike against Saddam Hussein." But when Kennedy stepped forward and answered that call for leadership, the *Post* devoted one sentence—36 words—to his address deep inside the A section. (Michael Getler, the *Washington Post*'s ombudsman, later took the paper to task for downplaying the speech.) On NBC's *Nightly News,* just 32 words from the Kennedy address were excerpted. On ABC's *World News Tonight,* it was 31 words. And on the CBS *Evening News,* 40 words.[10] Two days after the speech, Iraq was the main topic on the Sunday talk shows: NBC's *Meet the Press,* CBS's *Face the Nation* and ABC's *This Week.*[11] But Kennedy's speech never came up. The political press's enormous interest in Kennedy since the news of his brain tumor makes its snub of him in 2002 that much more haunting. The press, like many members of Congress and a majority of people across the country, were swept up in a patriotic fervor. A call to action had much more resonance than a call to measured inaction after 9/11. Senate majority leader Daschle summed up the mood of the country right before the vote when he said it was important "to speak with one voice at this critical moment." Many journalists would later defend their coverage during the buildup to war by claiming there wasn't much opposition to cover. Liberal Democrats like Kennedy were dismissed at the time as out of step, a waning force in American politics, a voice that didn't deserve as much credence apparently as the "expert" retired generals who populated so many of the cable news broadcasts during the lead-up to the war. MSNBC's Chris Matthews grouped Ted with several Hollywood stars when he reported on the speech: "Tonight on *Hardball* Barbra Streisand, Senator Ted Kennedy, and Tom Cruise speak out as debate picks up in Washington and in Hollywood over whether this country should attack Iraq."

"Looking back, a key turning point during that public rush to war was Kennedy's fervent and thoughtful speech," wrote political columnist Eric Boehlert. "It was a turning point because it highlighted, months before the invasion even took place, how the press was going to deal with high-profile, articulate critics of Bush's war policy. The press was going to downplay them, marginalize them and ignore them. Even if those critics included high-wattage political stars like Ted Kennedy."[12]

The prescience of Kennedy's stand against the rush to war seems that much more original in hindsight. None of the other Democratic leaders argued against the war as powerfully as Kennedy did. John Kerry, John Edwards, Hillary Clinton, Joe Biden, Steny Hoyer, Richard Gephardt, John Murtha and Tom Daschle all supported the Bush resolution, a choice most of them later regretted. Kennedy has no regrets about his stand.

Kennedy, Armed Services Committee Chairman Levin and Senator Bob Graham (D-FL) led the opening-day opposition to the White House–backed resolution. Senator John W. Warner of Virginia, the ranking Republican on the Armed Services Committee, was on the floor leading the charge for it. Kennedy tried unsuccessfully to set up a meeting of Senate Democrats to write a unified alternative proposal, but the effort fell on deaf ears. As the debate unspooled in the Senate over the course of the next week, Kennedy repeatedly took to the floor to make eloquent speeches about the gravity of making a decision to go to war. But the country was still in the grip of a post-9/11 fear, and attacking Iraq seemed to many people—and a majority of senators—the best way to lance that fear. At 1:15 A.M. on October 11, just a few hours after the House gave its assent, the Senate voted 77–23 to authorize President Bush to use the military "as he determines to be necessary and appropriate." Kennedy's own son, Representative Patrick Kennedy of Rhode Island, cast one of the pro-war votes in the House.

Eight Democratic senators had opposed the resolution before Kennedy's speech. That number rose to 23 on the day of the vote, a significant increase over the week, but far too little too late. "I think if . . . we had waited another ten days, I think you may have had a different story," Kennedy said.[13] "The sad aspect was that this administration, this president, insisted that we have the vote prior to the election." Kennedy was certain that Bush wanted to use the vote to help win the congressional elections in 2002, pointing out that Bush's father had waited until after the election to hold a vote on the Gulf War resolution in 1990. Less than a month after the vote, Republicans regained control of the Senate and expanded their majority in the House. "The Iraq card had been played successfully," Kennedy commented later.

Kennedy never ratcheted down his opposition to the war. "This is the wrong war at the wrong time," he said that spring at the National Press Club. "There was no imminent threat," Kennedy said on September 18, 2003, labeling the entire war "a fraud." "This was made up in Texas, announced in January to the Republican leadership that the war was going to take place and was going to be good politically." He accused the administration of "bribing" foreign nations to send troops to Iraq. In a speech on the Senate floor, Kennedy accused the administration of telling "lie after lie after lie after lie." In early 2004, Kennedy became the first senator to say the Iraq War was "George Bush's Vietnam." Later in 2004, he called Iraq "one of the worst blunders in the history of U.S. foreign policy." He also became one of the first senators to call for Defense Secretary Donald Rumsfeld's resignation.

The response Kennedy elicited was often scathing. "He's been saying some vicious and nasty stuff," former senator Alan Simpson, a Wyoming Republican and a close Kennedy friend, said at the time. "I'm appalled. These quotes are just plain nasty and, frankly, out of character for Ted." Columnist Charles Krauthammer wrote that "Kennedy's statement marks a new stage in losing it: transition to derangement." Noemie Emery, a contributing editor to the *The Weekly Standard*, linked Kennedy's views with those of his father when he was ambassador to England and supported a policy of appeasement with Hitler. "After a 60-year detour, Ted Kennedy has brought the famous family name back around to where his father disastrously left it: a name that stands for retreat and bad judgment," Emery wrote. "Appeasement, it seems, is a recessive gene that afflicts only some among family members. Ted Kennedy is not his brother's brother, but he is his father's son."

Kennedy was unfazed by the criticism and lack of support among fellow Democrats. He continued to speak out and press his views in press conferences, floor speeches and interviews. He wrote op-eds for the *Washington Post*, the *Los Angeles Times* and the *Boston Globe*. Kennedy's relentless opposition provided cover for other Democrats and war critics who gradually came out with softer critiques. Kennedy's constant tugging at the leading edge of dissent eventually widened the debate over the war, just as he hoped it would. He had a big microphone and he knew how to use it to push public opinion. In private, he warned other Democrats that their failure to strongly oppose Iraq could eventually cost them with voters. He was dead on.

U.S. missiles began raining down on Baghdad late on March 19, 2003. By April 24, Kennedy was already predicting that U.S. troops probably would need to stay in Iraq for "a minimum" of three to five years. Though Kennedy waged his opposition mostly in the court of public opinion during the war, he found incremental ways to legislate against Bush's Iraq policy once the war was under way. Days before the fighting began, Kennedy introduced a Senate resolution requiring Bush "to come back to Congress and present convincing evidence of an imminent threat before we send troops to war in Iraq." The vote failed, but Kennedy felt it laid the groundwork for future votes of its kind in later years. On July 16, Kennedy introduced an amendment in the Senate to order Bush to report to Congress within 30 days on his plans to internationalize postwar operations. Kennedy was one of only 12 senators to vote against the first, $87 billion supplemental to continue to fund the war, arguing that pulling the purse strings tight was the only way to force a change in Bush's policies. In September 2003, Kennedy drafted an amendment to cut off funds for military operations in Iraq and Afghanistan if the administration failed to give Congress a concrete plan for ending the occupation.

Some of Kennedy's efforts will improve oversight of future wars. At the end of 2005, Kennedy began working on an amendment to require portions of the top-secret Presidential Daily Briefs describing national security threats to be submitted to the congressional intelligence committees. Later, Kennedy pushed through an amendment that required an updated National Intelligence Estimate (NIE) on Iraq. The NIE collected together the conclusions of all 16 American intelligence services about the state of the war. When the NIE was released in early February 2006, it changed the public debate over Iraq. The report said Iraq was getting worse, not better, that the country was "in a rapid downward spiral toward chaos and anarchy." "The nation's intelligence experts have confirmed the nightmare scenario for our troops in Iraq," Kennedy said. "The country is sliding deeper into the abyss of civil war and our brave men and women are caught in the middle of it. . . . It's abundantly clear that what we need is not a troop surge, but a diplomatic surge, working closely with other countries in the region." Future senators and representatives are sure to demand updated NIE reports because of the precedent Kennedy set.

In late 2006 and early 2007, Kennedy also began to chair hearings on the massive Iraqi refugee crisis that developed during the war, demanding that the United States do more than take the 433 refugees it had allowed in since 2003. Less than a month after the hearings opened, the administration began developing a plan with the United Nations that would resettle 5,000 Iraqis in the United States.

On November 7, 2006, Kennedy won his eighth term in the Senate with just under 70 percent of the vote. "I'm going to keep running until I get the hang of it," he joked after casting his own vote. He punctuated his acceptance speech that night by declaring "I'll never give in until we change our course in Iraq." Fueled by anger over the costs of the Iraq War, voters across the country gave Democrats back control of the House and Senate that night. Kennedy's minority view had become the majority view. Normally hostile *Boston Herald* columnist Wayne Woodlief called Kennedy "the prophet."[14]

Kennedy had combined legislative activism with a forceful public relations campaign against the war, but he'd also been extraordinarily supportive of individual soldiers and their needs. No one else provided the same kind of sustained, multifaceted leadership against the war. Because of the catbird seat he occupies in Washington, Kennedy may have been the country's premier opposition leader during the period. But did it do any good?

Several Congress watchers believe Kennedy's articulate opposition may very well have been the flap of the butterfly wing that caused a major shift in public opinion against the war. Kennedy led the way out of a post-9/11 fear of challenging Bush to a much-needed national accounting for the war's failures. Kennedy saw what was coming earlier and with more clarity than nearly anyone else in a position of power in the country. Marcus Raskin, one of John F. Kennedy's national security aides, believes all three Kennedy brothers had a rare ability to see around corners when it came to issues of war and peace. "The Kennedys had the capacity of seeing the continuity of things and the moments of possible quantum leaps and change," said Raskin. "That is what is so astonishing about Ted Kennedy, and about the direction Jack and Bobby wanted to go." They all understood, Raskin believes, that the United States may have become too much of a warrior state at heart. The Kennedys all shared a fear that with so many foreign commitments to uphold, the country might forever be imprisoned by its military identity abroad. They all longed for a country defined more by its gentler, nobler attributes than by its

warrior ones. "Their opposition to war came out of an existential understanding of the pain of war," Raskin said. "What Bobby and Jack were feeling
existentially, Teddy was able to turn that into public policy and a stance."

Ted Kennedy ultimately may have regarded his stand against the Iraq
War as his finest moment because it neatly fit the definition of political
courage employed by someone he's always looked up to. "In whatever arena
of life one may meet the challenge of courage, whatever may be the sacrifices
he faces if he follows his conscience—the loss of his friends, his fortune, his
contentment, even the esteem of his fellow men—each man must decide for
himself the course he will follow," John Kennedy wrote in *Profiles in Courage*.
All of the examples of courage cited in his book are elected officials who, acting in accord with their conscience, pursued a larger vision of the national,
state or local interest in opposition to popular opinion or powerful pressures
from their constituents.

Jack probably meant someone like Ted.

16

THE FIGHT OF HIS LIFE

Of all the forms of inequality, injustice in health care is the most shocking and inhumane.

—Martin Luther King Jr.

On an ice-cold Boston evening in January 2008, Alan Khazei was desperately trying to buttonhole Ted Kennedy at a reception for ActBlue, a Democratic fund-raising organization. Khazei had known Kennedy for 20 years, ever since the idealistic Harvard grad had started a group called City Year, a youth service corps in Boston that later became the inspiration for the AmeriCorps volunteer service program Bill Clinton created in the 1990s. Sponsored largely by private businesses, City Year sent volunteer tutors and mentors into failing schools to try to turn them around. Kennedy had been a booster from the start. He was the commencement speaker at the group's very first graduation ceremony for 50 volunteers, held in an abandoned warehouse on the South Boston waterfront. Khazei had just started a new service organization, Be the Change, and he and his group had a big, new, idealistic idea to run up the flagpole with Kennedy. But a crowd of people still swarmed around the senator, each of whom was trying to grab a few minutes of face time. Khazei knew that if he got his chance he would only have a few minutes, and he'd better be persuasive. Finally the crowd parted ever so slightly and Khazei pulled Kennedy aside.

The senator remembered Khazei right away and asked him how his new organization was faring. Khazei told him the first thing his group wanted to do was a big campaign to try to bring together the country's national service programs and dramatically expand their scope. Khazei thought the time was ripe because millennials were volunteering in record numbers and JFK-inspired, civic-minded baby boomers were starting to retire. There were a million more volunteers in 2007 than in 2002. Khazei believed Americans wanted to do more than just shop in support of their country. The pendulum had swung, he told Kennedy. Public service was cool again.

"We think it would be terrific if you and Senator Hatch could partner on a new piece of legislation that could really take this whole thing to scale," Khazei pitched.

Kennedy stopped. There was a flash to his eyes. He squared his frame and focused completely in on Khazei, ignoring all the people around who were trying to get his attention.

"OK," he said emphatically. "This is great. I'm all for it. I'll do it. I want to move it. I've been wanting to do something new on service for a while. This is the right time. We won't be able to get this done until there's a new president but we have to get it moving now. I'd love to work with Orrin. He's a good friend of mine. He's a great partner on this. Call Michael Myers. And go see him right away."

Michael Myers was Kennedy's staff director on the Health, Education, Labor and Pensions Committee and a loyal adviser for 20 years. Khazei waited two days and then called for Myers and left a message. Myers called him right back.

"Well, I'm actually coming to Washington next week," Khazei said.

"Well, what time can you come in?" Myers asked.

"Well, since I'm gonna be there, can I come in at 11?"

"Sure," said Myers. "See you then."

And that was that. When Khazei went to see Michael two days later, two other fully briefed staff people were with him. "They were all teed up," remembers Khazei.

"We spoke to Senator Kennedy," Myers told Khazei. "Senator Kennedy wants to do this. What do you need? How do we get this done?"

Khazei laid out the whole premise of his campaign, that he hoped to hold a summit of service organizations in Boston and form a giant nation-wide coalition, ServiceNation, that inspired and encouraged thousands more people to engage in public service.

"But the heart of that strategy is getting this bill," Khazei told them, "because we need a vehicle to rally people around. So there is something tangible we can fight for."

There wasn't a briefing; there was no memo by his staff. "It was all just Boom. Boom. Boom. Boom. Boom. And then go," said Khazei, snapping his fingers as he recalls Kennedy's mode of operation. Khazei didn't really have to explain the idea at all, since it had been Kennedy's brother John who first proposed such a program. Service was a cause near and dear to the hearts of the Kennedys. For Ted, it was holy writ.

"Every battle is won or lost before it's fought," says Khazei, quoting Sun Tzu from *The Art of War*. "What Sun Tzu meant by that is it's not the actual fighting it's the preparation, it's the training, it's what kind of arms you have, all that, and that's Kennedy. He's thinking way ahead. He's thinking to the endgame, and he's way ahead of everybody. He's got a good sense of where the country's at and he understands the legislative process, and that it takes time."

Kennedy's staffers got together right away with Hatch's staff and started working on the beginning elements of a bill. Khazei and his staff started calling service groups, asking them: "Do you want to be part of this new Service-Nation coalition? Do you want to be part of this movement to bring service to scale? Do you want to be part of a service summit?"

Khazei's staff and Kennedy's staff worked hand in glove in the following months, meeting with a wide array of service groups to find out what they thought a national service bill should include.

"We asked service groups, 'What do you think?'" said Khazei. "What's the best way to do service learning? What are the best ideas to promote full-time service? What are the best ideas to promote volunteering?

"The great thing about Kennedy was, they didn't go off in a corner and say We're going to go figure this out. They said Give us your best thinking on this legislation."

Khazei saw Kennedy three times between January and May, and every time Kennedy sought Khazei out.

"I'm talking to Orrin," Kennedy told him. "We're moving it. We're negotiating now but it's going to get done."

Hatch and Kennedy incorporated many of the groups' ideas directly into the bill. They came up with a policy agenda that was endorsed by more than 100 organizations. They had buy-in, and a brand-new coalition behind it.

The key to the whole effort, Khazei said, was Kennedy's commitment. "Because I was able to go back to the coalition and say, 'We're going to have a new bill. It'll be Kennedy and Hatch. Senator Kennedy has made this a priority. He's gonna fight for it."

Because Kennedy had been working on national service for so many years, he had credibility with the groups. His long involvement gave him clout.

"People were saying, Kennedy's involved. This can really happen. Let's go," said Khazei.

Kennedys and their cohorts had been involved in every major effort over the last 40 years to create and expand national service programs. Acting on an idea of John Kennedy's, Eunice's husband, Sargent Shriver, founded a domestic version of the Peace Corps, Volunteers in Service to America (VISTA), while he was heading up President Johnson's War on Poverty in 1965. VISTA was later incorporated into the larger AmeriCorps network of service organizations created by Ted Kennedy and President Clinton in 1993. Shriver, father of California's first lady, Maria Shriver, also helped to found the HeadStart program in 1965 to give low-income children a chance to go to preschool.

National service went out of style for 20 years after the idealistic 1960s, until a Republican, President George H. W. Bush, took office in 1989. When Bush proposed his "Thousand Points of Light" program to encourage more volunteerism in the country, most Democrats scoffed. They ridiculed the proposal as empty rhetoric and a feeble substitute for government programs that served the needy. But Kennedy thought Bush was sincere.

"The old ideas are new again," Bush said on the campaign trail, "because they are not old, they are timeless: duty, sacrifice, commitment, and a patriotism that finds its expression in taking part and pitching in." Bush was singing Kennedy's tune. Kennedy reached out to the president, embracing the idea as a continuation of the tradition started by JFK and Shriver. Kennedy promised to try to win approval for the program in the Senate if Bush widened his net and linked Points of Light with other national service programs Kennedy cared about, such as City Year. With Kennedy's help, Bush set up a Points of Light nonprofit foundation and institute that supported volunteer-based organizations. The foundation created a network of volunteer centers around the country that acted as community hubs and clearinghouses for volunteers.

"That's when the modern national service movement began," said Khazei.

Building on the success of Points of Light, President Clinton created the Corporation for National and Community Service (CNCS) to provide grants that support service and volunteering. And again, Kennedy was the legislative leader. "Kennedy was the one who wrote the legislation, built the consensus to get it passed," said Khazei. "Obviously Clinton championed it as a presidential candidate and then as president. But again, it was Kennedy who put the legislation together. People don't even know this. He's not out there saying This is my bill. Because that's how he gets things done. If people actually knew . . . he wouldn't be as effective. He operates this way on everything. His fingerprints are everywhere."

CNCS became the umbrella program for service programs created by Kennedy, Bush and Clinton, including AmeriCorps, Learn and Serve America, Senior Corps and Freedom Corps. Harris Wofford, an adviser to John F. Kennedy who was instrumental in the creation of the Peace Corps, joined the Senate representing Pennsylvania in 1991 and helped to enact the legislation that created AmeriCorps, which employs 40,000 volunteers. A legacy had come back to life.

By 2008, Khazei was thinking big. He believed a national wave was building and Kennedy and Hatch were in a perfect position to ride it. He envisioned 200,000 people joining a national service program instead of 40,000. Maybe more. He envisioned universities building service into their students' experience. He imagined support for social entrepreneurs determined to do more than earn a buck. He saw corporations offering their employees paid leave for service.

The Serve America Act that Hatch and Kennedy came up with would provide $5 billion over five years for one-year stipends to people of all ages willing to do community service work in health, education, the environment and antipoverty efforts. Volunteers would also earn tuition credits for college.

The bill is essentially an expansion of AmeriCorps that creates five new distinct "corps": Education Corps, focused on mentoring to reduce dropout rates; Healthy Futures Corp, to spur enrollment in health-care programs and provide transportation for the sick and elderly; Clean Energy Service Corps, to help make the homes of low-income Americans more energy efficient; Opportunity Corps, to teach the unemployed new skills, through financial literacy programs and building new homes; and Reserve Corps, which would be called in to help out in the case of a disaster.

The Kennedy-Hatch bill would also encourage social entrepreneurs to create their own programs, allowing them to apply for "fellowships."

Both Barack Obama and John McCain promised Kennedy and Hatch they would be cosponsors, which meant the bill had a huge bipartisan shot at success in the next Congress no matter who won the presidency. "Service," Obama said, "will be the cause of my presidency."

Things were barreling along toward a grand fulfillment of John Kennedy's original vision in late spring of 2008. It had begun to look like national service was an idea whose time had come—or come back—and nothing would stand in its way. And then its greatest living champion, the one man who could guide it through the thickets of Congress to the promised land, suddenly collapsed on the floor of his home in Cape Cod.

★ ★ ★

Vicki Kennedy knew in a split second that something was gravely wrong that morning. She quickly dialed 911 on her cell phone, but she also knew the emergency call would tip off the media. Sitting at her husband's side, Vicki kept making calls as she waited for the ambulance, summoning her two children and Ted's three to the hospital so they would be there before the cameras arrived.[1] She also arranged for the senator to be transported from the hospital on the Cape to Massachusetts General Hospital in Boston by helicopter, and called Kennedy's Senate staff to put in place a crisis management team. And she called his closest friends.

During the course of the day, members of his family rushed quickly to Kennedy's side in Boston, pushing through the throngs of reporters and cameras outside the hospital or slipping into a side entrance by Storrow Drive. Ted Jr., Patrick and Kara were there almost immediately, as were Vicki's two children, Curran and Caroline Raclin, and Kennedy's niece, Caroline. Kennedy's sisters, Jean Kennedy Smith and Eunice Shriver, and his nephew, former Massachusetts congressman Joe Kennedy, were among the visitors. Many of Kennedy's grandchildren and grandnephews soon came calling, too.

Kennedy's personal physician, Dr. Larry Ronan, did preliminary tests and determined that Kennedy had not suffered a stroke. But he wasn't sure what had happened exactly, and ordered more tests. Within days Kennedy was diagnosed with a malignant glioma in the upper left portion of his brain. About 10,000 cases of the inoperable cancer are diagnosed each year in the United States, and only about half of those patients survive one year. After two years, perhaps 25 percent are still alive. The 76-year-old veteran of a thousand battles had a new one on his hands.

Kennedy faced the stark possibility of his own mortality the same way he had faced all the other deaths in his life: with both barrels blazing. In the days after he was diagnosed, he began planning his recovery much the same way he planned his legislative campaigns in the Senate.

First, as always, get the best staff available.

Kennedy enlisted Dr. Larry Horowitz, the Yale-trained doctor who originally joined his team in 1972 when he served as Kennedy's point person on health and medical research issues. Horowitz was later Kennedy's chief of staff, from 1981 to 1986. He also went to Moscow on Kennedy's behalf to grease the skids for a meeting with Mikhail Gorbachev, and has remained a close confidant. Horowitz helped Kennedy find the experimental treatment that saved the life of his son Teddy when he was diagnosed with bone cancer. He has also treated Patrick during asthma attacks.

Second, assemble a team to thoroughly research all the options.

Horowitz did just that, organizing a group of experts and former Kennedy staff members to scour medical literature and research experimental treatments.

Third, hold a forum to debate all the alternatives.

Horowitz and the Kennedys consulted experts from hospitals around the country, including Duke University Medical Center, which has a brain tumor research center that was conducting clinical trials on malignant glioma; M.D. Anderson Cancer Center in Houston; and a major brain tumor center at the University of California, San Francisco.

Vicki, Horowitz and a team of doctors at Massachusetts General decided that the best course of action was targeted surgery at Duke followed by chemotherapy and radiation.

The surgery had risks. It's often difficult to distinguish cancer cells from the surrounding brain tissue, and the tumor was close to parts of the brain that control motor function, speech and memory. After pulling back a flap of outer skin, the surgeons have to cut through the skull and the membrane surrounding the brain.

Kennedy was sedated during the surgery, but not put to sleep. Doctors needed to monitor his reactions as they located the motor and speech areas in the brain.

It's virtually impossible to remove all the cancerous cells during such a procedure, so aggressive radiation and chemotherapy come afterward.

Kennedy went under the knife on Monday, June 2, for three and a half hours, after which Dr. Allan Friedman, the neurosurgeon who performed the procedure, called the operation a success. Right afterward, Kennedy spoke with his wife: "I feel like a million bucks."

Kennedy returned to his Cape Cod home on June 9, a week after undergoing surgery, and soon began radiation and chemotherapy treatments at Massachusetts General. Vicki usually drove Ted up to Boston for treatments in the morning, and by afternoon he was out on Nantucket Sound in his schooner *Mya* with his dogs.

"I have drawn the line at sailing in thunderstorms, but other than that, he's out on the water just about every day," Vicki wrote in an e-mail to friends and family. Vicki said Ted was employing the same "grit and determination he's shown in his career" to fight the tumor. "He remained strong and was able to stay on schedule throughout this shock-and-awe phase of the treatment and his doctors—and we—are enormously pleased with his progress."

As he recovered back in Hyannis Port and slowly regained his strength during the summer, his thoughts quickly turned to legacy. Working by phone with Hatch and his staff, he put the finishing touches on the National Service bill he planned to offer to the new president in 2009.

"He has not skipped a beat," said Khazei. "Even with all the health care stuff he's dealing with, he's stayed on it, his staff has stayed on it. He's been making phone calls, keeping it moving."

The legislation was finished one week before the summit of service agencies in Boston in August 2008, where it was formally introduced to the world. Obama, McCain and Hatch were all there. Ted sent Caroline in his place.

During his summer vacation from the Senate, he also took time out from his treatments to record his biographical video for the Democratic National Convention and secretly practice his speech with Bob Shrum for three weeks.

He also formed a nonprofit group with friends to raise money and build an institute in Boston, next door to the John F. Kennedy Presidential Library, that will be dedicated to research and education about the U.S. Senate. He made dozens of phone calls to push his son Patrick's mental health parity bill forward.

And despite his condition, or more likely because of it, Kennedy began yet another full-court press for the elusive goal of making sure every person in the country had health insurance "as a right, not a privilege."

His public policy has always risen directly out of his own experience. His lifelong concern about the country's health care is really his private concern about the health of his family writ large. Kennedy is usually at his best when amplifying the personal into the public, both for his own good and the good of millions. The Kennedy drama has been the country's, both intimately and universally.

"It's very deep," Walter Mondale said of Kennedy's commitment to health care legislation. "My guess is that he's done some really deep thinking about, with maybe so little time left, how would he like to use his influence for a knockout blow on health care. And there will be tremendous emotional support for that. And if it's well thought through, I think it might have a chance."

Kennedy's sensitivity on the issue began with his sister Rosemary and continued unabated throughout his 76 years. "I knew even as a younger person about the challenges that she faced," Ted told author Burton Hersh. "And that probably made a subtle and not-so-subtle impression on me as a child who grew up in that family, and a consciousness just about some of the mysteries, you know, in terms of health care."

And then there were all John Kennedy's ailments: his bad back, his colitis, and his hidden Addison's disease. By the time he was president, Kennedy was on 10 to 12 medications a day. Bob Shrum remembers Ted telling him vivid stories about the deep impression Jack's illnesses made on him. "When JFK was wounded and came back from the war, he was in the bedroom in the first floor of the house in Hyannis Port, because going up the steps of the house was tough," said Shrum. "When Teddy was 12, John thought it would be fun, so they took turns reading John Brown's Body to each other."

Cancer first arrived to shadow Ted's life when his son lost his leg to it in 1973. "Can you imagine not having health insurance and having your son have cancer in the leg, as Teddy did?" asks former press secretary Tom Southwick. Shortly after fighting through his son Teddy's treatments, which cost $2,700 a day, Ted set about winning health insurance for 6 million children.

In 2003, Kennedy's daughter, Kara, was told she had inoperable lung cancer and only a year to live. Kennedy refused to believe the prognosis, and found a different doctor who operated on her—successfully.

Patrick, who has severe asthma and bipolar disorder, also had a noncancerous tumor removed from his spine when he was younger. Ted's first wife, Joan, was treated for breast cancer in 2005.

"One thing he did say to me is that as difficult as this is, it's nothing compared to the feelings he had when people told him his children had cancer," Horowitz told Matt Viser of the *Boston Globe*. "Hard as this is, it's a lot easier than hearing about your own children."

In response to it all, Kennedy has hammered a patients' bill of rights through the Senate, created portable health insurance, started community health centers, won dramatic improvements in medical education, toughened oversight of HMOs and secured stricter accountability for the Food and Drug Administration. Ted was there in 1965 to help birth Medicare, JFK's program to provide health care for the elderly.

On the day Kennedy won passage of the Americans with Disabilities Act, he said: "Many of us have been touched by others with disabilities. My sister Rosemary is retarded; my son lost a leg to cancer. And others who support the legislation believe in it for similar special reasons. I cannot be unmindful of the extraordinary contributions of those who have been lucky enough to have members of their families or children who are facing the same challenges and know what this legislation means."[2]

A complete summary of Kennedy's achievements in the Senate, compiled by his staff, is 50 single-spaced pages long, but it does not include the cause of his life, universal health care.

It would fall to Barack Obama to finish Ted Kennedy's last fight for him. Obama's commitment to comprehensive health care reform, which many Washington watchers thought was the wrong focus of Obama's first year in office, given the high unemployment in the country, stems from a direct promise he made to Kennedy as a condition of Kennedy's endorsement in January 2008. As Kennedy fought for his own life later in 2008, he quietly began orchestrating bipartisan, roundtable discussions aimed at forging that law. As health care costs have mounted, Kennedy thought he had his best chance in 13 years to try again.

As the ranking Republican on the Health, Education, Labor and Pensions committee, Senator Mike Enzi of Wyoming worked closely with Kennedy to forge some consensus on an initiative.

One of the reasons Kennedy and his team got a head start on the issue before a new president was elected was because of the lack of preparation they felt the Clintons had when they tried to hammer together comprehensive health care reform in 1993. Kennedy didn't want to make the same mistake twice. Enzi and several others involved in the new effort believe the best approach to reforming health care is going step by step, piece by piece, rather than offering up a comprehensive health insurance bill as the Clintons did. Enzi also said a big difference between the Kennedy and Clinton efforts is keeping the private market involved and reaching across the aisle. Others involved in the talks say the success and failures of state health care reforms, such as those in Massachusetts and California, provide relevant models to draw on this time around.

"The system is broken," Kennedy wrote in an November 9, 2008, editorial for the *Washington Post*. "And it's no longer just patients demanding change. Business, doctors and even many insurance companies are demanding it as well."

Kennedy staffers were working closely with Barack Obama's staffers on the initiative. Kennedy even appeared by videoconference from Massachusetts for a meeting on the legislation with members of the Health, Education, Labor and Pensions Committee.

In December of 2008, Kennedy relinquished his powerful post as chairman of the Senate Judiciary Committee to focus even more intensely on health care reform. "This is the opportunity of a lifetime, and I intend to make the most of it," Kennedy said at the time.

"It adds a great deal of poignancy to his recovery," said his son Patrick. "But that's how he sees it—he has to recover so he can get health care for the millions of people who don't have access to the care that we do."[3]

Nick Littlefield, a longtime Kennedy aide, made a prediction to author Burton Hersh back in 1994. "Long term, it may turn out that the failure of the Clinton healthcare bill ushered in the Republican landslide of 1994, and that landslide unleashed such extreme forces that it has turned the county against Republicanism for a generation and regalvanized the Democratic majority. . . . If that happens, then the last laugh on healthcare belongs to Kennedy, and we'll get it done next time."[4]

In Frank Capra's film *It's a Wonderful Life,* George Bailey never quite makes it out of the small town he longs his entire life to leave behind. Under the weight of his obligation to his family heritage and in the face of the machinations of the town's richest resident, George stays home to do his duty rather than follow his muse and travel the world. George's is not a larger-than-life life; it's a life-size life that makes a grand difference by making 100 small differences. Frank Capra made the movie to suggest that those life-sized lives and the difference they make, when they are added all together, deserve a large measure of appreciation they never really get.

Ted Kennedy was the same kind of politician when compared to his larger-than-life brothers: life-size. For 46 years, enduring setbacks and stumbles, he did the often-unglamorous, granular work of improving individual lives. You could call him the patron saint of the unsung, the guy who stuck with his duty as he perceived it despite the high price he and those around him paid emotionally. As Bobby Kennedy once pointed out, Ted could have sat at the pool his whole life sipping umbrella drinks. Certainly Kennedy has had his drunken, stupid moments, just as George Bailey did when he was contemplating suicide. And he will forever be responsible for the loss of Mary Jo Kopechne's life. But in spite of everything, Kennedy kept showing up. As a result, he has tacked a new message of inspiration onto the Kennedy legacy: A person *can* transcend his own limitations and live down his mistakes with an unceasing spirit of optimism and determination. Greatness doesn't always come wrapped in a pretty package.

At the end of *It's a Wonderful Life,* George's friends are alerted to his sudden financial straits and rush in on Christmas Eve to help, an outpouring that turns into a grand celebration of George's true worth as the town's best friend. Washington saw the same kind of outpouring in Kennedy's house— the Senate—when his brain tumor was announced in the spring of 2008. Hunched over in his wheelchair, Robert Byrd openly wept on the Senate floor as he read a tribute to Kennedy. Hundreds of phone calls, 19 bouquets and more than 2,500 e-mails reached Kennedy's office that day. King Abdullah II of Jordan sent an orchid. British prime minister Gordon Brown sent a get-well note, as did actors Glenn Close and Martin Sheen, rock musician Don Henley, Nancy Reagan and Al Gore, according to a Kennedy staff member.

In the chamber of the Senate, work simply stopped. "All of the oxygen went out of the room," said Senator Patty Murray (D-WA)[5] Dozens of senators said they couldn't quite imagine the place without Ted Kennedy, that he had come to symbolize the continuity and stability of the chamber. All his personal bumps had remarkably little effect on his life as a lawmaker. Ted's absence seemed to mark not only the end of an era in the family's history, but also the end of a more gentlemanly era in the Senate, as well.

The *Washington Post*'s Paul Kane made the point that several of the chamber's longest-serving and most able legislators retired, or were in ill health or were forced to leave office, in 2008, including Daniel Inouye, who started in 1963; Robert Byrd, 1959; Ted Stevens, 1968; and Pete Domenici, 1973. With them, the Senate is losing a certain breed of legislator who has long been willing to reach across the aisle to strike deals, keeping the Senate collegial in its practice of the art of legislation. Former senator Al Simpson feels the partisan and fractious nature of the House has infected the Senate as the club's old warhorses exit and new partisan warriors alight from the other chamber.

"When the institutional memory and experience of senators such as Kennedy, Byrd, Domenici, Stevens and Warner is gone, what will replace it?" Kane asked. "How many of the 10 senators elected in 2006, or the unknown number of freshmen who will begin service next January, will stay in the chamber for three or four decades? The breed of legislator that [Kennedy] represents may never return."

Yet just seven weeks later, the normally decorous chamber erupted in cheers of disbelief when the irrepressible Lion of the Senate did just that. The surprise, triumphant return moved many of his colleagues to tears; most had expected Kennedy never to come back.

Striding shoulder to shoulder with him that day through the double doors, above which is inscribed in gilt letters "Novus Ordo Seclorum" ("A New Order of the Ages")—were his son Patrick, the representative from Rhode Island; Senator Barack Obama, the presumptive Democratic presidential nominee; Christopher Dodd, Kennedy's best friend in the Senate; and Senator John F. Kerry of Massachusetts. The applause and hoorays were bipartisan as Kennedy made his way magisterially to the front, the pantheon of marble busts—John Adams, Thomas Jefferson and Aaron Burr—watching over the promenade from their honored niches above the gallery.

The matter at hand was health care, of course. Kennedy had returned to cast the deciding vote in favor of a bill that stopped a sharp cut in reimbursements for doctors treating Medicare patients. Forty-three years earlier, Kennedy had voted to bring his brother John's program into being. He wasn't about to see it diluted now.

Before Kennedy's arrival, Democrats could not muster the 60 votes needed to block a Republican filibuster on the bill. After, nine Republicans, swept along in the moment or just recognizing defeat, switched their votes to give the bill a veto-proof majority.

"Ted Kennedy wasn't going to let Medicare be destroyed," said Senator Reid of Nevada, the majority leader. "So he rose to the challenge, came to work."

He came to work. More than anything, those words describe what Ted did over the course of a 46-year career. As Woody Allen averred, 80 percent of success is showing up.

Kennedy's doctors "weren't terribly pleased" with his decision to make the trip, Senator Dodd told a reporter. "But Ted is not in the habit of listening to doctors."

When the din had subsided after his hallowed walk, Kennedy gazed up at the Senate clerk on the dais to do what he has done many thousands of times since he arrived in Washington in 1963. But at that moment the gesture carried the poignancy of a lifetime of perseverance.

This day, arms high in the air, Kennedy joyously shouted the vote he'd risk his life to cast:

"Aye," he roared.

After Ted Kennedy's death on August 25, 2009, his widow, Vicki, made the cause of his life the cause of her life. She received regular reports from House Speaker Nancy Pelosi, Senate Majority Leader Harry Reid and senior White House officials as President Obama's bill wended its way though Congress.[6] She visited the Capitol to meet one-on-one with wavering lawmakers, asking them to pass the legislation in memory of Ted. And she kept a promise to deliver a letter to President Obama after her husband was gone. "You will be the president who at long last signs into law the health care reform that is the great unfinished business of our society," Ted wrote in the letter. "For me, this cause stretched across decades; it has been disappointed, but never finally defeated. It was the cause of my life."[7]

On March 21, 2010, just seven months later, Vicki went to visit the simple white cross that mark's her husband's grave on a sloping hill in Section 45 at Arlington National Cemetery.[8] She wanted to spend a few hours with him as the House of Representatives—three and a half miles away straight up the National Mall—finally passed the health-care reform legislation that Ted had so longed to realize.

In an interview with CNN's John King the next day, Vicki said, "I thought yesterday was an important day to be there, because I had hope and confidence and certainly, you know, wish that the bill would pass. . . . You know Teddy always said that when we finally pass health-care reform and when people understand what's in the bill and what benefits there are for them, they are going to say 'What took you so long?'"[9]

In his floor speech in support of the bill on the day it passed, Rep. Patrick J. Kennedy talked about what the legislation meant to his father: "His heart and soul are in this bill."[10]

On the morning of Tuesday, March 23, members of Congress put on blue "TedStrong" wristbands in Kennedy's honor and posed for pictures with Patrick as they gathered in the East Room of the White House for President Obama's bill-signing ceremony. Caroline Kennedy, the senator's niece, sat in the front row for the ceremony with other members of the family. Vicki Kennedy came into the room with the bill's chief architects, Pelosi and Reid.

Obama received his biggest round of applause when he evoked Ted's memory in a brief speech. "I remember seeing Ted walk through that door in a summit in this room a year ago, one of his last public appearances," Obama said, "and it was hard for him to make it, but he was confident that we would do the right thing."[11]

When Obama signed the bill at 11:52 A.M., Patrick and Vicki Kennedy were standing behind him, watching over.

Ted didn't get to see the promise land himself, but now his last, biggest, hardest-fought dream was the law of the land. The Kennedy legacy was complete.

The morning after his son Patrick cast one of the decisive votes for the bill, he also visited his father's humble grave in Arlington National Cemetery. There, alone in Section 45, he placed a congressional note card at his father's footstone.

The note read: "7:50 A.M. March 22, 2010. Dad, the 'unfinished business' is done."[12]

EPILOGUE

THE DREAM LIVES ON

"The work continues, the cause endures, hope still lives and the dream shall never die."

—Ted Kennedy, speech at the 1980 Democratic convention

"The work begins anew, the hope rises again, and the dream lives on."

—Ted Kennedy, speech at the 2008 Democratic convention

On January 28, 2008, Ted, Patrick and Caroline Kennedy gift-wrapped the family's political and social legacy—with all its baggage and all its glow—and handed it off not to another Kennedy, but to underdog presidential candidate Barack Obama, who was all of one year old when Ted began his career.

In a rousing stem-winder of a speech at American University, Ted told the crowd, "Every time I've been asked over the past year who I would support in the Democratic primary my answer has always been the same. I'll support the candidate who inspires me, who inspires all of us, who can lift our vision and summon our hopes, and renew our beliefs that our country's best days are still to come. I found that candidate, and I think you have too."[1]

"He [Ted] was a monumental figure in the history of the campaign," David Axelrod, Obama's senior adviser, told POLITICO, saying that the weekend of Kennedy's endorsement "transformed the campaign. It was like being shot from a cannon." The day of the endorsement was, Obama told a Kennedy adviser at the time, the greatest day of his life.[2]

New York Times columnist David Brooks thought there was something "important and memorable" about the rapturous reception the 75-year-old

Kennedy received from a crowd 50 years younger.[3] He saw Kennedy's endorsement as a turning point in the political mood of the country—away from the hyper partisan politics that had dominated for so many years toward something sunnier and grander, something more . . . Kennedyesque. Walter Mondale noticed the same thing happening in 2008. "I've had people tell me, Kennedy's from another generation," he said. "This is not where the public is. To his credit he never backed off, and I think that history's coming around again to prove his ideas and philosophy were the right way to go."

In his speech, Kennedy made direct comparisons between Obama and his brother John. "There was another time, when another young candidate was running for President and challenging America to cross a New Frontier. He faced public criticism from the preceding Democratic President, who was widely respected in the party. Harry Truman said we needed 'someone with greater experience'—and added: 'May I urge you to be patient.' And John Kennedy replied: 'The world is changing. The old ways will not do . . . it is time for a new generation of leadership.'"

"So it is with Barack Obama. He has lit a spark of hope amid the fierce urgency of now. I believe that a wave of change is moving across America. If we do not turn aside, if we dare to set our course for the shores of hope, we together will go beyond the divisions of the past and find our place to build the America of the future."

Obama returned the compliment at the end of the day. "The Kennedy family, more than any other, has always stood for what's best about the Democratic Party, and about America," he said. "That each of us can make a difference and all of us ought to try."[4]

Ted Sorensen, JFK's speechwriter, points out that John Kennedy and Obama share an extraordinary number of similarities. Both went to Harvard, both rose to national attention almost overnight after appearances at the Democratic convention, both wrote bestselling political books, and both had a youthful appeal that engaged record numbers of new voters and young voters. The most striking similarity is the tenor of their speeches, which focus on the politics of hope rather than five-point programs or national malaise.

"He is clearly the most Kennedy-like candidate for President since the three Kennedy brothers themselves," said Sorensen. Just like John Kennedy, Sorensen says, "he is inspiring young people today to enter public service and politics through his idealistic and optimistic speeches."[5]

Ted and Caroline barnstormed the country for Obama in early 2008, and his victory owes so much to the Kennedy legacy that some pundits have begun to dub the Obama White House "Obamalot."

Just before he died in 1968, Bobby Kennedy was asked about the likely pace of civil rights progress in the future, and he predicted that it would be 40 years before a black man was elected president.

He was exactly right.

★ ★ ★

The Kennedy legacy is also carried on by hundreds of former Kennedy staff members and "Honorary Kennedys" who have since risen to the top of the Washington hierarchy. Many still keep in close touch with the Kennedy family, and jump at the chance to come to their aid if called upon.

"What you're seeing now is a second-generation effect," said Alan Khazei, the driving force behind Kennedy's national service legislation. "The people who got into government because of Kennedy now have the levers of power. So it's already starting to ripple out."

The Kennedy alumni include Supreme Court Justice Stephen Breyer, who served as chief counsel for Ted Kennedy in the 1970s, and Senator John Kerry, who volunteered on Kennedy's first Senate campaign. Ron Brown, Kennedy's deputy campaign manager during his presidential bid in 1980, went on to become chairman of the Democratic National Committee from 1989–92 and President Bill Clinton's secretary of commerce, the first African American to hold that post. Super-lawyer Greg Craig, a foreign policy adviser to Kennedy, was a close adviser to Obama before stepping down at the end of 2009. Dr. Larry Horowitz, who worked on Kennedy's staff in the 1970s and oversaw his brain tumor treatment plan, moonlights as a Hollywood and Broadway producer. Among his credits is *The Ted Kennedy Jr. Story.* Ken Feinberg, Kennedy's chief of staff in the late 1970s, oversaw the financial settlements for all 9/11 victims and serves as Obama's "pay czar," overseeing reforms to regulate bonuses for financial executives. Former Kennedy aide Stephanie Cutter is now Michelle Obama's chief of staff. Paul Kirk was the Democratic National Committee chairman in the 1980s, and now heads the John F. Kennedy Library Foundation. Mark Schneider was director of the Peace Corps from 1999 to 2001. David Burke became president of CBS News. James Guest is the president and CEO of *Consumer Reports.* Steve Scully is the host of C-Span's *Washington Journal.*

"Kennedy always had a brilliant staff," said Walter Mondale. "Long as I have known. He put a lot of time into picking really smart people." These men and women will continue to be a living legacy of Kennedy's for years.

★ ★ ★

Two days after Edward Kennedy's heart finally gave out in late August 2009, a few hundred people began to gather in front of the John F. Kennedy Presidential

Library and Museum in Boston. It was a buoyantly sunny day on Dorchester Bay, and the angular white building jutted into the cobalt sky above the crowd like an eight-story sail. Bostonians were assembling on the sidewalks and in the parking lots to await the motorcade that was to deliver Ted Kennedy to the library from the Kennedy compound in Hyannis Port. The late senator was to lie in repose at the library until his funeral Mass in Boston and burial at Arlington National Cemetery two days later. His procession was due at any minute, and the crowd wanted to see whether the passing of this Kennedy would be as poignant and wrenching as the deaths of his brothers. The sense of a great loss was present, but the mood of universal anguish over the assassinations was missing. Some began to wonder why the crowd wasn't larger, this being Boston's first chance to publicly mourn the passing of the last Kennedy brother. Even in death, Ted Kennedy could not escape the comparisons to John and Bobby.

Then a burst of emails and text messages lit up cell phones and BlackBerries, alerting the crowd that the motorcade was on the outskirts of Boston. The Kennedy family had set up a Twitter feed that announced they were about 15 minutes away. And suddenly, at the library, Bostonians arrived by the thousands. Busload after busload pulled up to the entrance in a steady stream, mourners filing out into a miles-long line snaking through the parking lots.

Thousands more people, many waving American flags and some wiping away tears, lined the 70-mile route from Hyannis Port, Massachusetts, to the city where the Kennedy family dynasty began. They gathered on roads and highways, crowded onto overpasses, and hung out of apartment windows to say goodbye to the man who served Massachusetts in the Senate for four decades.

The Reverend Jack Ahern, the onetime pastor of the Catholic parish in Brookline where Kennedy was baptized, drove into Boston just ahead of the procession. "Every bridge was packed with people," he said. "Every side road was full. Every inch of grass along the expressway was covered. It was the most moving thing I've ever seen in my life. It was this enormous outpouring of affection."

By early evening on August 27, the six books of condolences inside the library were filled with thousands of signatures. More than 10,000 people waited outside to add their names to the books and to become part of the historical record of the final chapter in Kennedy's remarkable life. Fifty thousand people would eventually come to the library. Among the family members keeping vigil inside was Kennedy's widow, Victoria, who greeted mourners with affectionate, grateful hugs—much to the chagrin of the security people who were trying to keep the line moving. "They tell me we're backing everything up!" she told a reporter as she adjusted to simple handshakes instead. The library kept its doors open into the night until every person waiting outside got to pay their respects.

Kennedy's death came a little more than a year after he was diagnosed with brain cancer. Through those months, he fought against his illness with a combination of the good humor that had long marked his buoyant personality and the cold-eyed realism of someone whose family has been touched repeatedly by tragedy and disappointment.

His passing triggered an outpouring of emotion from Senate colleagues from both parties, from the Bay State constituents he long served, and from people across the country and around the world who were touched by the Kennedy family's decades-long record of service and sacrifice. "I think it's the passing of an era," said Mort Zajac, a retired utility worker, after the procession moved past him near Hyannis. "It's a chip in the foundation."[6]

The day certainly had an end-of-an-era feel as the patriarch of the Kennedy family took his last, poignant journey. But many in the crowd expressed a thankfulness that this Kennedy had lived the full life that his brothers hadn't. They expressed an intimate appreciation for Ted the person rather than Ted the politician, or Ted the keeper of the Kennedy family flame. The tributes in Boston were for a single man, not a mystique.

"He has done something for all of us at one time or another," said Ahern while waiting in line to pay his condolences. "He took care of the sick and the poor."

★ ★ ★

"Seems like because of the tragedies in his own life, he could relate to the tragedy in other people's lives," said Jill Grossberg, who was spending her 42nd anniversary in line with her husband at the library that Thursday night. "Sometimes he was very unpopular, but he never wavered." Her husband, Bernard, said Kennedy's own foibles gave hope to other people that they could transcend their own. "If he could get through everything he's gotten through in his life, it made it easier for other people to get through theirs."

The day began with a private Mass at the Kennedy home, in a room overlooking the ocean where Kennedy spent so many of his days, including some of his last, sailing. The Reverend Donald MacMillan, a Catholic priest and minister at Boston College, was the celebrant. Among the more than 80 Kennedy family members present were Victoria; his children, Kara, Patrick and Ted Jr.; his sister Jean Kennedy Smith; and his brother-in-law Sargent Shriver.

After the family emerged from the house, Victoria and Jean, Ted's last surviving sibling of eight, stood in front of the other family members. They watched a military honor guard carry his flag-draped coffin from the house to the hearse to begin the deliberate journey to Boston.

In the city, the motorcade moved slowly past a succession of sites significant in Kennedy's life. They included historic Faneuil Hall, where he announced his unsuccessful bid for the White House in 1980; St. Stephen's Church, where his mother, Rose, was baptized and her funeral Mass was celebrated; the office on Bowdoin Street where Kennedy worked as a young assistant district attorney; and the skyscraper named for his brother, the slain president, which for decades has housed the senator's Boston headquarters. When the procession passed a waving group of people near Hyannis, Kennedy family members rolled down the windows of their black limousines to wave back.

Sue Kemmling, a nurse, wiped away tears as the cars passed her outside of Hyannis, saying "I thought it was very nice the Kennedys waved back to the crowd." She added: "He gave us civil rights. He gave us a lot of freedoms back in the '60s and '70s. Women's rights. Children with handicaps. I don't think there's anybody in the near future that'll be able to fill his shoes."

Kennedy's funeral took place at the Basilica of Our Lady of Perpetual Help in Boston's Mission Hill neighborhood, where new sidewalks were laid and a nearby building received a fresh coat of red paint in anticipation of the Mass. Kennedy often prayed at Our Lady in 2003 while his daughter, Kara, was being treated for lung cancer at a nearby hospital. Six years later, Kennedy visited the church again to ask for God's help in fighting his own tumor.

In his last days Ted had spoken of looking forward to resting beside his brothers in Arlington National Cemetery, of finally rejoining them. "Ted Kennedy has gone home now," President Obama said in his eulogy at the funeral, "guided by his faith and by the light of those that he has loved and lost. At last he is with them once more."[7]

At the funeral Ted Kennedy Jr., who lost a leg to cancer when he was 12, recalled his father's strength and inspiration as he struggled with his physical handicap. His voice choked with emotion, he remembered a sledding expedition on a snowy day not long after his leg was amputated. After he had fallen, his father helped him climb an icy hill when he doubted his own physical capacity to do so.

"We're going to climb that hill together, even if it takes us all day," the younger Kennedy said his father told him. He added: "You see, my father taught me that even our most profound losses are survivable, and that it is what we do with that loss, our ability to transform it into a positive event, that is one of my father's greatest lessons."[8]

Before the burial ceremony at Arlington later that day, the hearse carrying Kennedy stopped at the plaza on the East Front of the Capitol. There former Kennedy staffers, lawmakers, congressional aides and members of the public were gathered to pay their respects.

Kennedy's cortege to Arlington retraced the route taken during the funerals of his slain brothers—west from the Capitol along the broad boulevard of Constitution Avenue, around the north side of the Lincoln Memorial, where Robert Kennedy's motorcade paused in 1968, and then over Memorial Bridge to the hedge-lined Memorial Drive approach to Arlington.

By the time the funeral procession reached the cemetery, the sun had set and the gravesite was shrouded in darkness. Cardinal Theodore E. McCarrick, a friend of Kennedy's, presided and read from a letter the senator had written to Pope Benedict XVI, which Obama had delivered to the pontiff in Rome. In the letter, Kennedy wrote he had been "an imperfect human being but with the help of my faith I have tried to right my path."[9]

When Ted Kennedy's body was finally laid to rest 200 feet from the eternal flame that marks his brother John's grave and 100 feet from the single white cross that marks Bobby's, the story of a unique American brotherhood was brought full circle.

The prevailing emotion among the mourners gathered that day in August was that a great political dynasty was coming to an end. Many other events of 2009 and early 2010 would only serve to buttress that sense. Eunice Shriver, Ted's sister, had died less than a month before. John's daughter Caroline had shown a brief interest in trying to carry the family flame forward when she campaigned for an appointment to Hillary Clinton's Senate seat the previous January. But she abandoned her bid at the last minute after a fusillade of negative press questioned her qualifications and presumptiveness. When, in January 2010, a little-known Republican state senator, Scott Brown, won the Senate seat held for nearly a half-century by Ted Kennedy, questions began to arise about the endurance of the Kennedy legacy. Not long after, Patrick Kennedy announced his plans to retire from the House by the end of 2010, which meant that for the first time in half a century, no Kennedy would hold elected office in Washington.

Pundits have been wondering aloud whether there ever will be another Kennedy who can rise up to keep the Kennedy tradition alive.

"I don't think there is one," said Jack's friend Ben Bradlee.

Wendy Schiller, a political science professor at Brown University who has studied the Kennedys extensively, agrees. "I don't see that necessarily happening with any of the second-generation Kennedys now," she said. "Why would you even want to step into those shoes, let alone fill them?" she asked.

During his final weeks with his father, Patrick Kennedy talked about his desire to retire from politics, and his dad encouraged him to do what would make him happy, telling him that there are other avenues in which to make a difference—pointing to the legacy of Patrick's aunt, Eunice Kennedy Shriver, who founded the Special Olympics—and assuring him that he would love him regardless.

"For me, I had an audience of one," Patrick Kennedy told the *Washington Post*. "That was my dad."[10] The Kennedy legacy was, in many ways, more of a burden for Patrick than a help. White House adviser David Axelrod, a friend since Patrick's first congressional campaign, said: "There was a lot of tension, and Patrick was very focused on not disappointing [his father]. That's a heavy legacy to live with."[11]

Eunice's son, Tim Shriver, chairman of the Special Olympics, told a *Washington Post* reporter that he sees his generation gravitating more and more to "soft power," leveraging social causes and social media, rather than seeking the elected posts that brought his family glory and tragedy. "Maybe there's some dark psychic message in that," he said. "There's no more allure of Kennedy brothers. Camelot is pretty safely in the rearview mirror." He is reminded of a snatch of movie dialogue about the Boston Red Sox. "It's over," Shriver recites. "O-V-A. Over."[12]

Schiller seconds that assessment. "Kennedys can be effective in all sorts of arenas," she said. "They don't necessarily have to go to the Senate now. The Kennedys right now are really doing a lot of things outside the public sector that are having an impact," Schiller said. "They are reshaping and redrawing the Kennedy legacy in new ways, and expanding it."

In the future, Kennedys may follow Eunice's example of public service more than that of any of the famous brothers.

"Eunice is a perfect example of the power of public service outside of public office," Schiller said. Eunice has pushed the next generation of Kennedys to be as competitive about public service as they were about touch football. Every one of Eunice's five children is active in public service. Tim leads Special Olympics; Maria is first lady of California; Robert sits on the Santa Monica City Council and runs a company dedicated to philanthropy; Anthony Paul founded Best Buddies International, an organization that helps people with intellectual disabilities; and Mark manages U.S. programs for Save the Children.

★ ★ ★

Though he is leaving Congress, Patrick plans to continue his advocacy of the rights of the mentally ill from his home in Portsmouth, Rhode Island. He has decided that fighting discrimination against people with depression, schizo-phrenia and substance-abuse issues is every bit as important as the first civil rights battles his dad and uncles fought for African Americans.

"It's not like I went to my dad and said, 'I want to run for Congress be-cause I want to continue our civil rights legacy by taking up the issue of men-tal illness,'" said Patrick. "I couldn't see the forest for the trees, that this thing was a civil rights fight," he explained. "I was so ashamed of my own mental health problems and I felt it was not something that I was proud of, in terms of my own disease and the fact that I . . . felt like in my family, which is so competitive and prides itself on its 'strength' in so many ways, that I fell short of my family's ideal . . . because I'm ending up in rehab, I'm needing extra help, I've got to see a therapist, I have to take medications. I'm never going to make it politically because there's such a judgment on this. So I'm damaged goods politically. How could I have ever imagined that this subject, which I think is going to be my undoing, becomes the platform that connects me to my family's legacy? And continues it."

His own struggles with bipolar disorder and substance abuse made him more acutely aware of the need to champion the rights of those with mental illness. Patrick worked for 12 years to pass a mental health parity bill that would put insurance coverage of mental illness on the same footing as insur-ance coverage of physical illness. When he started his campaign, insurance companies charged higher deductibles for mental health care and paid less to reimburse doctors than they did for physical illnesses. Rhode Island already had a good parity law, and Patrick thought it could scale up for the whole country. Senators Paul Wellstone, D-Minnesota, and Pete Domenici, R-New Mexico, had teamed up on an earlier mental health coverage bill in 1996. (Wellstone had a brother who suffered from serious mental illness, and Domenici's daughter had schizophrenia.) But their early efforts didn't in-clude insurance coverage of alcoholism and addiction. Kennedy's bill did.

It wasn't until 2006 that things started moving for Patrick's bill. "It really wasn't until after my car accident, and the national exposure, and I thought I had hit kind of bottom," said Kennedy. "And then I came back."

First, then-Representative Jim Ramstad of Minnesota and Kennedy cre-ated an Addiction, Treatment and Recovery Caucus in the House to educate fellow members about the parity issue. In 2007, they launched a nationwide series of field hearings on mental-health insurance parity after Patrick came back. They passionately argued the case to patients, politicians and mental health-care professionals that everyone in the country ought to have access to the same mental healthcare coverage a Congressperson has. Out of those hearings they fashioned a new bill and presented it to the House.

In the process, Kennedy has become something of a poster child for recovery. He believes the stigma that surrounds alcoholism and mental illness
is akin to the prejudice experienced once upon a time by gay people, blacks,
even Irish Catholics.

"In our heads we knew better than to treat this as a second-class illness,"
Patrick said, "We just couldn't get over the prejudice. That nagging sense of
judgmentalism. Far be it for those winos, those people who are drunkards
that can't hold their liquor, to get treatment because they should be able to
pick themselves up by their bootstraps." For too long, Kennedy believes, alcoholics have been treated as if they have a moral defect of character.

"Frankly no one, *no one* can argue who has ever witnessed what I've seen
in my life, in terms of the tragic circumstances of people I've seen, who have
gone through this disease—friends, family and the like—that people would
actually put themselves through what they put themselves through," Patrick
added. "Voluntarily. You just don't do this to your life out of choice. *Out of
choice.* It's not a choice."

Mental-health parity became a father-and-son joint effort in 2006, and
the extra help from his dad made the difference. Ted teamed up with Senator
Pete Domenici, R-New Mexico, and Senator Mike Enzi, R-Wyoming, to quietly forge a broad bipartisan coalition with input from mental-health advocates, health-insurance industry representatives, and private businesses. The
Domenici-Kennedy-Enzi parity bill that resulted cleared the Senate with no
dissent in September 2007. It was Ted's careful oiling of the machinery of
Congress that got the bill through so quickly. "There aren't any coincidences
when it comes to the Senate with my dad around," Patrick said.

Patrick's more expansive bill passed the House six months later, in March
of 2008. House and Senate negotiators gradually hammered out compromises
on all the substantive policy issues in the bill, but then the legislation stalled
over differences on unrelated budget procedures. Patrick began to worry that
the bill wouldn't get finished in time for his father to see it happen. "I stressed
to him," said Patrick at the time, "even though we may pick up more seats in
the Senate and the House, and even if we recapture the White House, it's not
any guarantee that we're going to get a bill like this, because who knows what
the environment will be. You've got a whole set of other circumstances because you've got health care reform, too, and it could take a back seat to that.
So you gotta make the most of this situation right now."

Though he was still in Hyannis Port recovering from his chemotherapy
and radiation treatments, Ted got on the phone. He talked often to Senate
Majority Leader Harry Reid, Senator Chris Dodd and others, wheedling and
cajoling his way toward a compromise. "I think that there is a certain feeling

of collegial obligation" in Congress, Patrick said at a critical moment. "They know this is important to my dad, and that's why they're making an effort, too, because they know how hard he's worked to put the pieces together. He was down at the Cape but he was omnipresent in this whole process in helping behind the scenes."

As Congress rushed to adjourn in October of 2008, the bill's prospects looked hopeful. Then the bottom of the economy fell out, and all bets were off. Patrick was trying for one last "Hail Mary legislative pass" when Senate leaders out of the blue attached the bill to the huge emergency bailout package steaming its way toward passage in early October. Riding along on the bailout, the parity bill passed the Senate 75–24, and the only senator who wasn't there to vote on it was Ted. The House chamber broke into applause the next day at 1:22 P.M. when the bill polled a majority there. On the floor just before final passage, Jim Ramstad paid tribute to the power of Patrick Kennedy's candidness in winning the day. "Were Patrick's uncle, President Kennedy, still alive, and were he to write a sequel to his book, *Profiles in Courage,* President Kennedy's nephew Patrick would occupy a full chapter," he said.

Patrick had found the personal courage to face some of the emotional truths of his life that his father never had. It was a sign of hope for the whole family, that maybe, perhaps, some of the demons that had haunted them for so long could finally be purged.

Patrick sent a note to his father the night after the bill passed. "I just said I should be happy because of the substance of this bill and the fact that millions and millions of people will benefit from the coverage they'll now receive thanks to this legislation. But the person who I cared about the most in passing this bill, was you."

"Because in a sense," Patrick explained later, "in his fighting for it he was fighting for something that was not only important to me, personally, as a son, but he was fighting against the stigma and shame that I've always felt at being 'lesser than' because I've had this illness. And that meant the world to me."

The bill's success repeats a Kennedy family pattern that has endured for decades, going all the way back to Rosemary Kennedy's mental illness and Joe Junior's death in World War II: take a personal or family misfortune and turn into it into a political movement that on a much grander scale helps other people avoid some of the same pain and prejudice.

In achieving that metamorphosis of bad into good, personal into public in the parity victory, Patrick said he experienced an extraordinary twist of fate.

"Ironically, I grew up thinking, here I come from this amazing family involved in all this social justice and civil rights, you know, and that I was born at the wrong time." he said. "I wasn't part of anything! Couldn't be part of anything that was really happening. Those times were really before I was born."

Those regrets evaporated when Patrick came to realize that mental health parity was, in essence, a new civil rights battle. In fact, President John Kennedy, in what would be his last public bill signing in 1963, had authorized $3 billion to create the first national network of mental health facilities. But after Kennedy's assassination, the project languished and nothing was ever done to implement it.

Just as improving health care was his father's signature crusade, now mental health care has become Patrick's, and he says he can continue the work even if he isn't a Congressman.

In the coming years, he plans to try to address the lack of mental health assistance available from VA hospitals, which are far behind civilian hospitals in the sophistication of their research and treatment of mental illness. He hopes to assure Iraq veterans of better mental health care as they grow old. He plans to address the quality of mental health care for immigrants and those in prison, where more than 80 percent of the population has some mental illness. And he plans to fight for mental health care parity in Medicaid, the government healthcare program for the indigent. The parity bill, Patrick says, is only the first step.

★ ★ ★

Many other family members carry on the family legacy of public service in various ways. Right up until her death in 2009, Ted's sister Eunice maintained her involvement with the Special Olympics, which will continue to introduce hundreds of thousands of athletes with disabilities to the thrill of competition for years to come.

Ted's sister, Jean Kennedy Smith, is the last survivor of Joe and Rose Kennedy's famous nine children. She contributed to the family legacy as the ambassador to Ireland, helping to fashion an end to the violent despair of Northern Ireland.

Many of the children of that royal generation have found unique ways to carry on the family tradition of public service.

Ted's other son, Teddy Jr., who lost a leg to cancer when he was 12, has been a lifelong advocate for the disabled.

Though JFK's daughter, Caroline, cut short her own effort to win an appointment to fill Hillary Clinton's New York Senate seat, she continues her philanthropic work for New York City's public schools. She has tried to continue her father's legacy in the books she has written as well, including *Profiles in Courage for Our Time.*

Bobby's oldest son, former Congressman Joe Kennedy, left politics after a controversial divorce, but now runs Citizens Energy, a Boston company that provides heating oil to low-income families.

Bobby Jr., Robert's second-oldest son, is head of an alliance of environmental groups that keep watch over the cleanliness of rivers, bays and lakes. His political activism on environmental and progressive issues has occasionally landed him in prison over the years. He had hinted about running for Hillary Clinton's Senate seat if she had won the presidential nomination, and delivered a barn-burning speech at a Denver reception marking the 40th anniversary of his father's death. The fiery talk caught the attention of many in the audience, suggesting something more ambitious for Bobby Jr., and they wondered if it weren't an indication of a run for higher office soon. "We have to understand that this country is more than just a place where people can come," Bobby Jr. told the crowd. "And this is what my father was able to convince people. And that's why he was an effective politician. Because he was able to get them to transcend their narrow self-interest. And get them out in the community to say this isn't just a place where people can come and make their pile bigger and whoever dies with the most stuff wins. America means more."[13]

Kerry Kennedy—the seventh of Bobby's 11 children—is the founder of the human rights organization Speak Truth to Power, which awards what she describes as "the poor man's Pulitzers" to authors and journalists around the world who stand up to oppression. She also champions the Robert F. Kennedy Center for Human Rights, which identifies and supports defenders of justice around the globe, and authored a recent book, *Being Catholic Now*, which takes on many of the church's most controversial issues such as homosexuality and abortion.

Rory Kennedy, Bobby's youngest child, is a documentary filmmaker whose movies highlight pressing social issues, such as AIDS and poverty in Appalachia.

And there's a new generation of Kennedys emerging that is every bit as determined to carry on the family legacy. Maeve Townsend, the granddaughter of Robert Kennedy, told an ABC News reporter that, like those who came before her, she tries to live by the motto of the Kennedy family matriarch Rose Fitzgerald Kennedy: "To whom much is given, much is expected."

"I mean, what I've gotten from my life is, I am so lucky and I am so blessed and that I need to figure out [how] to take all these things and give back," Townsend said.[14]

Her younger sister Kerry Townsend plans to carry on Ted's commitment to health care by becoming the family's first female doctor.

But will any one in this new generation of Kennedy's aspire to public office?

Some Kennedy watchers are keeping a close eye on the Townsend girls' twin 29-year-old cousins, Matt and Joe Kennedy, who are also Robert Kennedy's grandchildren. The Harvard grads were front and center at the Democratic convention in 2008, and Joe is already following Uncle Ted's footsteps in one respect. Just as Ted did in Boston, Joe took his first real job working in a District Attorney's Office, this one in Barnstable, near his family's compound in Cape Cod. Rumors are already swirling that he may run for Congress some day, and Massachusetts residents already talk about how much presence he has at an early age.

Though he told a local newspaper reporter that "politics is one of the highest forms of public service," he hasn't said that he wants to run yet.[15]

He hasn't said he doesn't want to, either.

Ted Kennedy himself laid plans to ensure there are plenty of Kennedy-like senators in the future. Blueprints have been drawn up for a first-of-its-kind institute in Boston that will be dedicated to research and education about the Senate. Kennedy's vision includes a training program for incoming senators to learn about parliamentary procedures, organizing staff, and preserving paperwork. In other words, Kennedy's institutional knowledge of the body will be permanently available as a case study for any future senator. The institute will include a museum, classrooms, research rooms, exhibit space that will showcase excerpts from great Senate speeches, videos of historic hearings and a broadcast of the Senate floor in real time. The piece de resistance will be an exact replica of the Senate chambers.

"He will be gratified if things go forward as a salute to him and an institution he loves, at a place he loves," said Paul Kirk.[16]

"The United States Senate is one of our forefathers' most brilliant democratic inventions," Kennedy said in a statement before his death. "To preserve our vibrant democracy for future generations, I believe it is critical to have a place where citizens can go to learn first-hand about the Senate's important role in our system of government."[17] No other center for the study of the Senate exists.

Though Kennedy gave all his papers to the JFK Library, some will be on display at the institute. An oral history of his life will be housed both at the institute and at the University of Virginia, where Kennedy went to law school. The home where Ted lived out his last years will become a museum so Americans interested in paying homage to the Kennedy brothers can make pilgrimages to Hyannis Port at the same time they visit the institute.

The institute is Ted Kennedy's presidential library, in essence. It will be a shrine to the Senate and a temple to Ted right next door to his brother's presidential showcase, the John F. Kennedy Library and Museum. The Kennedy brothers compete into perpetuity.

★ ★ ★

Totaling up the cumulative legacy of the three Kennedy brothers, it's clear that Camelot was never really the right analogy. Theirs has not been one brief, shining moment, but rather a half-century of galvanizing public service that looks like it could well continue for another half century in new forms. The better analogy comes from Bobby. Each Kennedy contributes "a ripple of hope" to the legacy, he said, some large, some small, many skirting troubled waters, but all contributing to a current that beats endlessly at oppression and prejudice.

"For all my years in public life, I have believed that America must sail toward the shores of liberty and justice for all," Ted said at Harvard after receiving a rare honorary degree there in December of 2008. "There is no end to that journey, only the next great voyage. We know the future will outlast all of us, but I believe that all of us will live on in the future we make."[18]

Jack's inspiration and intelligence, coupled with the example of Bobby's commitment and the stick-to-itiveness of Ted's fighting spirit, have combined to create a force in America's political and cultural life that may be unparalleled. "It's the same spirit in different forms," said Harris Wofford. Senator Christopher J. Dodd, D-Connecticut, offered a similar observation about the famous brotherhood at a memorial for Ted just days after his death. "John Fitzgerald Kennedy inspired our America," Dodd said. "Robert challenged our America. Our Teddy changed America."[19]

And after 50 years, the Kennedy legacy continues to motivate. With each generation, that extravagant optimism—that we all can and should make a difference, and that we should never stop trying—begins anew. And the Kennedy brothers' dream lives on.

NOTES

A note on sources: No original interviews appear in these notes. All direct quotes that are not footnoted or attributed directly in the text come from interviews conducted by the author. Any sources such as newspapers, the Congressional Record or political speeches that are identified within the text are not repeated in these notes.

PROLOGUE

1.   All direct quotes that are not sourced or attributed directly in the text come from interviews conducted by the author.
2.   *Chicago Sun-Times*, September 19, 2008.
3.   *The New York Times*, August 26, 2008.
4.   *The Boston Globe*, August 26, 2008.
5.   Ibid.
6.   Thomas Oliphant, *The Boston Globe*, November 22, 1999.
7.   Adam Clymer, *Edward M. Kennedy: A Biography* (New York: William Morrow, 1999), back cover.
8.   David Shribman, *Daily News* (Salem, Massachusetts), Daily News, June 7, 2008.
9.   David Murray, *Berkshire Eagle*, February 4, 2002.

CHAPTER 1

1.   Edward M. Kennedy, *America Back on Track* (New York: Penguin, 2006), 2.
2.   Peter Collier and David Horowitz, *The Kennedys: An American Drama* (San Francisco: Encounter Books, 1984), 51.
3.   David Pitts, *Jack and Lem: John F. Kennedy and Lem Billings, the Untold Story of an Extraordinary Friendship* (New York: Carroll & Graf Publishers, 2007), 33.
4.   Kennedy, *America Back on Track*, 2.
5.   Ralph G. Martin, *Seeds of Destruction: Joe Kennedy and His Sons* (New York: G. P. Putnam's Sons, 1995), xviii.
6.   Michael O'Brien, *John F. Kennedy: A Biography* (New York: Thomas Dunne Books, 2005), 45.
7.   Ibid., 23.
8.   Pitts, *Jack and Lem*, 32.

9. O'Brien, *John F. Kennedy,* 46.
10. Ibid., 46.
11. Martin, *Seeds of Destruction,* 14.
12. O'Brien, *John F. Kennedy,* 46.
13. Burton Hersh, *The Education of Edward Kennedy: A Family Biography* (New York: William Morrow, 1972), 30.
14. Doris Kearns Goodwin, *The Fitzgeralds and the Kennedys: An American Saga* (New York: Simon & Schuster, 1987), 352.
15. O'Brien, *John F. Kennedy,* 46.
16. Martin, *Seeds of Destruction,* 579.
17. Goodwin, *The Fitzgeralds and the Kennedys,* 539.
18. *People,* August 16, 1999.
19. *MyFoxBoston* interview, 2006.
20. O'Brien, *John F. Kennedy,* 47.
21. Ibid., 12.
22. Ibid., 47.
23. Martin, *Seeds of Destruction,* 30.
24. Ibid., 29.
25. *The American Experience: The Kennedys,* PBS documentary, 2004.
26. Hersh, *The Education of Edward Kennedy,* 31.
27. *Boston Advertiser,* October 14, 1962.

CHAPTER 2

1. Laurence Leamer, *The Kennedy Women: The Saga of an American Family* (New York: Villard Books, 1994), 154.
2. O'Brien, *John F. Kennedy: A Biography,* 53.
3. Leamer, *The Kennedy Women,* 154.
4. Ibid., 148.
5. Pitts, *Jack and Lem,* 10.
6. Ted Kennedy's eulogy for Rose at St. Stephens Church in Boston, January 25, 1995.
7. Martin, *Seeds of Destruction,* 6–7.
8. *The Boston Globe,* September 12, 2008.
9. Ted Kennedy quoting his mother at Rose's funeral.
10. Leamer, *The Kennedy Women,* 154.
11. Kennedy, *America Back on Track,* 4.
12. Ibid., 5.
13. Goodwin, *The Fitzgeralds and the Kennedys,* 353.
14. Ibid., 754.
15. Leamer, *The Kennedy Women,* 147.
16. Martin, *The Seeds of Destruction,* 25.
17. Leamer, *The Kennedy Women,* 645.
18. Ibid., 679.
19. Martin, *Seeds of Destruction,* 25.
20. *New York Times Magazine,* June 17, 1979
21. Leamer, *The Kennedy Women,* 325.
22. Martin, *Seeds of Destruction,* 105.
23. Lester David, *Ted Kennedy: Triumphs and Tragedies* (New York: Grosset & Dunlap, 1971), 177
24. *The American Experience: The Kennedys,* PBS documentary, 2004.

25.   Goodwin, *The Fitzgeralds and the Kennedys,* 399.

26.   Kennedy, *America Back on Track,* 127.

27.   Burton Hersh, *The Shadow President: Ted Kennedy in Opposition* (South Royalton, VT: Steerforth Press, 1997), 191.

28.   Ronald Kessler, Newsmax.com, June 17, 2008. Kessler is also author of *The Sins of the Father: Joseph Kennedy and the Dynasty He Founded* (New York: Grand Central Publishing, 1996).

29.   Barbara Gibson's diaries are quoted at length in Hersh, *The Shadow President,* 192 on the topic of Rosemary's lobotomy.

CHAPTER 3

1.   "Kennedy Kids: America's Gift to Diplomacy," LIFE Magazine, April 11, 1938.

2.   Goodwin, *The Fitzgeralds and the Kennedys,* 524.

3.   Ibid., 525.

4.   Ibid., 539.

5.   Ibid.

6.   Martin, *Seeds of Destruction,* 69

7.   Interview with Louella Hennessy by Lester David, in *Good Ted, Bad Ted,* (New York: Birch Lane, 1993), 13–14.

8.   Ibid., 362.

9.   Nigel Hamilton, *JFK: Reckless Youth* (New York: Random House, 1992), 235–236.

10.   Ibid., 234.

11.   Ibid., 235.

12.   James M. Landis, draft manuscript for the unpublished diplomatic memoirs of former ambassador Joseph P. Kennedy, Library of Congress, chapter 1, 1.

13.   Goodwin, *The Fitzgeralds and the Kennedys,* 557.

14.   Ibid., 558.

15.   Ibid.

16.   Ibid. All the actions that were taken in response to the threat are excerpted from Goodwin, *The Fitzgeralds and the Kennedys.*

17.   Ibid., 559.

18.   Ibid., 560. The entire account of the scene in Parliament is excerpted from Goodwin, *The Fitzgeralds and the Kennedys,* 560–561.

19.   This review is drawn from a memo that was prepared by James Landis and Justin Feldman for campaign coordinator William Walton in October 1960, during the waning days of John F. Kennedy's campaign. It was never used in the campaign. The memo can be found in Joseph Kennedy's private papers at the JFK Library in Boston.

20.   James MacGregor Burns, *Edward Kennedy and the Camelot Legacy* (New York: W. W. Norton, 1976), 31.

21.   JPK private papers, JFK Library.

22.   Joseph P. Kennedy Jr. letter to Joseph P. Kennedy, January 25, 1939, JPK private papers, JFK Library.

23.   Joseph P. Kennedy Jr. letter to Joseph P. Kennedy, March 15, 1939, JPK private papers, JFK Library.

24.   Adam Clymer, *Edward M. Kennedy: A Biography* (New York: William Morrow, 1999), 13.

25.   Goodwin, *The Fitzgeralds and the Kennedys,* 587.

26.   Burns, *Edward Kennedy and the Camelot Legacy,* 36.

27. Ibid.
28. Leamer, *The Kennedy Women*, 286.
29. Letter to Ted from Joe is in the JPK private papers, JFK Library.
30. Martin, *Seeds of Destruction*, 93.
31. Ibid., 109.
32. Ibid., 116.
33. Letter from Joe Jr. to Joe Sr. and Rose, June 23, 1944, JPK private papers, JFK Library.
34. Letter from RFK to JPK Jr., July 7, 1944, JPK private papers, JKF Library.
35. Clymer, *Edward M. Kennedy*, 15.
36. Leamer, *The Kennedy Men*, 211.
37. Martin, *Seeds of Destruction*, 127.
38. Ibid., 122.
39. Collier and Horowitz, *The Kennedys*, 122.
40. Martin, *Seeds of Destruction*, xvii.
41. Ibid.,127.

CHAPTER 4

1. O'Brien, *John F. Kennedy*, 191.
2. Martin, *Seeds of Destruction*, 136.
3. Norman Mailer, *The Kennedys, Stories of Life and Death from an American Family* (New York: Thunder's Mouth Press, 2001), 9.
4. Martin, *Seeds of Destruction*, 132.
5. Ibid., 132.
6. Robert Dallek, *An Unfinished Life: John F. Kennedy, 1917–1963* (Boston: Little, Brown, 2003), 120.
7. David Talbot, *Brothers: The Hidden History of the Kennedy Years* (New York: Free Press, 2007), 35.
8. O'Brien, *John F. Kennedy*, 176.
9. Ibid., 177.
10. Martin, *Seeds of Destruction*, 130.
11. Ibid., 137.
12. O'Brien, *John F. Kennedy*, 191.
13. Dallek, *An Unfinished Life*, 119–120.
14. Martin, *Seeds of Destruction*, 129.
15. Ibid., 145.
16. Collier and Horowitz, *The Kennedys*, 131.
17. Kennedy, *America Back on Track*, 3.
18. Dallek, *An Unfinished Life*, 125.
19. Goodwin, *The Fitzgeralds and the Kennedys*, 716.
20. Ibid., 718.
21. Martin, *Seeds of Destruction*, 141.
22. O'Brien, *John F. Kennedy*, 197.
23. Collier and Horowitz, *The Kennedys*, 132.
24. O'Brien, *John F. Kennedy*, 204.
25. Martin, *Seeds of Destruction*, 140.
26. O'Brien, *The Kennedys*, 132.
27. Ibid., 132.
28. Martin, *Seeds of Destruction*, 148.
29. Ibid.

30. O'Brien, *John F. Kennedy*, 207.
31. Ibid., 223.
32. Charles Bartlett, "John F. Kennedy: The Man," in Kenneth W. Thompson, ed., *The Kennedy Presidency* (Latham, MD: University Press of America, 1985), 3.
33. Goodwin, *The Fitzgeralds and the Kennedys*, 753.
34. Ralph G. Martin, *A Hero for Our Time: An Intimate Story of the Kennedy Years* (New York: Macmillan, 1983), 57.
35. Martin, *Seeds of Destruction*, 168.
36. Ibid.
37. Ibid., 169.
38. Dallek, *An Unfinished Life*, 168.
39. O'Brien, *John F. Kennedy*, 248.
40. Ibid., 259.
41. Dallek, *An Unfinished Life*, 174.
42. O'Brien, *John F. Kennedy*, 249.
43. Ibid., 143.
44. Martin, *Seeds of Destruction*, 152.
45. Ibid., 152.
46. O'Brien, *John F. Kennedy*, 244.
47. Martin, *Seeds of Destruction*, 172.
48. O'Brien, *John F. Kennedy*, 240.
49. Ibid., 164.
50. Ibid.
51. Ibid., 174.
52. From a Doris Kearns Goodwin interview with Lem Billings in Goodwin, *The Fitzgeralds and the Kennedys*, 767.
53. Martin, *Seeds of Destruction*, 177.

CHAPTER 5

1.   Harris Wofford, *Of Kennedys and Kings: Making Sense of the Sixties* (Pittsburgh: University of Pittsburgh Press, 1992), 456.
2.   Dallek, *An Unfinished Life*, 230.
3.   Arthur M. Schlesinger, *A Thousand Days: John F. Kennedy in the White House* (New York: Houghton Mifflin, 1965), Preface.
4.   *Saturday Evening Post*, January. 23, 1960
5.   The Presidential Recordings: John F. Kennedy, Dictabelt series, Miller Center for Public Affairs, University of Virginia.
6.   Laurence Leamer, *Sons of Camelot: The Fate of an American Dynasty* (New York: HarperCollins, 2004), 6.
7.   Martin, *Seeds of Destruction*, 246.
8.   Ibid., 247.
9.   Ibid., 235.
10. Goodwin, *The Fitzgeralds and the Kennedys*, 795.
11. *New York Herald Tribune*, May 16, 1961.
12. Hersh, *The Education of Edward Kennedy*, 130.
13. Clymer, *Edward M. Kennedy*, 27.
14. *Saturday Evening Post*, January 23, 1960.
15. Martin, *Seeds of Destruction*, 251.
16. Dallek, *An Unfinished Life*, 253.

17. Ibid.
18. Martin, *Seeds of Destruction*, 252.
19. Ibid.
20. Goodwin, *The Fitzgeralds and the Kennedys*, 799.
21. Clymer, *Edward M. Kennedy*, 28.
22. The plane story is excerpted from Adam Clymer's account in *Edward M. Kennedy*, 29.
23. Martin, *Seeds of Destruction*, 268.
24. Ibid., 267.
25. Ibid., 256.
26. Burns, *Edward Kennedy and the Camelot Legacy*, 67.
27. Cited by Joe Klein, *Time*, April 9, 2006.
28. Wofford, *Of Kennedys and Kings*, 18.
29. David J. Garrow, *Bearing the Cross: Martin Luther King, Jr., and the Southern Christian Leadership Conference* (New York: HarperCollins, 2004), 144.
30. Martin, *Seeds of Destruction*, 271.
31. Ibid., 273.

CHAPTER 6

1. Richard Mahoney, *Sons and Brothers: The Days of Jack and Bobby Kennedy* (New York: Arcade, 1999), 85.
2. Martin, *Seeds of Destruction*, 283.
3. Oral history interview with John F. Kennedy by John Bartlow Martin, JFK Library.
4. Third interview with John Seigenthaler by Ronald Grele, February 22, 1966, JFK Library.
5. Ibid.
6. Ibid.
7. Ibid.
8. Martin, *Seeds of Destruction*, 286.
9. Robert Dallek, *An Unfinished Life*, page 327
10. Ibid., 290.
11. Ibid., 288.
12. Ibid., 311.
13. Wofford, *Of Kennedys and Kings*, 352.
14. Ibid., 364.
15. Ibid.
16. Ibid., 354.
17. Michael Dobbs, *One Minute to Midnight: Kennedy, Krushchev and Castro on the Brink of Nuclear War* (New York: Knopf, 2008), 10.
18. Martin, *Seeds of Destruction*, 310.
19. Dobbs, *One Minute to Midnight*, 11.
20. Ibid., 10.
21. Kennedy, *America Back on Track*, 55.
22. *Life*, January 26, 1962, 18.
23. Wofford, *Of Kennedys and Kings*, 407.
24. Ibid., 382.
25. Clymer, *Edward M. Kennedy*, 213.
26. Ibid., 331.
27. Ibid., 393.
28. Martin, *Seeds of Destruction*, 291.

29.   Thomas Cronin, *On the Presidency: Teacher, Soldier, Shaman, Pol* (Boulder, CO: Paradigm Publishers, 2009), 115.
30.   Ibid., 117
31.   Wofford, *Of Kennedys and Kings,* 339.
32.   Ibid., 340.

CHAPTER 7

1.   Clymer, *Edward M. Kennedy,* 31.
2.   Martin, *Seeds of Destruction,* 357.
3.   Ibid., 360.
4.   Ibid., 362.
5.   Ibid., 365.
6.   Hersh, *The Education of Edward Kennedy,* 110
7.   The scene at the Boston rally is excerpted from a description by Alsop in the *Saturday Evening Post,* October 27, 1962.
8.   Martin, *Seeds of Destruction,* 369.
9.   Clymer, *Edward M. Kennedy,* 36.
10.   Hersh, *The Education of Edward Kennedy,* 177.
11.   Ibid., 181. All debate quotes are excerpted from Hersh, *The Education of Edward Kennedy.*
12.   Ibid., 182.
13.   Burns, *Edward Kennedy and the Camelot Legacy,* 91.
14.   Martin, *Seeds of Destruction,* 419.
15.   Burns, *Edward Kennedy and the Camelot Legacy,* 98.
16.   Clymer, *Edward M. Kennedy,* 47.
17.   Mahoney, *Sons and Brothers,* 119.
18.   Clymer, *Edward M. Kennedy,* 49.
19.   Wofford, *Of Kennedys and Kings,* 404.
20.   Burns, *Edward Kennedy and the Camelot Legacy,* 98.
21.   Ibid., 103.
22.   Ibid.
23.   The entire bedroom scene is excerpted from Leamer, *The Kennedy Men,* 739.
24.   Ibid.
25.   Ibid., 741.

CHAPTER 8

1.   Martin, *Seeds of Destruction,* 467.
2.   Ibid., 467.
3.   Wofford, *Of Kennedys and Kings,* 411.
4.   Clymer, *Edward M. Kennedy,* 56.
5.   O'Brien, *John F. Kennedy,* xiii.
6.   Wofford, *Of Kennedys and Kings,* 418.
7.   Ibid., 416.
8.   Martin, *Seeds of Destruction,* 486.
9.   Burns, *Edward Kennedy and the Camelot Legacy, 120.*
10.   Clint Willis, ed., *The Kennedys, Stories of Life and Death from an American Family,* (New York: Thunder's Mouth Press, 2001), 125.
11.   Ibid., page 125.
12.   Ibid., 132.

13. Ibid., 136.
14. Burns, *Edward Kennedy and the Camelot Legacy*, 121.
15. Ibid.
16. Martin, *Seeds of Destruction*, 498.
17. Ibid., 499.
18. Burns, *Edward Kennedy and the Camelot Legacy*, 122.
19. Martin, *Seeds of Destruction*, 482.
20. Ibid., 483.
21. Wofford, *Of Kennedys and Kings*, 419.
22. Ibid., 421.
23. Burns, *Edward Kennedy and the Camelot Legacy*, 125.
24. Martin, *Seeds of Destruction*, 511.
25. Ibid., 512.
26. Clymer, *Edward M. Kennedy*, 72.
27. Ibid.
28. Ibid., 87.
29. Evan Thomas, *Robert Kennedy: His Life* (New York: Simon & Schuster, 2000), 323.
30. Martin, *Seeds of Destruction*, 527.
31. Wofford, *Of Kennedys and Kings*, 421.
32. Martin, *Seeds of Destruction*, 528.
33. Wofford, *Of Kennedys and Kings*, 423.
34. Ibid.

CHAPTER 9

1. All the observations about parallels between Jack's and Bobby's announcements are made by Thurston Clarke in *The Last Campaign: Robert Kennedy and 82 Days that Inspired America* (New York: Henry, Holt, 2008), 21.
2. Willis, *The Kennedys, Stories of Life and Death from an American Family*, 315.
3. Clymer, *Edward M. Kennedy*, 105.
4. Martin, *Seeds of Destruction*, 539.
5. Leamer, *The Kennedy Women*, 624.
6. Clarke, *The Last Campaign*, 37.
7. Ibid., 243.
8. Wofford, *Of Kennedys and Kings*, 424.
9. Martin, *Seeds of Destruction*, 536.
10. Clarke, *The Last Campaign*, 27.
11. Ibid., 243.
12. Wofford, *Of Kennedys and Kings*, 450.
13. Clarke, *The Last Campaign*, 52.
14. Ibid., 214.
15. Ibid., 55–56.
16. Ibid., 85.
17. Ibid., 86.
18. Ibid., 89.
19. Ibid., 90.
20. Klein's account of the rally in Indianapolis appeared in a column for *Time* magazine, April 9, 2006.
21. Martin, *Seeds of Destruction*, 550.
22. Clarke, *The Last Campaign*, 115.
23. Ibid., 117.

24. Ibid., 277.
25. Ted Sorensen, *Counselor: A Life at the Edge of History* (New York: HarperCollins, 2008).
26. Willis, *The Kennedys, Stories of Life and Death from an American Family,* 318.

CHAPTER 10

1. All the images of mourning can be found in Clarke, *The Last Campaign,* 4–5.
2. Clymer, *Edward M. Kennedy,* 119.
3. Clarke, *The Last Campaign,* 4.
4. *New York Newsday,* June 3, 1993, 63.
5. Martin, *Seeds of Destruction,* 576.
6. *People,* August 16, 1999.
7. Excerpted from the tribute video to Kennedy at the Democratic Convention in Denver.
8. Arthur M. Schlesinger, *Journals: 1952–2000* (New York: Penguin Press, 2007), 295.
9. Clymer, *Edward M. Kennedy,* 117.
10. Hersh, *The Shadow President,* 7.
11. Martin, *Seeds of Destruction,* 583.
12. Ibid., 582.
13. Ibid.
14. Harrison Rainie and John Quinn, *Growing Up Kennedy: The Third Wave Comes of Age* (New York: G.P. Putnam's Sons, 1983), 104.
15. Clymer, *Edward M. Kennedy,* 120.
16. Rainie and Quinn, *Growing Up Kennedy,* 104.
17. *People,* August 16, 1999.
18. Ibid.
19. Martin, *Seeds of Destruction,* 586.
20. *Time* magazine, January 10, 1969.

CHAPTER 11

1. Willis, *The Kennedys, Stories of Life and Death from an American Family,* 272.
2. Martin, *Seeds of Destruction,* 591.
3. Clymer, *Edward M. Kennedy,* 142.
4. Martin, *Seeds of Destruction,* 591.
5. Clymer, *Edward M. Kennedy,* 145.
6. Martin, *Seeds of Destruction,* 582.
7. Willis, *The Kennedys, Stories of Life and Death from an American Family,* 279.
8. Ibid., 287.
9. Ibid., 293.
10. Martin, *Seeds of Destruction,* 574.
11. Cited by Mel Ayton in *Crime* magazine, Oct. 17, 2005
12. Willis, *The Kennedys, Stories of Life and Death from an American Family,* 306.
13. Martin, *Seeds of Destruction,* 574.
14. Ibid., 594.
15. Mel Ayton, *Questions of Controversy: The Kennedy Brothers* (Houghton-le-Spring, England: Business Education Publishers, 2001), 328.
16. Willis, *The Kennedys, Stories of Life and Death from an American Family,* 340.
17. Ibid., 341.
18. Willis, *The Kennedys, Stories of Life and Death from an American Family,* 307–308.

19. *Washington Post Magazine*, April 29, 1990.
20. Ibid.
21. Ibid.
22. Ibid.
23. Clymer, *Edward M. Kennedy*, 142.
24. Ibid., 196.
25. Ibid., 159.
26. Ibid., 207.
27. Ibid.

CHAPTER 12

1. Clymer, *Edward M. Kennedy*, 290–291.
2. Ibid., 283.
3. Ibid.
4. Ibid., 307.
5. Hersh, *The Shadow President*, 44.
6. Clymer, *Edward M. Kennedy*, 293.
7. Hersh, *The Shadow President*, 155.
8. Gary Wills, *The Kennedy Imprisonment: A Meditation on Power* (New York: Atlantic/Little, Brown, 1982), 11.
9. Clymer, *Edward M. Kennedy*, 303.
10. Leamer, *Sons of Camelot*, 212.
11. *Rocky Mountain News*, August 24, 2008.
12. Hersh, *The Shadow President*, 51.
13. *Rocky Mountain News*, August 24, 2008.
14. Ibid.
15. *Boston Globe*, January 5, 2003.

CHAPTER 13

1. Leamer, *Sons of Camelot*, 215.
2. Clymer, *Edward M. Kennedy*, 325.
3. Leamer, *Sons of Camelot*, 209.
4. Orrin Hatch, *Square Peg: Confessions of a Citizen Senator* (New York: Basic Books, 2002), 112. The entire cigar smoke story appears in Hatch's book.
5. Hersh, *The Shadow President*, 86.
6. Hatch, *Square Peg*, 111.
7. Hersh, *The Shadow President*, 55.
8. Ibid., 58.
9. All quotes about weapons appear in ibid., 61.
10. *Boston Globe*, June 28, 1982.
11. Hersh, *The Shadow President*, 78.
12. A great deal of Kennedy's speech is reprinted in Clymer, *Edward M. Kennedy*, 369.
13. Hersh, *The Shadow President*, 77.
14. Viktor Chebrikov's letter and other documents relating to Ted Kennedy's outreach to the Soviets come from the Central Committee Archives of the Communist Party of the former Soviet Union, which were opened in the early 1990s by the Boris Yeltsin government, but closed after several inquiries. The document was found by a London *Times* reporter in early 1992, and the excerpts here come from his research. Historian Paul Kengor obtained a full copy of the document from Herb

Romerstein, a former staff member of the U.S. House Permanent Select Committee on Intelligence and a veteran cold war researcher. Kengor discusses the document at length in his book, *The Crusader: Ronald Reagan and the Fall of
Communism*, (New York: Harper Perennial, 2006).

15. Hersh, *The Shadow President*, 79.
16. Hearing before the House Committee on Education and Labor, July 10, 2007.
17. *Providence Journal* web site, audio interview of Patrick Kennedy, May 6, 2006.
18. All of Kennedy's misadventures cited here appear in a story by Rick Atkinson for
    the *Washington Post Magazine*, April 29, 1990.
19. Leamer, *Sons of Camelot*, 208.
20. Ibid., 209.
21. Hersh, *The Shadow President*, 70.

CHAPTER 14

1. *Boston Globe*, January 5, 2003.
2. Clymer, *Edward M. Kennedy*, 489.
3. Cited by Charles Pierce in *The Boston Globe*, Jan. 5, 2003.
4. *Washington Post*, May 30, 2008.
5. Quoted in ibid.
6. Clymer, *Edward M. Kennedy*, 541.
7. Ibid., 542.
8. Ibid., 553.
9. Hersh, *The Shadow President*, 136.
10. Robert Shrum, *No Excuses: Concessions of a Serial Campaigner* (New York: Simon
    & Schuster, 2007), 246.
11. Ibid., 248.
12. Ibid.
13. Ibid.
14. Ibid., 249.
15. Ibid.
16. Hersh, *The Shadow President*, 144.
17. Shrum, *No Excuses*, 249.
18. Hersh, *The Shadow President*, 147.
19. Shrum, *No Excuses*, 250.
20. Hersh, *The Shadow President*, 149.
22. Clymer, *Edward M. Kennedy*, 563.
22. Ibid., 603.

CHAPTER 15

1. The account of Kennedy's visit to the cemetery appears in an article by Mark Lei-
   bovich for the *Washington Post*, July 14, 2004.
2. WBUR Boston news report, July 21, 2008.
3. Sergeant Vanessa Turner's story is recounted by Edward Nesi in "Lion in Winter:
   Edward M. Kennedy in the Bush Years: A Study in Senate Leadership," a paper
   written for the political science department of Wheaton College in Norton, MA,
   May 19, 2007.
4. CNN report, August 30, 2002.
5. Nesi, "Lion in Winter," n. 174.
6. Kennedy, *America Back on Track*, 45–46.

7. *Larry King Live,* April 20, 2006.
8. Nesi, "Lion in Winter," n. 176.
9. Thomas Oliphant, *Utter Incompetents: Ego and Ideology in the Age of Bush* (New York: St. Martin's Griffin, 2007), 227.
10. All the word totals appear in a column by Eric Boehlert on the web site "Media Matters for America," May 28, 2002.
11. Ibid.
12. Ibid.
13. *Larry King Live,* April 20, 2006.
14. Nesi, "Lion in Winter," 167.

CHAPTER 16

1. Lois Romano, *The Washington Post,* May 30, 2008.
2. Clymer, *Edward M. Kennedy,* 472.
3. Associated Press, June 10, 2008.
4. Hersh, *The Shadow President,* 166.
5. *Seattle Times* wire services, May 21, 2008.
6. *The Washington Post,* March 24, 2010.
7. Ibid.
8. Ibid.
9. *John King USA,* CNN, March 22, 2010.
10. *Good Morning America* interview, March 22, 2010.
11. *The Washington Post,* March 24, 2010.
12. As seen in a photo taken by John M. Dicker and shared with the author by *Washington Post* reporter Phil Rucker.

EPILOGUE

1. *The Washington Post,* January 29, 2008.
2. *Politco,* August 27, 2009.
3. *The New York Times,* January 29, 2009.
4. *The Washington Post,* August 30, 2009.
5. Email to the author.
6. *The Washington Post,* August 27, 2009.
7. As heard by author at a Kennedy family reception at The Brown Palace Hotel, August 26, 2008.
8. *The Washington Post,* August 29, 2009.
9. Ibid.
10. *The Washington Post,* March 12, 2010.
11. Ibid.
12. *The Washington Post,* March 19, 2010.
13. *The Washington Post,* August 30, 2009.
14. ABC News Special, "Remembering Ted Kennedy." Aug. 26, 2009.
15. Cape Cod Times, February 10, 2010.
16. Boston Globe, August 12, 2008.
17. Ibid.
18. Harvard Gazette, December 1, 2008.
19. Dodd made his remarks at a memorial service for Ted Kennedy at JFK Library on August 28, 2009.

INDEX